Identity Parades

Identity Parades
Northern Irish Culture and Dissident Subjects

RICHARD KIRKLAND

LIVERPOOL UNIVERSITY PRESS

First published 2002

Liverpool University Press
4 Cambridge Street
Liverpool, L69 7ZU

British Library Cataloguing-in-Publication Data
A British Library CIP Record is available.

ISBN 0-85323-626-7 *cased*
      0-85323-636-4 *limp*

Set in Stone Serif and Sans by
Koinonia, Manchester
Printed in the European Union by
Bell and Bain Ltd, Glasgow

For Emily Nadira Jones, with love

Contents

Acknowledgments

I would like to thank the following people for their help, support and advice: David Alderson, Michael Allen, Simon Bainbridge, Emma Clery, Anne-Julie Crozier, Colin Graham, Conor Hanna, Ken Hirschkop, Eamonn Hughes, Edward Larrissy, Declan Long, Michael Parker, Shaun Richards and Helen Stoddart. Keele University's decision to grant me a junior research award was of immense help in the completion of this book and I owe a debt of gratitude to all the members of the English Department of that institution and to the members of the Keele/ Staffordshire University Irish Studies collaboration.

Much of my discussion of Northern Irish film derives from the experience of teaching a remarkable group of final-year Keele under-graduate students for a course on modern Irish cinema and I would particularly like to thank Sharon Collis, Jeanette Cutland, James Daniel, Oliver Mitchell, Helen Riddell and Sophie Rudkin for their scholarly perception, dedication and enthusiasm.

A section of Chapter 3 was originally published as 'Bourgeois Redemptions: the Fiction of Glenn Patterson and Robert McLiam Wilson', in Liam Harte and Michael Parker (eds), *Contemporary Irish Fiction: Themes, Tropes, Theories* (Macmillan Press Ltd, 2000), and is reproduced by permission of Palgrave. A section of Chapter 2 was originally published as 'Gender, nation, excess: reading *Hush-a-Bye Baby*', in Scott Brewster, Virginia Crossman, Fiona Becket and David Alderson (eds), *Ireland in Proximity: History, Gender, Space* (Routledge, 1999), and is reproduced by permission of Routledge. The publishers are also grateful to Faber & Faber for permission to quote from 'Off the Back of a Lorry' by Tom Paulin from *Liberty Tree* (Faber & Faber, 1983) and to Blackstaff Press for permission to quote from 'As You Like It' and 'Because I Paced my Thought' by John Hewitt from *The Collected Poems of John Hewitt* (ed. Frank Ormsby, Blackstaff Press,

1991). Every effort has been made to trace copyright owners and the publishers would be grateful to be informed of any errors or omissions.

Introduction

The question of 'speaking *as*' involves a distancing from oneself. The moment I have to think of the ways in which I will speak as an Indian, or as a feminist, the ways in which I will speak as a woman, what I am doing is trying to generalise myself, make myself a representative, trying to distance myself from some kind of inchoate speaking *as such*. There are many subject positions which one must inhabit; one is not just one thing. That is when a political consciousness comes in. So that in fact, for the person who does the 'speaking as' something, it is a problem of distancing from one's self, whatever that self might be.

Gayatri Chakravorty Spivak[1]

We live in an age in which it is practically impossible to speak of politics without speaking also of identity. Identity provides us with a sense of who we are, where we have come from, and, more importantly, where we are going. It mediates our personal memory in terms of collective inheritance and provides the platform from which we launch ourselves on an unsuspecting world. Understood in these terms, identity offers itself, almost uniquely, as a means of ordering the chaos of our experience. It can assimilate the unlikely event, the crisis-wracked history, the piece of outrageous good fortune and find in this material not merely a story but an explanation. Perhaps more importantly, within this function identity is *forgiving*; it justifies the visceral response, smoothes over the contradictions of our prejudices and constitutes the final refuge from which we can argue our case and vindicate our position.

At the same time, however, identity has its limits, not least in the fact that it never quite seems to coincide with the incoherences, the ambivalences and the gaps out of which we make ourselves. Indeed, Spivak's awareness of the 'distancing' involved in asserting any statement of identity is salutary in that it suggests something of the fundamental contradiction implicit in such utterances. As she notes, identity assumes this monolinear position because it is based not on the question 'who should speak?' but rather on the more pressing issue of 'who will listen?'. In its ideal form identity is a point of contact, a mediation between competing material forces and interests and, as such, is necessarily rooted in antagonism. It exists neither with the speaker nor with the presumed listener but occupies a site somewhere in between. There are possibilities as well as limitations identifiable in this positioning. While identity, in Spivak's terms, does not come close to answering the complexities of memory and affiliation at a personal level, its role as a strategy allows for the negotiation of political interests while protecting more vulnerable discontinuities. The essential 'thereness' of identity, the manner in which it dissolves any distinction between what already exists and what *should* exist, masks confrontation and becomes the point from which politics can emerge.

So why does identity – as Spivak's frustration suggests – never seem to come good on these promises? The essential unity of self and utterance it appears to offer at one level is never realised since both remain stubbornly in excess of identity's strategies of containment. For Terry Eagleton, the gap that emerges from this conjunction is painfully ironic because identity politics emerge from what he terms 'oppositional politics' and are thus 'ineluctably parasitic on their antagonists.'[2] Developing his argument, he notes: 'Our grudge against the ruling order is not only that it has oppressed us in our social, sexual or racial identities but that it has thereby forced us to lavish an extraordinary amount of attention on these things, which are not in the long run all that important.'[3] While Eagleton advocates embracing this irony as a strategy of resistance, at the same time this repeated investment in identity politics as a means of encountering, and some-times overcoming, opposition can also engender a certain exhaustion. Understood as such, identity becomes the darkling plain where the confused armies of competing interests clash by night.

A feeling of exhaustion is, of course, by no means uncommon for those who engage in the identity politics of Northern Ireland. As an example of identity's ability to disable communication just as it simul-taneously appears to enable it, the North has become a byword for all that is most restrictive, least constitutive and ultimately fossilised in cultural exchange. While such fatalism in itself indicates a certain fatigue, at the same time the fact that the normative 'two traditions' version of Northern Irish culture has proved incapable of reimagining the sectarian polarities of the province is now almost axiomatic. Indeed, when faced with the all-pervasive nature of identity politics in the North, it can be argued that the critical project that might chart a possible move beyond this totality has yet to begin. However, if one assumes that the only thing that can overcome identity is the inevitability of its own implicit lack, as Spivak perceives it, so the terms of any critical intervention are clearly revealed. Rather than search for the moment of revelation or propose an identitarian 'solution' through which the North can emerge into the daylight of a 'modern' sensibility, it is more productive to see such analyses as, in themselves, symptomatic of a form of theoretical despair: the critical equivalent of drawing a line in the sand beyond which anachronistic identity formations will not be allowed to pass. A more productive critical encounter, it can be argued, is one that encounters the cultural manifestations of identity politics not with the aim of locating their obsolescence but rather with the objective of tracing their implicit inner contradictions – Spivak's 'problem of distancing' – and it is with this imperative that *Identity Parades* seeks to make an intervention.

Firstly, however, other contexts need to be asserted. In arguing that symptoms of cultural and identitarian saturation in Northern Ireland do not derive from the inability to reconcile difference but rather have their genesis within the frame of competing interests through which such utterances are made possible, it becomes necessary to examine what can be termed the underlying totality of bourgeois ideology that gives expression to these seemingly antagonistic meanings. Taking this wider perspective, the status of bourgeois ideology in Northern Ireland cannot simply be reduced to the outlook and perceptions of a self-interested middle class, as Bill Rolston has argued,[4] but becomes rather the register through which all identitarian negotiations in the North take place. Bourgeois ideology provides the language for aggressive assertions of identity intended to challenge the dominant order just as it provides the means through which the state seeks to neutralise these threats. For this reason the cultural conflict in the North cannot be read in terms of an opposition in which a state-complicit liberalism seeks to promote a depoliticised sense of identity at the expense of sectarian or class-based solidarity, but rather should be understood in terms of the possibilities and deformations implicit in identitarian politics as a whole.[5] Such a model is reliant on Roland Barthes' perception of bourgeois ideology as an 'exnominating phenomenon',[6] the point at which 'all that is not bourgeois is obliged to *borrow* from the bourgeoisie. Bourgeois ideology can therefore spread over everything and in so doing lose its name without risk.'[7] Imagined in this way, bourgeois ideology's moment of triumph is the same moment at which it appears to be absent, while it is only rendered visible in its failures.

It is partly for this reason that the significance of bourgeois ideology in the constitution of Northern Irish cultural politics has been little considered. Indeed, perhaps the instinctive response when apprehending the relationship between the two is to think of the wilfully uncomprehending editorials of British broadsheet newspapers when faced with the latest crisis at Drumcree or an impasse in negotiations about prisoner releases. Such persistent tut-tutting is reducible in the final instance to the question Joseph Ruane and Jennifer Todd have critiqued in a perceptive essay: 'Why can't you get along with each other?'[8] There is, though, more at stake in this manoeuvre than the guilt complexes of British bourgeois ideology. The urge to perceive Northern Ireland as beyond the remit of bourgeois law is a strategy that not only protects the integrity of British political discourse but is also crucial to those Republican discourses within the North itself that seek to assert an ultimately irreducible difference. Equally anxious to sign up to this unlikely coalition is the discipline of Irish Studies, which, with its codifying energies, often defines the object of its study either as a pre-bourgeois enclave or, increasingly, as a location that has moved from the pre-bourgeois to the postmodern without having had cause to enmesh itself in the transitional period of the industrial bourgeois economy.[9] On this reading Northern Ireland offers itself as an implicit critique of both the bourgeois liberal British state and the triumph of the bourgeois-nationalist project in the Republic; it becomes the border beyond which these ideologies cease to have efficacy. As Kumkum Sangari has observed, 'the stifling monologues of self and other [...] remain the orderly discourses of the bourgeois subject'.[10]

The persistent strategy behind this manoeuvre is one that recognises the argument to which I have already referred. In circumscribing bourgeois ideology, the presence of the North simultaneously renders it visible and in so doing fatally weakens its powers. Similarly, on the rare occasions when the bourgeois is seen to declare itself *within* Northern Ireland the effect of its presence has to be anxiously policed. Ronan Bennett's Republican analysis of the role of bourgeois culture in the North in his essay 'Don't Mention the War: Culture in Northern Ireland'[11] is illustrative of this tendency:

In the North of Ireland it is possible to see *The Wind in the Willows* at the Lyric Players Theatre, *Oliver* at the Grand Opera House, *Romeo and Juliet* at the Arts Theatre, *A Room with a View* at the Queen's Film Theatre. You can see Ken Branagh's *Hamlet* at the Waterfront Hall, hear Handel's *Messiah* at the Ulster Hall, or watch the Duchess of Kent open Castleward, the North's cut-rate version of Glyndebourne. This is the culture of the affluent and educated citizenry; it is Belfast masquerading as Bristol or Leicester. Middle-class taste in the arts is what you would expect to find in any provincial centre. It is liberal, non-sectarian and draws heavily on metropolitan influences, those of London and, to a lesser extent, Dublin.

The 'Troubles' scarcely figure. Not in art, not in life. The neutral middle class can afford to be aloof. The North's well-to-do have managed to come through the conflict almost completely unscathed: they live in pleasant residential suburbs that see no rioting; they are not arrested or raided; they suffer no casualties.[12]

The disgusted rejection that gives momentum to Bennett's analysis at this point is based solely on the recognition that the Northern Irish middle classes are behaving in a middle-class manner. Moreover, the Northern bourgeois culture that they embody is seen not only as English but as an ersatz copy of Englishness at that. Their Belfast becomes a provincial location copying another provincial location. This indicates something of the extent of Bennett's disdain. Not only is the Northern Irish middle class repellent in itself, it is not even any good at being middle class. However, underlying Bennett's furious self-righteousness is a more profound sense of reassurance. The logic that drives his intervention is ultimately dependent upon an opposition between the readily identifiable symptoms of bourgeois culture – symptoms that are so self-evident as to require no further explication – and the North's social violence, which, as his argument develops, will metamorphose into 'the political'. As the latter is inimical to the former so the bourgeois is again circumscribed as little more than a few morbid symptoms. To return to Barthes, this dwelling on the traces of an ideology renders the bourgeois vulnerable to critique insofar as it seeks to render it visible and yet this strategy can only be achieved by subscribing to bourgeois ideology's own inability to declare itself as 'political'. Understood as such, 'Don't Mention the War' is an anti-bourgeois critique that articulates its argument in a thoroughly bourgeois manner; another manifestation of Sangari's 'stifling monologues of self and other'.

How, then, can this strict demarcation be complicated? What can be gained through a relocation of Northern Irish cultural politics in terms of the persistent strategies of bourgeois ideology when perceived as the frame through which even anti-bourgeois dissidence articulates itself? In the first and last instance such a critique has to take as its primary aim a desire to disrupt 'the orderly discourses of the bourgeois subject'. The persistent divisions of bourgeois ideology – divisions between thought and feeling, politics and culture, common sense and theory – have to be re-encountered and the various symptoms to which they give rise identified as part of an overall organising principle. This is a less gruelling activity than it first appears if only because of the quicksilver nature of bourgeois ideology itself. As the bourgeois, to return to Barthes, functions as an 'exnominating phenomenon' so it can be defined not by its uniformity but by its restlessness, its ability to assume ever more unlikely manifestations and to transgress into what may seem increasingly unpromising forms. This is a necessary process, for the moment at which the bourgeois ceases to reinvent itself is also the moment at which it is most vulnerable, the moment at which it can be recognised as such.

This suggests the critical trajectory of *Identity Parades* itself. While this book is primarily an analysis of bourgeois formations within Northern Irish cultural discourse – formations that invariably make themselves manifest through the tropes of identity – the range of texts it considers is more diverse, including indigenous and non-indigenous film, popular fiction, autobiography, critical analyses and government publications. Drawing these disparate texts together is a recognition of the shared aspects of their expressive form. The material considered is at once both concerned with identity and with explicating the meaning of identity in modern Northern Ireland, and, at the same time, unable to apprehend the frameworks of identitarian consciousness through which it signifies. In this respect, the perception of aesthetic activity in this book ultimately subscribes to David Lloyd's and Paul Thomas's broad awareness that 'from its inception, aesthetic culture defines a set of practices which at once define and moralize the bourgeois public sphere'.[13] This act of definition can, of course, never be completed and, indeed, it is tempting to argue that it is precisely because the exnominating function of bourgeois ideology is placed under such strain in Northern Ireland that its particular aesthetic manifestations are so polyvalent, insatiable, and very often fantastical.

Having defined the remit of the argument in these terms it may seem curious that *Identity Parades* omits any extended analysis of what is often considered to be the most significant cultural activity arising out of Northern Irish society: poetry. This is not because the complexities of the phenomenon known as the Northern Irish poet are somehow inimical to anti-bourgeois analysis; indeed the construction and then disavowal of 'Northern Irish poetry' as a meaningful category capable of explicating the complexities of poetic allegiance and aesthetic resonance accords closely with a perception of bourgeois ideology as able to contain and explicate dissidence within its own frameworks. Instead this omission arises from a wariness about the extent to which the paradigms of Northern Irish poetry have been allowed to function as a metonym for the wider strategies of the culture in recent analytical work. To take an obvious example, by this reading John Hewitt is perceived as the poetic voice of Protestant Ulster and Seamus Heaney as his Catholic counterpart,[14] and in this way they are not simply rendered as embodiments of a community but become mutually defining. That this critical preoccupation has led to the neglect of other forms of cultural activity in Northern Ireland is largely unarguable. However, what is, perhaps, more important is the extent to which this concentration on poetry has not merely overwhelmed the development of other modes of Northern Irish cultural analysis but has also imposed an interpretative template upon many of those wider analyses that do exist, imposing continuities where material interests suggest there should be fracture and finding through the workings of the individual text itself a mode of critical self-sufficiency. For this reason, then, *Identity Parades* is in dialogue with the frameworks established through criticism of Northern Irish poetry, but at the same time it seeks to suggest something of their ultimate obsolescence through a strategic relocation of focus.

An analysis that begins with the assumption of the pre-existence of bourgeois ideology has then a clear critical imperative: to stem what Barthes terms the 'unceasing haemorrhage'[15] of meaning from the concept of the bourgeois formation and to identify the various forms by which it has made itself known within identity politics. As will already be evident, the process of rereading identitarianism in *Identity Parades* gains its intellectual momentum and vocabulary from post-colonial theory's codification of the various subject positions that can be occupied in relation to the state, as it is through these procedures that identitarianism has been most thoroughly analysed. Alongside this, however, the desire to reduce cultural artefacts to little more than symptoms of irreducible liminality must be resisted, as must the temptation to reconfigure their significance as paradigmatic through the deployment of analogies. The faultlines between Irish Studies and postcolonial theory are never more clearly revealed than in the tendency of the former to cite decontextualised postcolonial paradigms (the very term being oxymoronic) in a manner reducible to that of 'use'. In this way, the appellation 'postcolonial theory and Ireland' is expressive of a presumed absence within the discourse of Irish Studies while being similarly indicative of irreducible difference. To express this differently: such a conjunction should not so much engage us in a debate as to Ireland's postcolonial status[16] (on the subject of which much energy has been expended) as force us to rethink how the post-colonial can be encountered through Ireland in the first instance. Aijaz Ahmad's assertion that 'we should speak not so much of colonialism or postcolonialism but of capitalist modernity, which takes the colonial form in particular places and at particular times'[17] is not, in these terms, merely an expression of annoyance with postcolonial theory's presumed refusal of materialist methodology, but a recognition of the necessary and welcome syntheses implicit in the development of cultural theory in its critique of subject positions.

If, in this way, it is possible to assert the necessity of cultural theory as a mode of analysis reinvented but not superseded by postcolonial theory, so there is an imperative to return to and update materialist critiques of bourgeois ideology and its persistent, although adaptable, governance of what gets said and what it is possible to say within Northern Irish cultural discourse. Here a greater silence is identifiable. While the (often highly self-conscious) importation of postcolonial theory into Irish Studies has provoked a unique version of the 'theory war' that dominated much of the debate as to the future of English Studies in Britain and the United States during the 1980s,[18] there has been no equivalent controversy about the possibilities and limitations of a critique of specifically Irish bourgeois subject positions and formations. This could be, of course, because few such studies exist.[19] While Irish literary criticism at least has proved willing to rethink its modes of analysis in terms of what can loosely be defined as Marxist orthodoxies, the assumption still remains that Ireland's uneven development in relation to capital prohibits more extended considerations (this despite the fact that Gramscian materialism is uniquely able to take account of and, indeed, make a virtue of such 'unevenness'). For this reason embryonic critical discourse on Ireland and postcolonial theory, despite the controversies implicit in the ethical reading of Ireland's status it demands, distorts rather than furthers a distinction between orthodox Marxism and postcoloniality understood as a *condition*. As Joe Cleary has observed: 'What one misses most in contemporary Irish discourse is any real assimilation of the rich heritage of Marxist critical theory which – at its best – has developed an altogether less one-sided and much more dialectical conception of modernity, one which attempts to sort out the matrix of oppressive and emancipatory forces involved.'[20]

It is, however, equally necessary to be suspicious of any strict demarcation between what can be seen as previously assured critical orthodoxies and 'new' modes of analysis. In a recent waspish moment, John Goodby criticised nascent Irish postcolonial criticism for its 'monotonous dependence on Friel, Heaney and Banville', implying that, despite such theory's 'iconoclastic pretensions', it still finds itself most comfortable with 'a narrow range of canonical works and authors'.[21] The point is persuasively argued and it can be suggested that a similar 'monotonous dependence' is observable in Northern Irish Cultural Studies as it groups its analyses obsessively around such texts as *The Crying Game*, the popular thrillers of Colin Bateman and the series of Northern Ireland Office television advertisements from 1994 designed to encourage the use of its confidential telephone line service. *Identity Parades* is guilty of revisiting the first two of these clichés but does so in the hope that new contexts can be asserted. The self-reflexivity of Cultural Studies, the manner in which it can redefine itself as a discipline according to the object of its study, is at once its most attractive and yet its most frustrating characteristic. To put this another way, while, as Barthes remarked, 'literature' is 'what gets taught',[22] there has always been the nascent possibility in Cultural Studies that it can form itself around 'what gets said', and this should remain its organising principle.

To express these reservations is not, then, to agree with David Miller's recent bizarre assertion that 'the standard of academic, media, and popular commentary on the Northern Ireland conflict remains abysmal'.[23] While it has become common to find academics and cultural commentators declaring in moments of vexation that the North has become over-researched and over-analysed (or over-agonised) and that some academic version of a fishing quota should be applied in order to protect stocks of increasingly rare research material, the state of Northern Irish Studies in all of its various disciplinary formations has never looked so vigorous nor so diverse. That said, the requirement for any new critical work to shoulder a space for itself within what is an increasingly crowded field is obvious and I hope that the interventionist aspirations and theoretical ancestry of many of the ideas explored in *Identity Parades* are clear. Most significantly, the work of the *Cahiers* collective within film studies has been a constant touchstone, since its reworking of Lacanian 'misrecognition' to describe the subject's misunderstanding of his or her relationship to actual material forces provides a powerful and adaptable critique of what can be considered the identitarian moment. Similarly I make no apologies for the deployment of what are, at times, traditional Althusserian analyses if only because Louis Althusser's preoccupation with the frame within which individual cultural acts take place allows for a flexibility that can encompass not only the discreet strategies of bourgeois ideology itself but also the institutional frame within which critiques of such ideology take place.

For this reason I feel it is appropriate that *Identity Parades* concludes with an extended consideration of what happens when the internal contradictions of identity's strategies of engagement overwhelm its own delicate structures – the point at which the implicit desire to declare for a particular affiliation reveals other resonances that trouble the binary assertions on which the declaration was originally founded. It is in this way that texts become dissident – become a camp critique of their own identitarian earnestness – as they are rendered not merely oppositional but also transgressive of the discourse on which the original opposition is based. Identifying the 'subversive and popular' nature of camp, Tom Paulin has asked 'Where are the lengthy critical studies called *Camp and Shopping in the Age of Mass Culture*, *The Semiotics of Camp*, *Late Bourgeois Camp*?',[24] the implication being, perhaps, that such is the joylessness of much modern cultural theory that it is unable to capture anything of camp's quicksilver nature and thus dismisses it as so much triviality. The point is well made and, with this in mind, my final chapter on Northern Irish camp in a 'late bourgeois' society approaches its subject with a certain timidity. Similarly, it takes cognisance of Susan Sontag's awareness that it is 'embarrassing to be solemn and treatise-like about Camp. One runs the risk of having, oneself, produced a very inferior piece of Camp.'[25] Whether this is the unfortunate fate of my final chapter is for others to judge but insofar as *Identity Parades* attempts to map a cultural progression, so it locates in the camp moment the ultimate destination of much identitarian positioning and as a result sketches some of the forms that identity's implicit critique takes. It is through this act that I hope a different mode of oppositional critique begins to emerge. As I have previously suggested, there is no 'solution' to the conflicts of identity in Northern Ireland or anywhere else, but equally there is an imperative to be more than simply a spectator of the faction fight.

1

Cultural Identity and the Bourgeois Spectacle

On Thursday 2 July 1998 the Grand Orange Lodge of Ireland published an open letter in Northern Ireland's two morning newspapers:

Dear Fellow Citizens

I am sure, in common with members of the Orange Institution, you are concerned about events over the coming days in respect of traditional Orange parades. In order to assist understanding of our historic culture and noble traditions we wish to outline certain facts which are relevant to the situation.

The disputed parades occur along main arterial roads which are shared by all communities. All are traditional routes, none have been concocted or organised to cause offence. We are not engaged in coat trailing, or triumphalism. We simply want to celebrate our culture and identity peacefully and with dignity. [...]

The restricting of loyal order parades along main roads creates cultural apartheid, where one community has a veto on another community's expression of identity and heritage. Banning and re-routing Orange parades from shared road and village main streets will only lead to further segregation of our respective communities. This is not the way to build a future where there is mutual respect and tolerance. Ethnic segregation is morally wrong. It did not work in South Africa and the United States. It must not be allowed to work in Northern Ireland.

In a democratic, divided society accommodation is the only way to build a future where people of differing traditions can peacefully co-exist. Toleration needs to be the approach when matters of tradition and heritage are expressed. While much of gaelic and nationalist culture is politicised, the unionist community does not go out of its way to be offended or obstructive. We may not identify with gaelic and nationalist culture, but we do not attempt to censure it. All we ask for is the same in return for our Protestant heritage and unionist identity.

We would especially appeal to all free-thinking people in the nationalist community to consider the parading issue carefully. Are your views based on toleration and mutual respect? Have you thought about the time it takes a parade to pass along these so-called contentious routes, and the changes which parade organisers have made? Or are your views based on bigotry and an anti-British mindset in which there is no place for those from the unionist tradition? What we celebrate through our traditional parades is civil and religious liberty for all; not just for Protestants, not just for dissenters. But civil rights for all, regardless of race, creed, denomination, or gender, and special privileges for none.

Tradition, heritage, rights: the triumvirate through which identity is paraded, or, to use the more accepted term, 'celebrated' in Northern Ireland. For the Grand Orange Lodge, the desire 'to celebrate our culture and identity peacefully and with dignity' is placed in opposition to the 'cultural apartheid' of previous restrictions and, with this, a future is posited of 'peaceful co-existence' far from the sectarian divisions of the past. This intervention into the crisis known as 'Drumcree IV' was described by the Nationalist *Irish News*[1] as 'largely predictable' but it did note that 'what was of considerable significance was the fact that the message was written in the first place'. Acknowledging the desire of the Grand Orange Lodge to find a common language in which such contentious issues could be discussed, the newspaper suggested that 'Nationalists have a duty to make an imaginative and generous response'. Such a gesture, however, was always going to be unlikely. In the early hours of the same day of the letter's publication eleven Catholic churches were destroyed or damaged in a wave of arson attacks by North Antrim Loyalists. Visiting one of the burnt-out shells in Crumlin, Co. Antrim, the British prime minister, Tony Blair, said: 'This is the past in Northern Ireland and we are trying to give people a future.' For Loyalists, the protest of Drumcree IV was understood as the inevitable response to a series of compromises and defeats. The new independent Parades Commission had ruled on 29 June that the Drumcree parade should be rerouted from the Garvaghy Road and so away from Nationalist housing estates – a decree that the Orange Order intended to defy. Alongside this and Loyalist displeasure at the Good Friday Agreement signed earlier in the year, Portadown Loyalists had other, more specific grievances. In December 1997 Billy Wright, a local Loyalist leader and terrorist, had been murdered in the Maze Prison by Republicans while in February Portadown town itself was bombed. Although the local Orange Lodge, like the Grand Orange Lodge of Ireland as a whole, was eager to dissociate itself from Loyalist violence, it found itself, as in the past, hopelessly enmeshed in the contexts of perceived and imminent betrayal.

How then can we understand the role of identity politics within such a crisis? It is tempting to see the Grand Orange Lodge's letter, in Blair's terms, as symbolically poised between the past and the future: a construction that perceives that which has been as little more than atavism, irrationality and communal hatred and suggests, in turn, a future of democracy, tolerance and a new language of cultural pluralism. Indeed, such a construction would be more convincing had not so many similarly emblematic moments been posited in Northern Ireland's past.[2] Despite this, it is still possible to agree with the assessment of the *Irish News* that the Orange Order's assumption of the language of cultural tolerance is, in itself, a progressive development: that the relativism implicit in the notion of a 'cultural identity' does at least allow for the possibility of mutual recognition. However, such an argument must also be aware of the chameleon-like nature of cultural identity, its ability to remake itself according to strategic interests. As Terry Eagleton has observed: 'One can make rational choices between forms of politics, but not for the most part between forms of cultures, so that to redefine the political in cultural terms – to call Orange marches a celebration of one's cultural heritage, for example – is to render one's politics far less vulnerable to critique.'[3]

The (false) opposition between culture and politics that Eagleton identifies here is seductively similar to the opposition of the past and the future previously identified and it has been Northern Ireland's monotonous fate since its inception to be forced to confront both of these binaries repeatedly. Moreover, it has been the curious role of 'identity', understood as both the problem and the solution, to act as the trope through which such choices have been mediated. The various annual manifestations of the Drumcree stand-off have, if nothing else, signified the limits of a government policy, codified since 1985, that has underwritten the creation of (or modified) many quasi-institutional structures[4] based on a pluralist notion of the state and it has been through a radicalised notion of tradition as diverse and performative that this agenda has gained its specific momentum. The perception of identity as reducible to a 'cultural tradition' relinquishes the idea of a homogeneous society and allows instead the celebration of a number of different (if carefully delineated) traditions. In turn the expression of these beliefs is commodified under the sign of diversity – a flexibility that allows for dissidence as well as adherence to the codes of the society itself.

Some consideration of the reasons why identity, in its persistence, can maintain such adaptability is necessary at this point. Gerry Smyth in *The Novel and the Nation*[5] identifies what he terms the '"identitarian" imperative' as a central constituent of decolonising strategies, and locates it as a response to a series of insistent questions: 'Who am I in relation to the groups and the beliefs and the political affiliations I perceive around me? Who am I in relation to the past from which I believe myself to have emerged and the future towards which I believe myself to be moving?' Understood in this way, identitarianism becomes a symptom of historical uncertainty, a lingering 'fidelity to a past structured in terms of clearly defined stories about *us* and *them*' and, in the final analysis, a 'malign influence'.[6] Similarly, although writing from a very different ideological perspective, the poet and critic Peter McDonald identifies this aspect of identity's troubled function within the political and cultural life of Northern Ireland as it is manifest in the Northern Irish identitarian text *par excellence*, *A Citizens' Inquiry: The Opsahl Report on Northern Ireland*:[7] '"Identities",' he writes, 'seem the cause of the problem; old notions of identity have been "shattered"; and yet the problem continues to be discussed as one resolvable through identity.' In these terms, identity is at once a symptom of cultural sickness and its remedy. As he further states:

> Political analysis (like actual politics) cannot take the possibilities of identity in Northern Ireland very far, since any conclusions are fated to come down to a 'new' offer of identity. As long as the problems of Northern Ireland are framed as problems of identity, solutions will always end up as identity-prescriptions of one kind or another; and these, by offering a fresh sense of identity, will not displace but tend further to entrench the identities already in place.[8]

While McDonald's response to these issues would not be mine (indeed he would be likely to see an extended analysis of identity such as this as another example of the obsession with 'identity prescription'), the symptoms he identifies are recognisably within a perception of identity as an ideological response to temporal uncertainty: identity becomes process as well as symptom, and, as such, a means of articulating a provisional political agenda. It is in this way that 'constructs of identity', as Judith Butler notes, 'serve as the points of epistemic departure from which theory emerges and politics itself is shaped',[9] while Stuart Hall's similar recognition draws attention to the contradictions implicit in this dual function:

> Cultural identities are the points of identification, the unstable points of identification or suture, which are made, within the discourses of history

and culture. Not an essence but a positioning. Hence, there is always a politics of identity, a politics of position, which has no absolute guarantee in an unproblematic, transcendental 'law of origin'.[10]

Whereas McDonald sees essentialist identities proliferating in response to perceived absences within the pre-existing identitarian formations in Northern Ireland, Hall perceives the tendency of identity to multiply and reshape itself as a function of its relationship to political and cultural hegemony. In many ways there are close similarities in these two interpretations; where they differ is in the positional critique they demand: the former seeks to escape from the tautologies of identity and find another way of representing subject position, the latter perceives such tautologies as an inevitability and therefore the most suitable point of departure for a materialist analysis. As Butler summarises: 'In other words, the "coherence" and "continuity" of "the person" are not logical or analytic features of personhood, but, rather, socially instituted and maintained norms of intelligibility.'[11]

Any analysis of Northern Irish identity politics would do well to draw both on the spirit of McDonald's frustration with the repeated investment made in identitarianism in Northern Irish social discourse and on the imperative implicit in Hall's and Butler's awareness that identity can only be viewed through the frame of competing, and often incompatible, discourses. However, as I have already noted, identitarianism is not just a determined attempt to construct difference but is an expression of difference negotiated through a framework of bourgeois ideology. While it is almost a truism to note that the narratives of competing identity formations within, for instance, nationalism are intimately tied to the progress (and, usually, eventual triumph) of the bourgeoisie, the status of this latter phenomenon has often been assumed and yet elided in accounts of identitarian struggle. This is not simply because bourgeois ideological formations are notoriously difficult to identify with any degree of confidence (although this is the case), but also because of an understandable suspicion about the seeming persistence of a social formation that has endured for such a lengthy period and taken so many different forms.[12] For this reason the assumption of a bourgeois presence as a constituent aspect within identity construction seems to run counter to the specificity demanded by such analyses. One can, however, argue that these difficulties tend to resolve each other. Bourgeois ideology remains a fleeting presence within identitarianism *because* of its ability to adapt, remake and disguise itself in ways appropriate to contingent situations.

As Maria Ossowska notes: 'The word "bourgeoisie" is used then to refer to different categories. But even when it is applied more rigorously to one category alone, this category itself can vary strikingly from one country to another. [...] The English or French petty bourgeois is not at all like his German counterpart, who amounts to a caricature. The same goes for the Norwegian bourgeois, who has a very different history behind him.'[13] In these terms, the identification of a specifically Northern Irish bourgeois ideology becomes an act of sensitive context-ualisation rather than the imposition of a theoretical template. Indeed, the degree of specificity the bourgeois can assume is such that often it can only be recognised *as* bourgeois not through signification but in the manner in which it asserts relationships between diverse ideological phenomena. In order to identify the elusive features of bourgeois ideology as it is manifest in Northern Ireland, then, it is necessary to have recourse to specific analyses of the bourgeoisie undertaken by French Marxist structuralism, since it is through these texts that this situational aspect has been most thoroughly considered.

As this suggests, Roland Barthes' assessment of the bourgeoisie as 'joint-stock company' remains highly relevant to such a project and a useful place to begin in a consideration of cultural identity and its relationship to economic power:

> Whatever the accidents, the compromises, the concessions and the political advantages, whatever the technical, economic, or even social changes which history brings us, our society is still a bourgeois society. I am not forgetting that since 1789, in France, several types of bourgeoisie have succeeded one another in power; but the same status – a certain regime of ownership, a certain order, a certain ideology – remains at a deeper level. Now a remarkable phenomenon occurs in the matter of naming this regime: as an economic fact, the bourgeoisie is *named* without any difficulty: capital-ism is openly professed. As a political fact, the bourgeoisie has some difficulty in acknowledging itself: there are no bourgeois parties in the chamber.[14]

Barthes' brief glance at the political history of post-Revolution France here insists not just on the durability of the bourgeoisie but, more crucially, on its ability to adapt itself to the various formations of capital as they succeed each other. As I have previously suggested, this plasticity is not simply the means through which the bourgeoisie maintains itself while it accumulates capital but the feature that both defines it and makes such accumulation possible. It is at this point that the bourgeoisie's relationship to cultural identity becomes important. As Barthes notes, while the economic formation of the bourgeoisie can be recognised and named as capitalism, its *political* identity is elusive. This, we might argue, is not because such identity is non-existent (for if this were so the bourgeoisie could not maintain its relationship with the economic base) but because it has the ability to empty itself of meaning while adopting and assimilating the persistent threats to its status from other economic formations. As I will discuss further, it is for this reason that the economic formations of a society and the cultural identities that make themselves manifest within it often fail to tally. Understood as such, identitarianism is nothing more than the process through which the bourgeoisie assimilates threats to its economic status. Barthes develops this argument thus:

> The bourgeoisie has obliterated its name in passing from reality to repre-
> sentation, from economic man to mental man. It comes to an agreement
> with the facts, but does not compromise about values, it makes its status
> undergo a real *ex-nominating* operation: the bourgeoisie is defined as *the
> social class which does not want to be named*. 'Bourgeois', 'petit-bourgeois',
> 'capitalism', 'proletariat' are the locus of an unceasing haemorrhage:
> meaning flows out of them until their very name becomes unnecessary.[15]

Those features of the economic landscape around which class struggle can congregate are laid waste by the depoliticising strategies of the bourgeoisie and the terrain, in turn, is populated by identities and formations whose ultimate role can only be that of further extending the dominant economic power of the class that has rendered itself invisible. Central to this act of political erasure is the concept of the nation.[16] As with the general theory of the sign as Barthes elucidates it, the nation adopts an amorphous form that can be expanded or contracted in order to include or exclude dissident elements, and it is in this way that it has the ability to minimise the disruptive effects of economic disparity. In these terms, the nation operates as the space in which conflicting class interests are negotiated or, more usually, elided under the sign of 'universality'. This totalising project extends to all aspects of everyday life or, as Barthes expresses it, 'the unwritten norms of interrelationships in a bourgeois society',[17] and it is from this aware-ness that the *Mythologies* adventure gains its exhilarating momentum. More specifically for our purposes, Barthes' insistence upon the contin-uum between 'our remarks about the weather, a murder trial, a touching wedding'[18] and the inexorable progress of the nation itself allows for a materialist critique able to operate at all levels of ideological signification and one that prefigures Benedict Anderson's similar perception about the mediation of the nation narrative in his *Imagined Communities*.[19]

The conclusion that this inevitably suggests is that identitarianism in Northern Ireland, rather than being expressive of an anomalous situation within European capitalism, can be seen as part of the homogenisation of the commodity in which sameness (the operation of spectacle as opposition) is cloaked in difference (the competing claims of the conflicting identities). As Guy Debord notes in his *Society of the Spectacle*, 'the struggle of powers constituted for the management of the same socio-economic system is disseminated as the official contradiction but is in fact part of the real unity'.[20] Debord's awareness – that difference can be presented as a manageable contradiction within a society just as long as the systematic expression of that difference adheres to criteria contained within the bourgeois state – is illuminating in that it provides a mode of analysis that can account for the manner in which seemingly dissident aspects of identity politics in Northern Ireland are, at the same instant, unable to theorise themselves beyond the parameters established by the nation-concept itself. For this reason, it is appropriate to refigure identitarianism as spectacle in that, as Debord develops his argument, 'diverse oppositions can be passed off in the spectacle as absolutely distinct forms of society (by means of any number of different criteria). But in actual fact, the truth of the uniqueness of all these specific sectors resides in the universal system that contains them.'[21] Here some care needs to be exercised. The recognition of identity in terms of spectacle seems to orientate us effortlessly towards a concentration on these elements of identitarianism in Northern Ireland that self-consciously offer themselves *as* spectacle: most obviously Loyalist and Nationalist parades and the various reclamations of territory implicit in these activities. However, while such activities can be placed within the realm of the spectacle, their full significance can only be understood if the emphasis is placed on the way such events are consumed. It is not, we might argue, the fact that parades embody difference – a critical practice that claimed as much would be vulnerable to accusations of exoticism – but rather that the consumption of, say, an Orange Order parade seems to tell us that this is *all we need to know* about the culture made manifest through it. It is the totalising aspect of the spectacle, its metonymic function, that typifies the phenomenon, as the frame of bourgeois ideology renders difference as something which can be contained, understood and assimilated. As Hall notes, identity is 'a "production" which is never complete, always in process, and always constituted within, not outside, representation'.[22] From this awareness only a short step is needed to take us to Butler's well-known formulation of (in this case, gendered) identity as 'performative', a perception that involves its own implicit critique:

> According to the understanding of identification as an enacted fantasy or incorporation [...] it is clear that coherence is desired, wished for, idealized, and that this idealization is an effect of a corporeal signification. In other words, acts, gestures, and desire produce the effect of an internal core or substance, but produce this *on the surface* of the body, through the play of signifying absences that suggest, but never reveal, the organizing principle of identity as a cause. Such acts, gestures, enactments, generally construed, are *performative* in the sense that the essence or identity that they purport to express are *fabrications* manufactured and sustained through corporeal signs and other discursive means.[23]

It is, then, in identitarianism's articulation of difference – its specific purpose – that difference is elided. However, the conclusion that this implies – that identity politics are inevitably and irreducibly foreclosed by the systematic forms of expression available – is not, in itself, necessarily a politically retrograde awareness. While the continuing and repeated expression of identity politics may constitute a ritualistic parade it is at the same time the most obvious mode through which social reformation is effected: an evolutionary procedure that corresponds to what Antonio Gramsci famously identifies as the progress of the subaltern and 'their active or passive affiliation to the dominant political formations, their attempts to influence the programmes of these formations in order to press claims of their own, and the consequences of these attempts in determining processes of decomposition, renovation or neo-formation'.[24] Such a procedure, understood in these terms, does not disturb what Barthes terms 'the amorphous universe'[25] of the bourgeois norm in that it can only gesture towards the absence of a properly realised class politics long since drained of representation.

As this suggests, there is in the continuous play of identity a perpetual negotiation of competing interests but such is the power of the spectacle to mask this negotiation through the expression of singular difference that little of this subtler tendency can be identified. Indeed the expressions of despair usually resorted to in response to identity's stubborn reliance upon difference have themselves become clichés as the critic or theorist gazes at the nature of Northern Irish society and pronounces it to be saturated with the symbols, tokens and meanings of identitarian struggle, which are irredeemably antagonistic. David Butler, speaking at a Cultural Traditions Group Symposium in 1991, illustrates well the intellectual progression such a perception impels. Noting that 'there cannot be a settlement to the dispute, in either the political or cultural terrains, because both protagonists reject the legitimacy of the other's terms of reference', he suggests:

> By the same token there can be no neutral language, verbal or visual, no uncontested images, and certainly no unifying imagery. Every signifier is spoken for. This, it seems to me, accounts for why the iconography of the Troubles is so stale and predictable. In one respect it is nobody's fault. The perpetual stand-off between Orange and Green orthodoxies not only obstructs feasibly non-sectarian formations from emerging, but it has also petrified political ideologies and cultural practices in outmoded seventeenth and nineteenth century (i.e. pre- or early modern) forms. Reliance on cliché and second-hand motifs is nearly unavoidable, marring all but the most imaginative and critically informed of representations.[26]

Written at a time when it appeared that, to put it bluntly, the violence would never end, it is possible to have some sympathy with the terms of this analysis, and yet such a reading also constitutes a form of abdication. While Butler's analysis remains locked into the 'two traditions' model of Northern Irish society, the theoretical limits he identifies within it do not prompt rereading but rather the desire for a grim recognition of the sheer nastiness of the oppositions revealed. As he notes: 'The way forward, it seems to me, lies in representing in words and pictures the contradictions as they actually are, however ugly or irreconcilable. Better for all to realise what's going on around us than to make the mistake of misrecognition, of mis-representation.'[27] In these terms such despair is also oddly comforting as it both posits cultural practice as something that *can* be recognised, excavated and explicated, and assumes, in turn, a safe critical distance between 'us' and the menacing 'what's going on' endemic everywhere else in the North.

Culture, one is tempted to comment, does not work like this. The difficulty with Butler's analysis is that, for all its desire to return to a form of year zero in its recognition of 'ugliness', it is also a mode of fantasy built upon the dream of cultural 'solution'. However, the terms of his analysis are by no means unusual. A constant, and often disabling, element of cultural theory and criticism when it turns its attention to Northern Ireland is the desire to place perceived cultural stasis in opposition to a longed-for resolution of conflict. This is an understandable reaction if one acknowledges a despair similar to Butler's but the manner in which it prevents a perception of culture as in *process*, something ultimately not reconcilable to the problem/ solution opposition, forces, in turn, a passivity on cultural practice that prevents recognition of its own dissonance, its own implicit critique. More to the point, the actual form such a solution, resolution or settlement may take is nearly always hidden somewhere off-stage. In this context, while 'resolution' clearly constitutes a rejection of the usual suspects, those 'outmoded seventeenth and nineteenth century (i.e. pre- or early modern) forms' that Butler identifies, it is more coy about its own manifestation.

Perhaps then a critique of dominant Northern Irish cultural analysis has to begin by revealing the implicit solutions longed for rather than fixing its gaze on perceptions of existing cultural sickness. To rephrase this in terms of the similarly disabling archaic/modern opposition through which Northern Ireland is also often encountered, we should ask: what might a Northern Irish 'modern' look like? An obvious answer is that it would look rather like everywhere else in Western Europe: a bourgeois society, in which identity and identity formation are not obliterated but are, rather, neutralised, purged of their psychopathic tendencies and contained within the parameters of state institutions. While this, in itself, is a dangerous fantasy, more pointedly the progression that it suggests prevents any recognition of the extent to which 'the ugly or irreconcilable' elements of current cultural practice are already securely located within bourgeois frameworks of identification and response.

Such a perception goes some way towards indicating the agonised degree of self-consciousness that can be attendant upon identitarianism, a process that involves what Seamus Deane has referred to as 'an inevitable monotony' in the 'endless search for a lost communal or even personal identity'.[28] In this context, identitarianism conducts itself knowingly, fully aware that the available positions of resistance have been previously validated by that which is opposed. This version of strategic essentialism suggests that identity politics exist as a complex series of negotiations between knowingness (or cynicism) and naïvety, or, to use Eagleton's opposition, 'irony' and 'commitment'.[29] As I have already observed, for Eagleton 'oppositional politics' are 'ineluctably parasitic on their antagonists'[30] and have to be encoded in ways that at least have the potential to reveal ultimately their inner contradictions. This, however, is also a gamble: just as identitarianism functions as part of the socio-economic structure it seemingly critiques so its articulation of difference also reorders (if not transforms) that structure in a manner advantageous to the economic and social interests unified by the identitarian spectacle. As I will argue in my analysis of recent fiction from Northern Ireland, the flexibility that this imputes to the structure of bourgeois cultural formations is not merely a coincidental phenomenon but a fundamental aspect of its peculiar longevity as it endlessly assimilates seemingly dissident elements. Such awareness accounts for the adaptability of the ritual process itself. For as Neil Jarman insists in his analysis of Northern Irish parades and visual displays, *Material Conflicts*, the flexibility of ritual is almost its defining characteristic. As he notes, 'Even when the form [of ritual] remains stable it does not imply that the meaning is static: in fact discontinuity between form and meaning may contribute to the persistence of a ritual by increasing the multivocality of the event and thereby its ambiguity, and in turn, its vitality.'[31]

It is at this point that cognisance needs to be taken of David Lloyd's call for an 'anti-identitarian' project[32] as a means of resisting the universalising claims of those 'bourgeoisified' formations within nationalism that elide class difference through the assertion of national identity. For Lloyd, such resistance must begin with the 'struggle against domination at the material level' but it also involves recognition of a 'narrative mode which refuses any single model of integration (or even of oppositional positioning)'. Such narrative modes are subversive not simply through their refusal to acknowledge the 'inauthenticity enforced upon the colonial subject' but, more crucially, in their refusal to 'substitute any authenticity in its place'. For Lloyd it is Samuel Beckett's narrative structures of non-identity that provide 'the most exhaustive dismantling we have of the logic of identity'[33] and this necessarily conscious mode of resistance is one that he returns to repeatedly through the course of *Anomalous States*, locating paradigmatic texts and cultural phenomena that reveal the contradictions implicit in 'the post-colonial moment'. While anti-identitarianism as Lloyd recognises it is similarly central to the analyses undertaken in this study, *Anomalous States* has a different focus in its concentration upon the 'oppositional positioning' that Lloyd identifies as an inherent (if paradoxical) part of the narrative progress towards integration. This is particularly appropriate to an analysis of current Northern Irish cultural formations, which invariably manifest themselves as spectacles of oppositional positioning, with the state seemingly able to maintain a relative fluidity in relation to (or in between) these politics of discontent.

For this reason it becomes possible – indeed necessary – to countenance the formation of an 'identitarian moment': the point at which economic formations are transformed into assertions of self-conscious inheritance as new alliances are formed and, to return to Gramsci, 'processes of decomposition, renovation or neo-formation' gain momentum. This identification requires a critical stance that can, in the words of Homi Bhabha, 'think beyond narratives of originary and initial subjectivities and [can] focus on those moments or processes that are produced in the articulation of cultural differences'.[34] Such a practice can be described as 'situational', not just in its refusal to begin with the assumption of sovereign subjectivity, but also in its perception of difference as a negotiated reality. As Bhabha develops this argument:

> These 'in-between' spaces provide the terrain for elaborating strategies of selfhood – singular or communal – that initiate new signs of identity, and innovative sites of collaboration, and contestation, in the act of defining the idea of society itself.
>
> It is in the emergence of these interstices – the overlap and displacement of domains of difference – that the intersubjective and collective experience of *nationness*, community interest, or cultural value are negotiated.

In these terms, the 'interstices' of identitarian moments are signified by the emergence of new self/utterance paradigms in which strategic self-interest is seen to be indivisible from both the act of being and the sense of belonging to a historically located community. Indeed, it is this indivisibility that must conceal the provisional, temporal nature of the alliances formed. The logic of integration that such a manoeuvre insists upon (bearing in mind Lloyd's awareness that such logic can encompass oppositional forms) is constitutive, in turn, of insistent narratives that demand their own integral legitimacy. A situational critique that refuses this imperative is one able to identify both the inevitable strains and fissures attendant upon the self/utterance unity and the fleeting presence of bourgeois ideology through which it is manifest.

What, then, are the implications of a critical practice that asserts and then maintains this structural model as a means of accounting for social difference? In some ways, it can be seen as open to accusations of an inevitable passivity; as a practice capable of observing the repetitious play of difference within a system but able to do little more than gloomily predict the next manifestation of an essence seemingly implicit in the social order. Indeed, if this was all that could be said about identity politics then the act of critical recognition would not simply be incidental but would also be constitutive of those meta-morphoses that it might, strategically, wish to oppose. However, identitarianism is *not* entirely contained by the structural framework as I have outlined it. While the manifestation of identity as *spectacle* is necessarily a procession of 'play', it is in the structures through which such spectacle is made possible that contradiction makes itself evident. Judith Butler's analysis of identitarianism's role within gender formation well describes the political possibilities of such a strategy through its identification of what she terms 'the foundationalist frame':

> The deconstruction of identity is not the deconstruction of politics; rather, it establishes as political the very terms through which identity is articulated. This kind of critique brings into question the foundationalist frame in which feminism as an identity politics has been articulated. The internal paradox of this foundationalism is that it presumes, fixes, and constrains the very 'subjects' that it hopes to represent and liberate.[35]

This turn towards a consideration of the frame through which identity makes itself known is, then, a necessary aspect of any identity critique wishing to do more than merely repeat the symptoms it observes. To express this in another way, if identity as spectacle is ultimately expressive of difference as sameness, so the structures through which spectacle operates can be understood as a seeming sameness ultimately constitutive of a fundamental, irreducible, difference.

Perceived in this way, identity politics, rather than being simply a reflection of the antagonist's position through the parasitism that Eagleton identifies, assert a mode of resistance through what Bhabha terms the 'almost the same, *but not quite*'[36] nature of the structural relationship. It is in this way that Bhabha's account of mimicry pivots upon 'the sign of the inappropriate'. As he notes in consideration of anti-colonising strategies:

> It is as if the very emergence of the 'colonial' is dependent for its repre-sentations upon some strategic limitation of or prohibition *within* the authoritative discourse itself. The success of colonial appropriation depends on a proliferation of inappropriate objects that ensure its strategic failure, so that mimicry is at once resemblance and menace.[37]

Leela Gandhi has usefully glossed this perception of mimicry as a 'sly [...] ambivalent mixture of deference and disobedience'[38] that appro-priates the logic of opposition only to misappropriate, to misread, and to misinterpret. Such a process is, in turn, not contained by the oppositions through which the authoritative discourse makes itself known but is fundamentally in excess of them, left unresolved within the relationship. As postcolonial literary criticism has argued in its foregrounding of formal ambivalence in the anti-colonial novel, these manoeuvres can be highly self-conscious – a mode of resistance 'sly' in its deployment, and subsequent misrecognition, of inherited authoritative literary forms. This accords with Bill Ashcroft's perception that 'excess performs the function of shouldering a space for oneself in the world'.[39] However, at the risk of tautology, it should be noted that excess is always in excess of excess itself: as Hall argues, 'meaning continues to unfold [...] beyond the arbitrary closure which makes it, at any moment, possible. It is always either over- or under-determined, either an excess or a supplement. There is always something "left over".'[40] Similarly, the monolithic nature attributed to 'authoritative discourse' in this opposition, even if perceived as containing 'strategic limitation', hardly accounts for the prevalence, persistence and, most crucially, amorphousness of bourgeois ideology as it lodges itself within discourses of opposition even at the point of their germination. For this reason it is perhaps more profitable for this argument to understand mimicry and the excess to which it gives rise as Eagleton perceives a conception of the present: 'in the alienations of its desire, in its persistent inability ever quite to coincide with itself'.[41] Excess, identified as such, cannot be a phenomenon celebrated unquestioningly but rather becomes a troubling supplement that can be as inhibiting as it can be emancipatory: a process similar to what Judith Butler identifies in her analysis of gender formation as 'the cultural emergence of those "incoherent" or "discontinuous" gendered beings who appear to be persons but who fail to conform to the gendered norms of cultural intelligibility by which persons are defined'.[42]

This reading of identitarianism ultimately finds it to be self-obsessed, less interested in asserting difference as a means of opposition than in mobilising difference as a way of addressing an irreducible absence within itself. Indeed, it not difficult to locate the many examples of identity politics in Northern Irish culture in which the implicit desire to declare for a particular affiliation inevitably reveals other resonances that trouble the binary assertions on which the declaration was originally founded. Indeed, although it is a zero-sum argument, it should be recognised that a statement or assertion of identity in itself casts doubt upon its own foundation as its call for self-recognition contradicts the self-evident premise upon which it is ideally based. From this primary moment of contradiction, identity is unable to reconcile the 'alienations of its desire'. As this study will argue, the ultimate teleological location of identitarianism from this moment onwards is that of bourgeois camp, as identitarianism's failure ever quite to connect with material self-interest leads to increasingly desperate assertions of selfhood that ultimately deconstruct the self/ utterance unity on which it is based. Camp becomes at once both the excess of previously over-determined identity formation and a constitutive part of subsequent spectacles. As this form of camp fails to know itself as such so the identitarianism from which it derives becomes dissident, not just in terms of the authoritative discourse against which it defines itself, but also in its transgression of the limits through which it seeks to make itself known.

At this stage of the argument it is tempting to assert that the only thing that can overcome identitarianism is itself; that within identity's self-perception is carried the germ of its own obsolescence, realised in its working through and ultimate exhaustion of the tropes and oppositions by which it is sustained. However, such strict teleology should be resisted. As the example of nationalism's relationship to the state it creates indicates, the energies of identity formation do not dissipate once realised in a tangible expression of citizenship but rather persist, in residual forms, within that state as a stubborn form of excess. As Deane notes:

> One of the most enduring characteristics of a postcolonial state is the presence within it of remaindered communities, formations that cannot be incorporated politically and must therefore be sustained culturally by the life-support machine of the aesthetic or the touristic, two intimately related practices. These display both the power and the failure of a system of representation that can only effect its purposes by a process of peripheralisation for those elements within the national state system that are presumed to have served their historical purpose [...].[43]

This perception is acute, although the passivity that it imputes to those 'remaindered communities' argues that such formations have passed from dynamism to silence, sustained as a guilty secret by the modernising state, which is unable to accommodate them in any other way. As Deane further notes, 'these peripheralities conceive of themselves [...] as a form of authenticity environed by inauthenticity, as an élite group environed by a mob, as history incarnated in a group that has been cast away as no longer belonging to the present'. In this way, the binary oppositions of modernity/residual, authenticity/ inauthenticity, rationality/irrationality around which Deane's narrative is based are a recognisable development of Frantz Fanon's mistrust of the postcolonial state; a formation in which epic revolutionary energies give way to bourgeois tedium:

> A bourgeoisie that provides nationalism alone as food for the masses fails in its mission and gets caught up in a whole series of mishaps. But if nationalism is not made explicit, if it is not enriched and deepened by a very rapid transformation into a consciousness of social and political needs, in other words, into humanism, it leads up a blind alley. The bourgeois leaders of under-developed countries imprison national conscious- ness in sterile formalism.[44]

Contextualised in these terms, the forces that led to the founding of national identity in the first instance have to be rechannelled, or 'enriched', in order to preserve their political relevance as a counter to the monotony of the new state's narrative. For both Deane and Fanon, the issue at stake becomes not so much one of political expediency but rather one of betrayal in that they assume that the bourgeoisie will inevitably rise to dominance from within national agitation and jettison that which is in excess of its primary purpose: the accumulation of capital.

However, while indicative of the cultural boredom that is, more properly, the object of Deane's analysis in this essay, his reading underplays the extent to which such forces continue to exert, through the very authenticity he identifies, an ethical pressure upon the state that has superseded them. This latter argument is close to, if not a duplication of, Lloyd's perception that nationalism, by virtue of its inherently disruptive energies, is ultimately unable to reconcile itself to the structures of the nation state, which it creates.[45] As a result such forces are not enclosed within the touristic and aesthetic but remain active, disruptive voices seeking redress and influencing the progress of the state by asserting an opposition reducible to that of the state against the people-nation. In this way, to reorganise the terms of Deane's initial analysis, the cultural sustenance the new state is obliged to provide impacts inevitably upon the political frameworks from which the residual is perceived to be excluded.

Deane's extension of his thesis to Northern Ireland is, in these terms, initially puzzling:

> If this is true in the Republic, it is much more harshly true of the two communities in the north, both of whom wish to speak the same language

of economic development while also adhering to different cultural languages. And both experience the same plight – of being told that their communities must surrender the archaic language of difference – because it is irrational, improvident, insusceptible to civilization – and surrender it to a more controlled and controlling language of ecumenism that will permit economic development to proceed and a sad history to be left behind as nothing more than an object of touristic pleasure.[46]

While this negotiation is rightly considered a form of 'specious combat', the perception of identity politics in Northern Ireland as roughly reducible to the fate of residual formations in the Republic implies that a new form of arrangement (if not settlement) is now identifiable. In itself such an assertion might be supportable but from Deane it is a peculiar perspective, considering the extent to which he has previously insisted on the provisional nature of the political landscape in the North as a means of giving urgency to the Field Day Theatre Company's cultural intervention. Moreover, while it is possible to identify the institutional forms that the 'controlling language of ecumenism' has taken in Deane's narrative of the South since independence, their equivalent manifestation in the North is less easily recognised. What this suggests is that the progression from archaism to modernity, or from nationalist pre-history to the bourgeois present, implicit in this particular postcolonial narrative is unable to explicate the more provisional web of loyalties and negotiations that typifies Northern Ireland. Instead, and in order to balance the equation, some account has to be made of the persistence of a bourgeois ideology that did not rise from amidst the ruins of identitarian struggle but had an existence preceding – and gave form to – such nativist energies. To reshape Lloyd's awareness of nationalism as excessive of the containing discourses of the state, it can be argued that cultural identity in Northern Ireland, even as a residual force, remains – *as it has been from the first instance* – a product of bourgeois ideology, and as such adapts to its reduced circumstances with the same flexibility it had previously exercised. In Deane's analysis such ideology is as elusive a presence as Barthes found it to be in 1960s France.

To conclude this part of the discussion, a recognition of the concept of identitarianism as providing a meaningful critique of cultural practice offers a way of understanding the various cultural alliances forged between capitalism and nationalism and an identification of the ultimate repository of such values within bourgeois cultural forms. In this, it forms a bridgehead between materialist analyses of the subject and postcolonial theory's rigorous impatience with humanism's denial of alterity. As this suggests, because an analysis of the identitarian moment must take much of its methodology from French Marxist structuralism's critique of the bourgeois state, so it can ultimately propose itself as another route from Gramsci's conception of the subaltern to postcolonial theory. Some of the dangers of such a methodology are self-evident: most importantly anti-identitarianism must resist the temptation to perceive cultural identity as a means of unifying isolated subject positions. Rather, the materialist inheritance of the anti-identitarian project insists that social and economic formations *are* existent but are not necessarily interchangeable with the cultural identities formulated within the bourgeois-nationalist project. This distinction is crucial, since the formation of these subsequent identities tends inevitably towards the revelation of bourgeois ideology as normative through its capacity to exoticise or assimilate the limited forms of oppositional politics that it enables to emerge. As one might comment when faced with the brutal opposition of bourgeois Irish Nationalism on one hand and bourgeois progressive Unionism on the other: 'what kind of a choice is that?'

2

Identity, Image and Ideology in Film

> This society which eliminates geographical distance reproduces distance internally as spectacular separation.
>
> Guy Debord[1]

Bemoaning the inability of recent films about Northern Ireland to 'advance understanding', John Hill, writing in 1988, ended his consideration of 'images of violence' in Irish cinema with the following remarks:

> This is not to suggest that there is then a 'correct' interpretation of the conflicts which films about Ireland should be supporting. What it does imply, however, is that the ability to respond intelligently to history, and the willingness to engage with economic, political and cultural complexity, would need to be considerably greater than that which cinema has so far demonstrated.[2]

This perceived absence is one that Hill's book *Cinema and Ireland* (co-written with Kevin Rockett and Luke Gibbons) returns to repeatedly. While this text is, in many ways, a key work of definition and codification, its prevailing tone is one of regret for missed opportunities and a slight fatigue with the manner in which films about Ireland, both North and South, circulate obsessively around tired oppositions and implicit prejudices. In these terms the history of Irish film-making, as *Cinema and Ireland* charts it, conforms to a more general lament often found in materialist film criticism. As Annette Michelson in her essay 'Film and the Radical Aspiration' proclaims with understandable frustration: 'The history of cinema is, like that of revolution in our time, a chronicle of hopes and expectations, aroused and suspended, tested and deceived.'[3] Hill's complaint, then, can perhaps be perceived as a symptom of what Jean-Pierre Oudart refers to as 'the utopia of a Marxist cinema': a cultural practice unrealised and possibly unrealisable but one that is 'very precious in so far as it is the only representation available to us today for imagining a cinema different from that which we criticise'.[4] As present cultural practice is unsatisfactory, so the assertion of a utopia gains ethical force as the only possible way of maintaining a critical position founded in opposition. And yet, as the unrealised nature of Oudart's project suggests, such a utopia is inevitably imagined in terms of that which already exists; both the definition and purpose of it arise from current bourgeois cultural hegemony.

The circularity of this theorising, then, is a relevant, if exasperating, place to begin in any consideration of recent representations of Northern Ireland in film. While it indicates most obviously the distance between current film practice and critical assessments of that practice – granting to Hill, Gibbons and Rockett something of the status of a government in exile awaiting the overthrow of the present corrupt order – it also renders explicit the frustrations of such a position as criticism turns in disgust from bourgeois cinema and yet is unable to posit an alternative mode of representation. As this suggests, it is important to recognise that any critique of bourgeois practices in film-making must conform to more general principles implicit in materialist critiques of bourgeois practice. Identification of the formal fragment, the moment of interpellation, is not in itself constitutive of such a critique unless it also maintains the ability to balance such analysis with a perception of the entire unfolding picture of the bourgeois world-view. As Brian Henderson notes in reference to his discussion of 'flatness' in Jean-Luc Godard's tracking shots: 'The nature of the bourgeois totality and the project of criticizing it require that it never be lost from view, or broken up into parts and aspects, but always be kept before the viewer as single and whole.'[5] This critical refusal to isolate what can be termed 'elements of significance' is essential as a means of combating bourgeois ideology's own tendency to fragment, to identify meaning in the particular or the individual and, in so doing, to render amorphous and apolitical the wider social terrain. Such an awareness is clearly apposite to a consideration of the bewilderment that Hill expresses in his survey of Northern Irish film violence. In suggesting that there is a pre-existent 'economic, political and cultural complexity' to Northern Irish society which can be apprehended as a whole and which is, in turn, travestied and simplified by cinematic representations (which are usually made from non-indigenous perspectives – or at least funded with non-indigenous capital), Hill's perception is granted a seductive coherence not least because it conclusively identifies blame. The critical position is in sympathy with the reality of life in Northern Ireland and the negotiations between various political, cultural and economic imperatives that it demands and, with this, locates the creation of stereotypes as a purely external perception. This version of base and superstructure, even accounting for its assertion of 'complexity', does not, however, address the peculiar longevity of these stereotypes, their persistence within the culture, or indeed, the manner in which they are, in turn, constitutive of the Northern Irish bourgeois totality. In short it can be argued that Irish materialist film criticism is, in itself, an unfeasible project, as its existence is predicated on the identification of fragments of the totality, missed opportunities and hopeful aspirations.

Returning to the terms of Hill's analysis more than ten years on does, however, indicate how the landscape of Northern Irish cinema has been transformed in the intervening period. While *Cinema and Ireland* was published at a time when the North was finally receiving some attention from film-makers and a specifically Northern Irish film criticism was developing as a result, during the 1990s a distinct historical turn can be recognised in cinematic representations of the North to a degree so startling that it is hard not to see the overall tendency as a mode of redress. Films such as Ken Loach's *Hidden Agenda* (1990), Jim Sheridan's *In the Name of the Father* (1994) and Terry George's *Some Mother's Son* (1996) all propose a re-examination of recent political events, while Neil Jordan's *The Crying Game* (1992), Thaddeus O'Sullivan's *Nothing Personal* (1995) and Marc Evans's *Resurrection Man* (1997), although not so tightly bound to a historical perspective, also offer themselves, at least in part, as analyses of the complexities of cultural identity. Moreover, for Brian Neve, this historicisation has been allied to a greater formal sophistication and a willingness to subvert stereotyped narratives of conflict. As he notes, 'Recent work for the cinema exhibits a degree of self-consciousness amongst film-makers about the formal concerns John Hill and other writers on the tradition of "Troubles" films have brought to prominence.'[6] However, while the importation of 'history' into Northern Irish film has provided a new audience and a sense of creative momentum, it can be argued that it has not challenged the fundamental identitarianism upon which these films are constructed. The formal sophistication that Neve identifies has been limited to a means of explicating the complexities of identity itself (such as in *The Crying*

Game or *Resurrection Man*) and, moreover, it should be noted that 'complexity' and 'history' are by no means synonymous. Perhaps for this reason it is difficult not to be sceptical about the optimism that, for Neve, this tendency engenders as he suggests that 'foregrounding the politics, or at least the sociology of violence is arguably a step towards confronting a solution'.[7] The teleological momentum of this analysis is a typical feature of many bourgeois analyses of the relationship of culture to history as it finds within the complexities of the cultural artefact a model for the complex series of negotiations necessary for a final (and presumably permanent) solution to difference. In this way Neve's ideal of 'confronting a solution' chimes with Hill's perception that cinema should 'respond intelligently to history' in that both assert a central feature of bourgeois ideology: that culture *should be of some use*.

A materialist analysis that can account for recent developments in Northern Irish cinema, take cognisance of Hill's earlier demands, but avoid the utopian circlings implicit in the 'what exists/what should exist' opposition is then required, and it is here that the critical frameworks established by Jean-Louis Comolli, Jean-Pierre Oudart and Jean Narboni in the journal *Cahiers du Cinéma*[8] remain of central significance. In a series of exhilarating essays and dialogues, the writers of *Cahiers* proposed, through fundamentally Althusserian methodology, a critique of bourgeois ideology's ability to mediate meaning and representation within capitalism as much through its silences and ellipses as through those moments when it declares itself present. As Nick Browne comments:

> Taken together, these essays undertake to demonstrate a number of interlocked and characteristic effects: transparency of image to referent, naturalisation of the truth of the protagonist – whether man or woman – by means of mythologization of narrative, whose currency is closely allied to the general system of production and social power, and the construction of spectator misunderstanding about the terms of the functioning of the film.[9]

Although the ambition of the *Cahiers* project was only half-realised, it is in these terms that its relevance continues as its ability to reconcile analyses of the image with what Henderson refers to as 'the bourgeois totality' within which the image operates gestures towards the possibility of a historical materialism able to identify the naturalising tendencies of bourgeois ideology itself. When considering recent films from and about Northern Ireland the obvious significance of this is that it provides the preconditions for an analysis that can interrogate the self-evident nature of cultural identity – the manner in which it displays itself as already pre-existent – as a specific effect of bourgeois ideology. Just as the usual role of political conflict in films about Northern Ireland has been to function as a backdrop against which issues of individual wills and ethics could be negotiated, so the fetishisation of that 'political' element has allowed for a concomitant naturalisation of identity that has often remained stubbornly beyond analysis.

Against this mythologisation, the *Cahiers* project redefined and developed the concept of 'militant cinema' as an assertion of possibility, a form of cinema that must 'rigorously and clearly place itself within the context of production and reception and [...] provide an account of its own process of meaning'.[10] Defined as such, it is possible that the kind of Northern Irish cinema called for by Hill, a cinema that would 'engage with economic, political and cultural complexity', can be envisaged as a form of militant cinema, with the condition that, for *Cahiers*, the terms of militant cinema constitute not just a critical utopianism but arise as a specific critique of the existing dominant cinematic practice. With this imperative, the militant film 'refers to the real social and economic contradictions outside the film, as pre-texts to which it refers, and seeks to place itself with reference to its historical conditions by re-marking the formative and productive processes that constitute the text'.[11] In this way militant cinema interrogates both bourgeois codes of representation and its own methods of representation, and through this self-consciousness reasserts a historical context. *Cahiers*' codification of *La Vie est à nous* as a militant film in terms of its two political discourses ('the pattern of the historical-social configuration of that moment' and the 'particularization of this general discourse in a series of exemplary scenes') is helpful at this point:

> The articulation of these two modes, which is what organizes *La Vie est à nous* as a political discourse, ensures that it both fulfils exactly the condition of all militant film – propagating a single political signified, a univocal message – but avoids an effect generally fatal to the militant film, that of being no more than the transparent enunciation of a single political signified. This is the stumbling block for all 'committed' discourse which does not think through its expository process. *La Vie est à nous* escapes this fate precisely because the articulation of the two modes provokes a complex reading of the single political signified. Instead of being merely its

énoncé, the film reflects the conditions of its *énonciation*; it poses the question, not of its meaning (which is given – single and unchangeable – at the beginning of the film), but of its 'effects of meaning' – that is, the interference of the question of the recipient of the message in the filmic process of production of meaning.[12]

In this process (which can be understood, in Browne's terms, as a 'transformation of the status of the image: from the "real" to the "apparent"'[13]) the ultimate identification of the political is seen to reside in the formal articulation of a film's political message rather than in its recognition of the political-social context itself. This means, of course, that many films that offer what *Cahiers* terms 'a univocal message' are, at the same time unable to fulfil the conditions of militant cinema – despite their espousal of 'militancy' – because of their reliance on formal transparency. Such films tend to attract *Cahiers'* most aggressive condemnation, as it is through this lack of self-reflexivity that bourgeois ideology reinscribes its presence. Deployed in these terms, the concept of militant cinema, despite the rarity of its manifestation in an individual text, provides a theoretical framework through which the 'political' or 'historical' film can be critiqued.

The following analysis does not, then, attempt to provide a comprehensive survey of Northern Irish cinema but instead seeks to account for the 'historical turn' of recent films about Northern Ireland through the frameworks established by *Cahiers*. Not the least useful aspect of *Cahiers'* methodology as revisited in this way is the possibility it offers to re-imagine what can be understood as explicit socio-sectarian 'bias' on the part of the director and producer – a factor that has disabled the theoretical momentum of some recent work in this field.[14] Instead, the significance of such 'bias' can be seen as strictly limited to little more than the construction of the univocal message. This does not mean that a film's explicit Nationalism or Unionism can be simply dismissed as bourgeois (although such a dismissal certainly has its attractions) but rather that the construction of such a univocal message rarely leads to a film addressing its 'effects of meaning'. What *is* revealed in viewing Northern Irish cinema through the *Cahiers* lens is the persistence not of stereotypical characters and situations but of the transparency of the ideology of identitarianism as the natural, preordained area of inquiry and dilemma. Lest it appear, however, that Northern Irish cinema is incapable of offering anything other than such identitarian texts, this chapter will also consider the one instance of a Northern Irish film that, I would argue, does achieve the status of 'militant cinema': Margo Harkin's *Hush-a-Bye Baby* (1989). In its emergence and disappearance, this film's presence, in itself, inevitably recontextualises and critiques the other films that constitute the tradition of representation.

In the Name of the Father (dir. Jim Sheridan, 1993)

A central component of the *Cahiers* critique of bourgeois cinema, returned to repeatedly by Comolli, Oudart and Narboni, is its revelation of what Browne refers to as the 'naturalization of the truth of the protagonist': the means by which the particular values of the central character are rendered normative and, to a large extent, unquestionable. Such naturalisation, it is at least possible to argue, has ideological uses beyond the classic interpellation of bourgeois subjects, and yet it is within the framework of such interpellation that this process has its greatest power as it is incorporated into bourgeois realism's effortless rendering of formal structure as transparent. For this reason, naturalisation has to be understood in terms of Comolli's perception of the 'logic of identity';[15] an awareness that leads to an important (if slightly tortuous) denunciation:

> A film which has not examined its place in the relations of production, the economic-cultural status of the conditions and means of its specific practice – a film, that is, which has not thought through its writing and its reading, at the same time as its production and its diffusion, *in a relation of contradiction* with the economic cultural norms of the dominant social system and its ideology – can do nothing other than reproduce both the economic norms and the cultural norms of production, and thus, in the moment of its fabrication, can only reduplicate the modes of formulation/ inculcation of the dominant ideology. So much so that even if at the level of its declared 'political message' the film believes it is not restating the themes of this ideology, it reintroduces them in masked form, the form of their greatest violence, by reintroducing the ideology's modes of formulation and inculcation.[16]

While this critique underwrites all the analyses of Northern Irish films undertaken in this chapter it is worth considering it specifically in terms of Jim Sheridan's *In the Name of the Father* if only because this film most obviously locates naturalisation within the logic of identity. Based loosely on Gerry Conlon's autobiography *Proved Innocent*,[17] the film tells the story of Gerry (Daniel Day-Lewis) and his father Giuseppe (Pete Postlethwaite) following their wrongful arrest and imprisonment for the bombing of a bar in Guildford in 1974 – the event with which the film begins. As the title suggests, it is the relationship between these two characters, rather then the miscarriage of justice itself, that dominates the film as Gerry repudiates and then ultimately embraces the values of the decent, if victimised, Giuseppe. As Julie Nugent notes, by the conclusion of the film 'the virtues [Gerry] displays are the true Christian ones: a forgiveness which is not an apology for injustice; strength and courage in the face of adversity; and, above all, a sense of compassion'.[18] In a similar manner, Neve recognises the film's necessary connection of 'Conlon's personal redemption' to his ultimate 'triumph over British oppression'.[19]

It is, however, in the reconciliation of these two narratives (the search for the father and the search for justice) that the film, to return to Comolli, 'reduplicate[s] the modes of formulation/inculcation of the dominant ideology'. While critics such as Martin McLoone[20] and Brian McIlroy[21] have identified the necessary repudiation of violence (represented by the brutal, if politically motivated, IRA leader Joe McAndrew [Don Baker]) Gerry undertakes while in prison, such a transformation is understood in terms of a shift in the film's ideological consciousness away from violent Republicanism and towards a form of constitutional Nationalism. In these terms, Gerry rejects the false father, McAndrew, and learns to embrace the humane values of his biological father, Giuseppe. Indeed, for McIlroy, this manoeuvre 'mirrors in an uncanny way the Sinn Féin doctrine of fighting with both the Armalite and the ballot-box',[22] a tactic that, as he notes, 'eventually produces results'. Such a perception is acute but it is underwritten by the assumption of intentionality on the part of Sheridan: that this is a film able to make specific choices about the form of its representation and one that chooses to locate itself at a precise position within broadly Nationalist ideology. In short, what it does not account for is the narrative imperative at work in the film and the manner in which Gerry's reconciliation is an unavoidable aspect of his naturalisation within bourgeois codes. It is in this way that the establishment of a 'univocal message' in the film is contradicted. Allied to this is the significance of what can be termed the pressure of the real: *In the Name of the Father* tells a true story, Gerry ultimately must be released and the British system of justice must be seen to continue in a familiar, if slightly chastened, form. While, in obvious ways, this may be said to limit the narrative possibilities available to Sheridan – in that Gerry's release cannot be seen as revolutionising the institution that incarcerated him – what it tends to do in actuality is deflect attention from the other similarly preordained aspects of the narrative that focus on the socialisation of Gerry as a fully individuated human agent. In other words, while Gerry has to be released, the film frames this release within a conversion narrative that ensures that the event is seen as a form of reward: a symbol of his attainment of a fully human status.

This process is encapsulated in a fifteen-minute section. Gerry is initially drawn to Joe McAndrew as a new father, an attachment that the film frames as a form of political awakening. As Gerry's voice-over comments: 'Joe explained things to me. He explained how the Brits never left anywhere without a fight. How they had to be beaten out of every country they ever occupied. How this prison was just an extension of their system.' Such sentiments develop the film's interest in exploring postcolonial analogies and are clearly juxtaposed with Giuseppe's indignant refusal to accept any help or support from McAndrew or, by extension, the IRA. While in prison, McAndrew mobilises the other prisoners (who, in their status as social outcasts, are perceived as having an identity analogous to the Irish in Britain) and masterminds a sadistic attack on prison warden Barker (John Benfield); a figure who immediately prior to the event had formed a fragile emotional link with Giuseppe. Gerry witnesses this attack with horror, tries to help Barker, and realises instinctively that McAndrew's ways cannot be his. At this point the film jumps forward and Gerry recognises that he must help Giuseppe with his letter-writing campaign. Presented as such, the 'political awakening' stage of Gerry's development is perceived not just as a form of juvenilia but also as something that must be ultimately repudiated if salvation (and, by implication, freedom) is to be achieved. In these terms, the rejection is framed within the opposition of ideology (McAndrew's teaching of Gerry) and action (the burning of Barker) and it is Gerry's refusal to see an implicit connection between the two that leads to his acceptance that only constitutional activity will have any effect.

In these ways the political ideology of *In the Name of the Father* becomes explicable. To return to Comolli, while the film clearly seeks to repudiate a dominant ideology 'at the level of its declared "political message"', the ideology is reintroduced through its 'modes of formulation and inculcation'; in other words, the narrative of Gerry's humanisation through his suffering. In this way, prison is an improving experience for Gerry; a necessary, almost unavoidable, process. As

David Lloyd has observed, 'the verisimilitude of realism resides in its capacity to make such narratives of self-formation normative'.[23] The film's adoption of *Bildungsroman* as its dominant mode therefore enables the more troubling aspects of the political contradictions Gerry faces to be evaded. While, at one level, the film proposes itself as a thorough critique of the institution of British justice, at the same time it demonstrates how that same institution is able to heal itself through the integrity and, more properly, the *determination* of the Conlons' defence lawyers. Understood as such, this restricted critique of institutional power can be seen as a function of bourgeois realist film's structural and formal limitations. As with Ken Loach's earlier *Hidden Agenda* (1990), *In the Name of the Father* suggests that there is something close to an absolute corruption in place within British state institutions and yet it withdraws from an examination of the implications of this awareness, since such an examination would destabilise the structural balance of oppositions around which the narrative of Gerry's humanisation is built. The institution ultimately must remain intact, since it is against this that the values of the Conlons and their saintly advocate Gareth Pierce (Emma Thompson) are rendered explicable. It is not, however, correct to suggest that the film is compromised by this perceived timidity. Instead such a manoeuvre is an unavoidable symptom of the film's failure to place itself, in Comolli's words, '*in a relation of contradiction* with the econo-mic cultural norms of the dominant social system and its ideology'; a failure that is ultimately nothing more than an issue of structure. Either way, the inevitability of this strategy within the film, the manner in which it must eventually be made manifest, questions the ultimate triumph it seeks to assert. The essentialising terms of Nugent's analysis of this conclusion are, therefore, morbidly appropriate: 'But the final image of the film is a positive one. As the vindicated enter into freedom – through the front entrance not the suggested back door – they symbolise a pride in being Irish, whatever formation that identity might take, which persists despite it all.'[24]

Hidden Agenda (dir. Ken Loach, 1990)

While in *Hidden Agenda* there is no ostensible attempt to project the individuation of a bourgeois subject in the manner of *In the Name of the Father*, the film's political consciousness can similarly be said to reside in its formal structure. The story of a vast conspiracy theory built around John Stalker's aborted 'Shoot to Kill' inquiry but extended to include MI5's attempts to subvert Harold Wilson's Labour administration of the 1970s, the film's plot revolves around Kerrigan (Brian Cox), an English policeman detailed to investigate the mysterious death of an American civil rights lawyer, Paul Sullivan (Brad Dourif), and Sullivan's girlfriend, Ingrid (Frances McDormand), another American civil rights activist. It is soon revealed that a team of British intelligence operatives has assassinated Sullivan because he was in possession of a tape made by a former British agent, Harris (Maurice Roeves), which contains conclusive evidence of state corruption. The plot of the film revolves around Ingrid's attempts to gain a copy of the tape and to make contact with the elusive Harris, and Kerrigan's ethical dilemma in deciding what are the proper limits of his investigation. A half-hearted alliance between the two develops but this is cut short firstly by the fact that Kerrigan is blackmailed by British intelligence (in an obvious echo of the Stalker affair) and, towards the end of the film, with the murder of Harris by British agents. The film concludes with an awareness of weakness: rather then investigate the full implications of the conspiracy, Kerrigan prepares to submit a partial report and returns to England to continue his life as a 'career policeman', while Ingrid, it is assumed, will try to publicise the revelations contained on Harris's tape but without the vital corroboration of Harris himself as a witness.

Although it can be argued that the existence of the film, in itself, is an indication of the success of this publicity (in that it is a public document), the inconclusive note of failed possibilities that the conclusion of the film strikes indicates a deeper pessimism about the potential of testimony to correct corruption. It is possible to argue that *Hidden Agenda*, a film relentless in its pursuit of narrative drive, encapsulates many of the weaknesses in the British Left's thinking about Northern Ireland during this period. Although the film's release coincided with the removal of Margaret Thatcher and the installation of John Major as prime minister, the film's narrative despairs of the possibility of overcoming the right-wing political hegemony the film details and offers instead a future consisting only of further state subversion. This political exhaustion is reflected in the film's structure. Despite the best efforts of the film's publicity to construct the text as a thriller,[25] its actual capacity to create suspense is nominal because the forces ranged against Ingrid and Kerrigan are represented as virtually invincible. For this reason, the film should more properly be viewed (in line with Loach's other work) as a docudrama, a fable that leads to knowledge but not to ideological closure.[26]

Moreover, *Hidden Agenda* well illustrates other aspects of the British Left's half-hearted intervention in Northern Ireland during this period. While the film evinces a utopian Republicanism throughout, its actual engagement with Irish politics is marginal in that it serves only as a means of introducing the film's more obvious object of inquiry, the infiltration of the British state by far-right ideologues. For this reason it is significant that Kerrigan and Ingrid, the two figures in the film who at least offer the possibility of political redress, are English and American respectively. Just as the opening of the film pays homage to the opening of Carol Reed's *Odd Man Out* (1947) in its huge sweep over the cityscape of Belfast, so Loach follows Reed in using the political structure of Northern Ireland as a means of engaging with other issues.[27] At the opening of *Hidden Agenda*, Ingrid gazes upon a passing Orange march and murmurs 'tribal rites', a perception that the rest of the film does nothing to question.

To return to Comolli's proposition, then, it can again be argued that in *Hidden Agenda* the dominant ideology's 'modes of formulation and inculcation' reassert themselves despite the fact that what Comolli refers to as the 'declared "political message"' of the film is one that constructs it as an oppositional text. Unable to reach closure within either the genre of the thriller or that of the docudrama, the inconclusiveness of the ending does not suggest a potential for action but rather indicates the totalitarian nature of the institutions it wishes to critique. In a similar manner, while the film is Republican at the level of its 'declared message', it refuses to present Irish characters as active political agents. In an incidental (and therefore revealing) scene towards the film's conclusion, Ingrid's desperate attempt to escape from Dublin with the tape while pursued by British operatives is delayed by a prevaricating, slow-witted taxi driver. The viewer's urgent empathy with Ingrid's predicament at this point impels its own unique form of anti-Irish prejudice.

Angel (dir. Neil Jordan, 1982)

While, in these terms, *Hidden Agenda* is ultimately less interested in Northern Ireland than it appears to be, the issue of contemporary films presenting the province as little more than a location of ancient hatreds and, in turn, 'using' this as a means of discussing other issues is a more complex matter than it initially appears. Although it is necessary to take cognisance of Luke Gibbons' awareness in his response to *Odd Man Out* that 'the charged political environment of a city like Belfast cannot be treated as simply an expressive foil for individual characters, however much this may lend itself to narrative cohesion',[28] as with the more general history of Irish film, a criticism of celluloid representations of Northern Ireland as one-dimensional is not, in itself, a recognition of political inadequacy. Instead, it should be recognised that, ultimately, representation is sublimated to structure in that the mode of representation employed must enable closure via the working-through of its inner dynamics. In this way the accusations of political simplicity that have been levelled at the genre are responses only to structural imperatives and it is at this level that a political critique must begin.

Such an awareness is particularly apposite when considering Neil Jordan's *Angel*, a film that deploys a strictly linear quest structure in its analysis of violence. As Danny (Stephen Rea), the film's protagonist, revenges himself on the Protestant paramilitaries responsible for the murder of a deaf mute girl, so the quest becomes both a search for the guilty parties and, more ineffably, a desire to understand why the initial act of violence was necessary. Strictly speaking, this latter aspect of the film's agenda is spurious in that the film ensures, from the initial moment of the murder onwards, that it will be impossible to understand the act as anything other than futile. For this reason, Danny's quest becomes a journey into increasing mystification as an unknowable, but seemingly remorseless, evil asserts itself as the basis for the murders that ensue. Conceived as such, the endemic violence becomes infectious, seamlessly transforming Danny from a musician to a killer, just as the territory of the conflict as a whole is charged with the symbolic rituals of retribution. As Bloom (Ray McAnally), the police chief, asserts, 'everyone's guilty'.

This strict framework of innocence/guilt provides the focus through which *Angel*'s experimentation with cinematic form should be viewed. While, in many ways, it is appropriate to see the film as an exploration of the different ways in which Northern Irish violence can be represented (an achievement described by McIlroy as 'truly remarkable'[29]), such exploration is necessarily foreclosed by its overall insistence on the necessary futility of violence as a political tool; a point repeated with increasing frequency as the ideological limits of the film's structure are revealed. Danny's quest concludes where it begins,[30] in the now burnt-out shell of the Dreamland ballroom and the final confrontation between Danny and a corrupt policeman who controls the extortion operation (and who is ultimately shot in the back by Bloom). The film, then, asserts a conditional form of closure although, as is appropriate to the thriller form with which *Angel* engages, the underlying conditions that created the specific situation are left unaffected. In this way, the film imagines the North as a political wilderness, a blank page onto which Danny and the other major characters will inscribe meaning, and so it is not for nothing that it also gestures towards the genre of the Western. *Angel* emphasises this perception in a number of ways: the opening titles are rendered in a recognisably 'Western' font while the long opening shot of the ballroom suggests a frontier town isolated in the desert. The generic expectations this initial defamiliarisation prompts are most obviously satisfied in Danny's narrative progress. While the lonely retributive quest on which he is engaged broadly takes its cues from the Western genre, more specifically, his encounter with Mary, a single woman managing an isolated farm, and the closing (highly stylised) 'duel' draw on recognisably Western thematic tropes. It can be argued that the logic behind this construction derives from the familiar perception of South Armagh as 'border' or 'bandit' country, a frontier beyond the control of stable institutions, but while the evocation of this comparative ethical landscape might appear ingenious, it ultimately serves only to (re)present the depoliticised strategies of individual will and political fatalism coherent with a humanist perception of the conflict. More pointedly, *Angel*'s assumption of a pre-existent social reality that proposes that all terrorist violence is not just wrong but also criminal (in that the terrorists are engaged in no more than an extortion racket) inevitably locates the film within the zero-sum oppositions surrounding the hunger strikes of the period immediately prior to the film's release. In this way, the film's prioritisation of the mythic over the 'historical' enmeshes the work in those very discourses that such mythologisation seeks to transcend.

Angel, then, can be apprehended in the same way that Oudart, Narboni and Comolli apprehend the work of Miklos Jancsó,[31] as an example of 'static structuralism'. Such a concept is typified by films that, in the words of Browne, demonstrate 'the play of certain formal parameters that display the mechanisms of modern productive activity but fail to account for the text's actual determinations'.[32] To put this another way, such works can articulate the fetishes of modern alienated society but cannot account for how they have come to assume their particular force in relation to history. As a result, and as Narboni insists:

> History capitalized, elevated or elided to the status of an unreasoned Cause (in which one recognises the mythic narrative, a dimension constantly present in Jancsó's films), untiringly renewing the cycle of eternal returns, locus of all discord and division, motor of the arbitrary on which it impresses its law in order to give it an order – that History passes itself off as an abstract, transcendental, universal Law, always and everywhere valid.[33]

In a similar way, the political consciousness of *Angel* can be located in the relationship it asserts between 'real' social conditions and the aestheticised version of this 'real' presented in the film. As the latter refers to the former in a purely metonymic way, so the *effects* of this construction, the recognition that this is an aesthetic artefact referring to real social conditions, create an opposition that naturalises the equally conditional 'social reality'. For this reason, a film such as *Angel* can propose itself as an exploration, or contextualisation, of a pre-existent social reality that is simultaneously rendered recognisable and sacrosanct. As all energies are expended on the aesthetic labour of the metonymic effect, the act of decoding implicit in the work, so the film's formal innovation has no other consequence than to refer the viewer back to *that which is already known*. This can be illustrated by the film's preoccupation with physical and mental disability. Just as the initial victim in the film is deaf and mute,[34] so one of the killers wears an orthopaedic shoe, the one aspect of his appearance Danny can notice from his vantage point curled up in a nearby drainage pipe. As the shoe becomes a metonym for the (literally) unbalanced killer, so the paramilitary becomes a metonym for a society that is similarly unbalanced by its emotional and social disabilities. This metonymic logic is relentless and is reinforced later in the film as Danny's band performs in a psychiatric hospital for the benefit of the patients. As Danny remarks, he is 'nuts like them'. In this way, metonymy insists on the connection between signifier and signified while the sign that emerges from this conjunction both draws attention to its aesthetic origin and disguises the forced violence of the coupling.

Cal (dir. Pat O'Connor, 1984)

A consideration of Pat O'Connor's *Cal* (1984) is useful at this point as it is a work that seeks to develop the possibilities implicit in *Angel*'s strategies of engagement while revisiting many of the themes and images of Northern Irish violence commonly found in other films from this period. Like Danny, the main character in *Angel*, Cal (John Lynch) is a sensitive young man from a small Northern Irish town implicated inevitably, if reluctantly, in violence. As a member of a local IRA cell, Cal is an accomplice to the murder of a police officer. A year later he finds his life becoming inextricably linked with that of the victim's widow, Marcella (Helen Mirren), and a brief affair ensues. His arrest following the capture of his IRA colleagues at a British Army roadblock brings the film, and (presumably) his involvement in Marcella's life, to an end. There is, then, much here that is familiar: Cal's musical talents suggest an artistic nature unsuited to the perpetration of violence in the same way that Danny cannot reconcile his saxophone and his gun, while they share a personal charisma and a tendency to brooding self-examination that gives both narratives their particular trajectory. As both films open with acts of violence, so it is the resultant search for reparation and/or redemption that conditions the length and structure of what follows. It is for this reason that *Cal*, again as with *Angel*, is so monolinear in its structure: the integrity of Cal's quest for redemption becomes indivisible from the agonised revelation of plot. However, as Cal is unable to direct his own fate in any meaningful way this revelation becomes an exercise in alienation: Cal is unable to achieve a realised individuation, unable to gain self-knowledge or indeed knowledge of the structures that oppress him. For this reason the film does not present the viewer with a narrative curve that culminates in the achievement of a full humanity (as in *In the Name of the Father* or *Some Mother's Son*) but instead achieves closure only through the mechanical resolution of the various structural oppositions implicit in the plot itself. In these terms, what passes for Cal's 'humanisation' is the expiation of his guilt, which, it is assumed, takes place after the conclusion of the film through the punishment he will receive at the hands of the British judicial system. As Cal is unable to change his situation through personal intervention so it is appropriate that responsibility for his atonement must also pass to the hands of others. As John Hill astutely observes: '*Cal* imposes a religious interpretation on the meaning of political violence ("sin") to which it then offers a religious, rather than political, solution ("redemption" through masochistic suffering).'[35]

As this suggests, there is perhaps little point in repeating the accusation that *Cal* fails to provide a coherent political or social rationale for the violence that engulfs the community depicted,[36] although it is worth noting that one of the effects of such an avoidance is that one is left with very little else that can be said. While Brian McIlroy identifies in *Cal* 'a bias against the Protestant community' and suggests, therefore, that the film is a 'Catholic narrative voice in search of a Catholic reader',[37] the speculative nature of such accusations is, in itself, indicative of a cultural practice that reduces the viewer to an enforced passivity; trapped, like Cal himself, in a downward spiral towards narrative fulfilment. Such enforced passivity can be seen as a particularly violent effect of *Cal*'s own form of static structuralism. As history in the film is read only as an 'abstract, transcendental, universal Law' so a viewing practice can do little more in response to the film than identify the working-through of its symbolic order. This process of observation is immediately established at the film's opening with the juxtaposition of extreme violence, an Irish rural landscape, and the dominance of the church, as a local preacher (Tom Hickey) nails a sign to a tree proclaiming 'the wages of sin is death'. The momentum that this creates is reinforced by a cut to Cal walking through a bloody abattoir[38] searching for his father. From this point onwards the unity of the film's political symbolic strategy is not questioned. Like Cal himself, the viewer moves from one paradigmatic sectarian moment to another and it is in this way that the film's particularly bleak vision of social despair is gradually generated.

One way of accounting for this process is to regard the world presented in *Cal* as one that is pre-existent, a world that is complete in its totality and one, therefore, that has already made itself in a series of static forms. Understood as such, the film's fetishisation of Cal's progress only draws attention to the underlying repleteness of its frame of sectarian relationships. The effect of such a process creates, in many ways, a narcissistic viewing strategy in that a 'successful' viewing of the film is one entirely dependent on the ability of the viewer to identify the significance of the various symbols of socio-sectarianism deployed through the film. A 'correct' identification of the totality of these symbolic relationships is all that constitutes the 'political' element of the film as an appreciation of formal and aesthetic coherence merges with the recognition of the self-contained sectarian symbol.

Such a technique is comforting in that it reassures the viewer that his or her knowledge of socio-sectarianism in Northern Ireland encompasses the entirety of the society itself, while, simultaneously, it invites these local signifiers to be read as a manifestation of a universal malaise.

The Long Good Friday (dir. John MacKenzie, 1979)

Reading *Cal* and *Angel* in these terms suggests that it is the purposefully self-evident nature of the sectarian image itself that inhibits the political vision of these films, and indeed it can be argued that it would not be until 1989's *Hush-a-Bye Baby* that an alternative mode of addressing political division in the North and its subsequent violence would be found. Perhaps then it is necessary to approach the issue of representation of Northern Irish violence during the 1970s and early 1980s from a slightly more oblique angle. Of all the films that featured Northern Irish violence during this period one of the most interesting in illustrating the complex web of paranoias and stereotypes implicit in British–Irish relationships barely concerns itself with political motivations, or indeed Ireland, at all. In John MacKenzie's *The Long Good Friday* (1979), Britain is represented as an entirely homogeneous, if entirely corrupt, system of capitalism. As a lawyer for an American Mafia organisation hoping to get involved in this system states: 'This country's a worse risk than Cuba was, it's a banana republic, you're a mess.' A London gangland leader, Harold Shand (Bob Hoskins), has established a 'sweet' operation of illegal and vaguely legal businesses that extend to the centre of the British establishment, implicating high-ranking policemen through a series of property deals that will, as the film predicts, entirely transform London over the next decade. In the same manner, it is upon this corruption that it is assumed Britain's inevitable gravitation towards Europe is predicated, as well as the future of Anglo-American business relationships. It is into this totalitarian system of capital, a system in which everybody seemingly has a role and which generates no surplus, that the IRA intrudes as an invincible force, ruthlessly and systematically destroying Harold's empire in revenge for a failed deal. For this reason, the IRA has a function in the film of greater significance than that of merely providing a mode of oppositional force. While the terror and mystification its intervention inspires unite existing disparate elements within British society, the film's refusal to individuate the motivations of the

IRA through characterisation prevents such fears being rationalised. For this reason the inexorable progress of the IRA is seen not just as a mode of excess on the margins of a regulated system but as an excess that is not reducible to a supplement by its own defeat. Indeed, it is the IRA that will ultimately infect and destroy the system itself. As the corrupt police officer in the pay of Harold, Parky, comments: 'If that bomb's Irish it's a different game. Those boyos don't know the rules.'

The mystery that, in these terms, surrounds the political motivation of the IRA in the film was not innovative, nor was the presentation of that organisation as an absolute (if criminalised) other to late capitalist society. However, what is more interesting about *The Long Good Friday* is the manner in which the film itself refuses to be complicit with this construction, presenting Harold's ignorance about the IRA and its aspirations as the fatal flaw that will ultimately lead to his presumed destruction as he is captured and driven away by terrorists at the culmination of the plot. Hill, in a perceptive account of the film, recognises this possibility but notes that 'insofar as the film inscribes its own distance from the IRA characters, denying us any sense of interior relation with them, so it also confirms, rather than queries, the apparent inexplicability of their actions'.[39] The point is well made but it is a charge that can be more effectively levelled at those Irish/British thrillers (most obviously *The Crying Game*) that feel obliged to articulate the IRA's motivations and yet, because of the structural limitations of the genre as I have previously identified them, can only do so fleetingly and through the tropes of individual cultural and political identity. By comparison, *The Long Good Friday*'s refusal to countenance identity politics by having no commitment to the presentation or articulation of otherness reveals more starkly the spurious nature of the oppositions by which Harold maintains his political ideology while preventing the viewer from achieving a comfortable distance from such prejudice. It is for this reason that 'Ireland' makes itself known in the film almost entirely through traces and symbols: the various bombs and bodies that are scattered across London are the most obvious manifestations of its presence and it is through this activity that Ireland shoulders a space for itself within Harold's ideal economic triangle of Britain, the United States and continental Europe. As he notes:

> Our country's not an island anymore, we are a leading European State, and I believe that this is the decade in which London will become Europe's capital having cleared away the outdated [...] and that is why Charlie and

Tony are here today, our American friends, to endorse the global nature of
this venture. Let's hear it, ladies and gentlemen, hands across the ocean.

This relationship, when seen in the light of the film's conclusion
(memorably structured around a lingering close-up of Harold's face as
he sits in the back of his own car – now commandeered by the
terrorists – and gradually becomes aware of the full significance and
irony of what has happened) bears its own powerful resonances.
Through the course of the film Harold's learning curve is steep.
Beginning with the mystified query 'what have the Irish got to do
with me?' he is soon forced to recognise that the purging, almost
puritanical, nature of the IRA's violence will brook no opposition: in
response to Harold's assertion 'I run London', Parky replies, 'Not now,
Harold, they're taking it away from you.' As Harold is the dominant
economic force in the film so he is prone to casting wistful looks back
to the residual economic Britain of Empire and stability (an interpretation reinforced by the American perception of the current state as
a banana republic). However, as the film concludes so Harold and the
values he represents will in turn be superseded not by the hoped-for
coalition of multi-national criminals, but instead by the presumed
atavism of nationalist violence. In this way, the IRA represents the
return of the repressed in Harold's economic-state nexus. While through
the course of the film Harold frequently mobilises the concept of
nation as a way of justifying and furthering his own economic
expansion, the violence that is enacted upon him serves as a reminder
of the essentialist momentum concealed within nationalism – a force
that Harold had previously suppressed to a purely strategic role in the
accumulation of capital. Read in these terms, the fact that the film's
release coincided with the first stirrings of what would become the
Thatcherite market revolution (based largely on the same fetishisation
of property that so obsesses Harold) is something more than
accidental. As in Carol Churchill's *Top Girls*,[40] a play that is concerned
with the same transformations of capital in this period, diagnosis,
prophecy and prescription interweave to create an unsettling vision of
possibilities and frustrations.

What a consideration of *The Long Good Friday* in these terms reveals
is not so much the inability of films concerned with Irish political
culture to explicate the complex motivations of, say, Republican
violence, but rather the issues surrounding why such articulation is so
often deemed necessary. By analysing a film that reduces the role of
political motivation to a pure cipher, subsequent attempts to (re)place

contextual motivations within Northern Irish film can be more clearly assessed. Moreover, despite its conspicuous lack of 'Irish' subject matter, *The Long Good Friday* was an important precursor for later Irish films in other significant ways. Both Hoskins (*The Woman Who Married Clark Gable*, Thaddeus O'Sullivan, 1985 and *The Lonely Passion of Judith Hearne*, Jack Clayton, 1987) and Helen Mirren (*Cal* and *Some Mother's Son*, Terry George, 1996), who played Harold's wife, went on to have significant presences in Irish cinema. Hoskins also played the lead male role in Jordan's *Mona Lisa* (1986), a film that pays homage to *The Long Good Friday* in its vision of a labyrinthine London, poised between residual and emergent capital, that defies the best efforts of those individuals lost within it to explicate its complex workings. In turn Jordan revisited the themes of *Mona Lisa*, particularly the triangular structure of the main relationship, for *The Crying Game* – a film that might also be said to bear other traces of *The Long Good Friday* in its perception of London as a city in which the contesting claims of fear, violence and truth can be negotiated.

Nothing Personal (dir. Thaddeus O'Sullivan, 1995) and *Resurrection Man* (dir. Marc Evans, 1997)

While the sectarian affiliation of the terrorists presented in *Angel* is, in many ways, strictly incidental to the progression of Danny's narrative, Jordan's decision to locate them within the Protestant community is significant if only because representations of Loyalist paramilitary activity remain relatively infrequent in films about Northern Ireland. However, what is remarkable about those representations that do exist is the speed with which they have codified into a series of instantly recognisable tropes and figures quite distinct from representations of Republican violence. Thaddeus O'Sullivan's *Nothing Personal*, a film of central importance in the identification of this process, revisits the terrain of *Angel* and the inexplicable nature of its violence. Set in 1975 in the aftermath of the Ulster Workers' Council strike and during the IRA cease-fire of that year, the film depicts a 24-hour period in the lives of local Loyalist leader Kenny (James Frain) and his sadistic sidekick Ginger (Ian Hart). Searching for a random Catholic they chance upon Liam (John Lynch), a childhood friend of Kenny's, who, coincidentally, is returning from the house of Kenny's estranged wife, Ann (Maria Doyle Kennedy), bearing injuries from a sectarian beating that occurred previously in the evening. Despite Kenny's assertions that he 'has no friends' and that his interrogation and torture of Liam is 'nothing personal', sentiment prevents him from allowing Ginger to kill Liam and he is returned to his home area. At this point plot and subplot are resolved. Ginger, anxious still to kill Liam, is shot in the knee by Kenny, and Liam's daughter, Kathleen (Jeni Courtney), is accidentally killed by her friend, Michael (Gareth O'Hare), as she attempts to prevent him exacting revenge for the torture of Liam by shooting Kenny. Fleeing from the scene of the horror, Kenny, Ginger and the rest of his gang are ambushed by the British Army – an event seemingly co-ordinated by Kenny's superior Leonard (Michael Gambon) – and, with the exception of naïve gang member Tommy (Ruaidhri Conroy) who escapes, they are all killed. The film ends with the funerals of Kathleen and Kenny taking place simultaneously in the same cemetery. Liam and Ann meet, embrace, and part – although a final glance and smile from Ann suggest future possibilities of tolerance.

As this summary suggests, the tragedy narrative of *Nothing Personal* owes more to melodrama than to the thriller, hence what is perceived as the specific futility of the political trajectory of Loyalism is enclosed within the inevitabilities of the melodramatic moral code: violence must be repaid, the innocent will be destroyed and evil will arise from good intentions (in this case Kenny's decision to spare Liam). For this reason, a comparison of *Nothing Personal* with Marc Evans' *Resurrection Man* is instructive. While both films reconsider 1970s Belfast Loyalist terrorism from the perspective of the late 1990s and in this take their inspiration from the activities of Lenny Murphy and his gang (the 'Shankill Butchers'[41]), the films differ markedly in their assumption of guilt. While *Nothing Personal* appears almost paranoid in its desire to assert the possibility of uncontaminated spaces (most usually the homes of Liam and Ann) and people (women and children) beyond the reach of the violence, *Resurrection Man* is more insistent in its assumption of a widespread guilt beyond the activities of the 'Resurrection Man' himself, Victor Kelly[42] (Stuart Townsend). This, however, is far from *Angel*'s bland assumption that 'everyone's guilty'. In *Nothing Personal*, as with *Angel*, it is women who reject the fetishisation of weaponry central to the men's lives and who assert values of mutual tolerance and the economic imperatives of life rather then the rituals of death. For this reason, the discovery by Gloria (Lynne James) of a gun in Tommy's pocket threatens to end their teenage love affair almost before it has begun. Similarly, children in the film are portrayed as in a state of innocence, living constantly with the threat of entanglement in the surrounding violence. Because of this segregation, the only horror that the film's major characters express at any single event comes when Michael shoots Kathleen in the film's climactic closing moments. As a result of these strict oppositions, the set-piece scenes of explicit violence depicted in the film (the assassination of a presumably innocent man by Ginger, the setting fire to a Catholic during a sectarian riot and the torture of Liam by Kenny's gang) are rendered less horrific by being counterposed to the existence of a fragile decency that ultimately allows for a tentative optimism as Protestant Ann and Catholic Liam embrace at the film's conclusion. This opposition, which is false insofar as the values of liberal decency ranged on one side are deemed to be as unquenchable as the human spirit itself, is rejected in *Resurrection Man*. Here women such as Victor Kelly's girlfriend, Heather (Geraldine O'Rawe), witness uncritically the beating and ultimate mutilation of a random Catholic victim, while Victor's mother, Dorcas (Brenda Fricker), is seen as the embodiment of a malign, if uncomprehending, Protestantism. Similarly, the home is not perceived as a protected space but becomes another location for violent abuse; the place where Ryan (James Nesbitt) beats his wife. In this context Victor's explicit murders do not function as originary acts of evil but as part of a wider conception of violence in the community, which encompasses linguistic violence, domestic violence and the ethical violence implicit in the representation of a death in a news story.

These observations, however, should not prevent a recognition of the many shared images and tropes found within these films – similarities that suggest the emergence of a coherent mythology of Loyalist violence quite distinct from representations of Republican terrorism. Indeed, far from understanding all Northern Irish violence as in some way psychopathic, the contrast insisted on between the different forms of Loyalist and Republican violence has become one of the major oppositions through which these narratives of conflict are sustained. An early essay by Seamus Deane provides a resonant summary of the assumptions that both constitute and are constitutive of this ideology:

> It is more difficult to characterise Northern Protestant populism, not because it is more, but because it is ultimately less complicated than the IRA form. For its evangelical hatred of Catholicism makes it as much a religious as a political movement. It cannot be satiated by political triumph, but must always be reiteratively gratified by the memory or the repetition of it. It is a pathological condition in that its paranoia needs enemies to

justify its existence and needs the idea of mass slaughter as something to anticipate, like a gruesome Last Judgement. But for such a group the death of the enemy is really a disappointment, for it also means the death of its own raison d'être. Witness the sadistic nature of Protestant murders. The victim, so long as he is Catholic, does not matter. They are ghastly initiation rites for the murderers into the fraternity of hatred. The IRA, on the other hand, kills with efficiency and despatch, because that is the 'style' of the professional guerilla army.[43]

Written from the perspective of 1974, a period of triumphalism for such Protestant populism and a period when the physical details of the worst excesses of sectarian violence were only dimly perceived, the theoretical bewilderment identifiable here is understandable. However, this desperate assertion of a theoretical framework capable of unifying such disparate events draws on an older perception: the sense of working-class Loyalism as essentially reactive and, by definition, reactionary. Consequently, the 'sadistic', perhaps self-mutilating, nature of Loyalist violence becomes a cry of anguish, an event without a narrative, while the 'efficiency and despatch' of IRA killings has its own momentum. This cultural opposition has become dominant in representations of violence from both parties. The invincible IRA that sweeps all before it in *The Long Good Friday* gains its particular force from the structural, rather than personal, nature of its operation, while Loyalist violence, as in *Angel*, is committed for personal gain rather than towards an overall political objective. Similarly, *Nothing Personal* revisits the terms of Deane's analysis in a striking manner. Not only are the two communities in working-class Belfast perceived as mirror images of each other – ensuring that the violence of Ginger is seen as a hatred of his own reflected image – but it is the aesthetic power of what Deane terms 'ghastly initiation rites' that enables Belfast to be portrayed as a classic noir city,[44] devoid of everyday life and populated only by those in search of what is seen as the Loyalist trinity: alcohol, sex and violence. For this reason, the predetermined moral landscape of noir chimes with the depoliticising strategies of the liberal ideology manifest in *Nothing Personal*. Janey Place's definition of the relationship of the noir city to the individual character is, in these terms, instructive:

> The dominant world view expressed in film noir is paranoid, claustrophobic, hopeless, doomed, predetermined by the past, without clear moral or personal identity. Man has been inexplicably uprooted from those values, beliefs and endeavours that offer him meaning and stability, and in

the almost exclusively urban landscape of film noir (in pointed contrast to the pastoral, idealised, remembered past) he is struggling for a foothold in a maze of right and wrong. He has no reference points, no moral base from which to confidently operate.[45]

Deane's early analysis of the fate of Loyalist terrorism takes on a noir hue through its insistence on reading it as a 'pathological condition', while the image of the urban maze is fetishised in both *Nothing Personal* and *Resurrection Man*. Here Belfast is presented as a city devoid of recognisable landmarks, a place of endless terraced streets that diverge, join and extend in a manner that defies the best efforts of the victim inhabitants (usually Catholics such as Liam in *Nothing Personal*) to find structure, direction or meaning. Searching the labyrinth, and embodying its malign presence, is of course, the Minotaur – the lone car of the Loyalist hitmen, which is possessed of an instinctive ability to navigate the physical and ethical confusion (indeed Victor in *Resurrection Man* can navigate Belfast with his eyes closed).

This shared noir inheritance leads to other fundamental similarities in the films' representation of Loyalist violence. In both works, a Catholic victim[46] is found wandering the maze and is taken by car to the place of interrogation. In both instances this is a bar, deserted in *Nothing Personal*, crowded in *Resurrection Man*. In both films this interrogation is clearly coded as an initiation rite: for the inhabitants of the bar in *Resurrection Man* it is a celebration of communal power (confirmed by Victor's cry that it is 'showtime!'), for Tommy in *Nothing Personal* it is the event that will confirm his progression from child to terrorist – a test he fails miserably. As this suggests, in these films the bar becomes the location of all that is ultimately most horrific in the Loyalist mindset, a symbol of moral squalor where fragile, alcohol-fuelled myths of community are rehearsed and where sectarian ideology is transformed into physical essence. Controlling and shaping this process is the narcissistic leader of each gang (Kenny in *Nothing Personal*, Victor in *Resurrection Man*), who does not actually take part in the physical abuse but who is responsible for identifying and confirming the religion of the victim he has ensnared. The relationship of the leader to the actual violence is, then, mediated through others, although in each instance the camera's lingering gaze on the demonic physical beauty of the leader ensures that he is seen as the ultimate source of what ensues. This slightly crude interpellation of the viewer is contextualised by the relatively less frequent use of victim point-of-view shots, although in both films the timidity of this strategy appears to gesture more towards an unwillingness to construct the victim in terms of an absolute commodification. While *Resurrection Man* travels further down this path in presenting the Catholic victim as entirely without agency, Liam, the victim in *Nothing Personal*, resists his attackers more stoutly – as befits his status as a major character in the film as a whole. Liam's sarcastic commentary on the violence and its perpetrators repeatedly attacks the supposed sexual inadequacy of the gang members and in so doing further confirms the psycho-sexual explanation for Loyalist violence that both films continually allude to:

> *Eddie*: My girlfriend said I could poke her tonight.
> *Liam*: Who hasn't poked your girlfriend?
> *[Ginger laughs]*
> *Eddie*: You for a start. She wouldn't let a Catholic near her.
> *Ginger*: She wouldn't know the difference with the lights out.
> *Liam*: Oh, she'd know the difference all right.
> *[Eddie attacks Liam, pushing him off his chair]*

Liam's insistence on the relationship of the violence he endures to the sexual inadequacy of his perpetrators is repeated through the rest of the scene, culminating in his sarcastic assumption that the gun Ginger forces into the back of his head is, in fact, Ginger's erect penis.[47] Significantly the gang members have no response to Liam's accusations other than increased violence – a failure that confirms the possible truth of Liam's assertions while reinforcing the viewer's perception that the violence enacted on Liam throughout the film is almost masochistically desired.[48] The torture scene in *Resurrection Man* similarly confuses sectarian and sexual violence, as an unnamed protagonist comments to the sub-intelligent gang member Hacksaw, 'You can come round to my place anytime. Give the wife one of them kicks.' As Victor is perceived as the point of origin for all the violence in the film (or as the film's publicity would have it, 'the source of the fear') so it is appropriate that such confusion also has its genesis in Victor's sexual ambivalence and his homoerotic Nazi fantasies, eagerly fuelled by the sinister McClure (Sean McGinley). It is in these ways that Deane's perception of Loyalism as 'pathological' gains celluloid manifestation.

It is through a consideration of these moments that the limits of the films' representation of Loyalism in the 1970s are revealed. While it is tempting to assert that their focus on Loyalism in itself goes some way towards redressing the balance of representation (and indeed, one might suggest that *any* form of consideration, no matter how one-dimensional, is at least an acknowledgment of existence), at the same time we should note that for both films, located as they are in the aftermath of the successful UWC strike of 1974, this period is perceived as representing the high point of a Loyalist political strategy that has subsequently declined. Indeed, both films suggest that there is no other aspiration within Loyalist culture during this period than to maintain the situation as it exists and it is for this reason that the major characters' only emotional and political development is towards disillusionment.[49] In this way, the internal squabbles and betrayals that typify both films' presentation of the terrorists anticipate the more widespread factionalisation of the movement that would take place during the 1980s. If nothing else, such a perception accords closely with that of Andy Tyrie, leader of the Ulster Defence Association during this period, who has noted that 'the British Government stopped taking the Loyalist community seriously after 1977 because they saw them so divided'.[50]

However, the intense focus on the *particular* futility of Loyalist violence as it is presented in these films implicitly gestures to the possibility of other forms of violence in Northern Ireland having less negative results. It is the British Army that ultimately brings Kenny's chaotic reign of terror to an end in *Nothing Personal* (just as it is the RUC that releases Danny from his revenge quest in *Angel* as Bloom kills the corrupt terrorist/policeman), while a coalition of Loyalist leaders, the IRA and the British Army conspire in the ultimate destruction of Victor Kelly in *Resurrection Man*. Importantly, this conclusion does not necessarily accord with those more general perceptions of representations of violence in Northern Irish culture that assert that British violence is persistently rendered acceptable while indigenous violence is portrayed as reactionary. Instead both films, despite their determined focus on Loyalism in the period (or what Deane terms 'Northern Protestant populism'), remain mystified by the subject under scrutiny and privilege any form of violence that has some ideological or institutional justification above it. The persistent strategy in Northern Irish film of reducing socio-economic struggle to the emotional interplay between two or three carefully defined characters is, at least in these films, not then simply an avoidance of complex abstraction but rather an acknowledgment of defeat – an assumption that there is no ideology behind Loyalism that can be reimagined in this way. Understood in these terms Loyalist politics begin and end with pathology, Victor Kelly is the cause rather than the effect and Kenny's anguished question to Ginger after yet another seemingly senseless act of violence ('Why did you do it?') can be answered in only one possible way: 'How the fuck do I know?'

Hush-a-Bye Baby (dir. Margo Harkin, 1989)

Sir, If sewage is a part of any community then the film *Hush-a-Bye Baby* is a septic tank. Apart from the low moral tone and gratuitous foul language, this infectious little film included the oddity of a Brit speaking bizarre Irish. Most people I know, when checked by the security forces, feel the reality of endurance, caution or humiliation. More important, this fulsome film seemed to condone the holocaust of abortion, while the undignified behaviour of the protagonists in making the drama, scandalised both themselves and the people who finance such scatology.

Average Punter[51]

As an antidote to what can appear the exhausted repetition of identitarian tropes and images in so many of the films discussed in this chapter it is worth considering in some detail the mode of response – and resistance – to identity politics in the North adopted by *Hush-a-Bye Baby*, a film by the Derry Film and Video Workshop. In the response of 'Average Punter' to the 1990 television broadcast of the film moral disgust is combined with Nationalist sentiment to create a dizzying explosion of furious self-righteousness. While this, in itself, is not an unusual combination, what is more noteworthy is the inability of the writer entirely to disassociate herself or himself from the film itself. To develop the implications of the opening metaphor, the 'septic tank' that is *Hush-a-Bye Baby* simply contains that which the community would rather not acknowledge, regardless of whether it is 'infectious', scandalous or merely 'undignified'. In this context, the 'sewage' responsible for the film constitutes a form of excess: it is that which is left over, that which cannot be incorporated into the discourse of (in this instance) traditional Derry Nationalism. For this reason, the film becomes both 'little' and 'fulsome': 'little' in that it is peripheral to the major narrative of oppression outlined in the letter, 'fulsome' because it is, at the same time, over-abundant, gross, somehow *too much*. The offence that the film commits is not one of fabrication but rather of presentation; the writer does not deny that 'the holocaust of abortion' takes place within the community but would prefer it to go unreported. Through its condemnation the letter articulates an intimacy with the film that is ultimately both disconcerting and yet integral to the work's significance. The energies of excess as displayed in *Hush-a-Bye Baby* are always present within a discourse yet, we can argue, always lie beyond it. More pertinently, and as 'Average Punter' seems to recognise, it is within excess that resistance begins.

To account for the significance of *Hush-a-Bye Baby* requires an acknowledgment of this intimacy, of its status within the Derry Catholic community, and of the nature of the excess it subsequently generates. Working within the paradigms of Northern Irish identitarian politics, the film locates itself at the intersection of class, nation and gender and through this both advances a conception of identity and simultaneously denies any thorough analysis of that condition. For the film's major character Goretti Friel (played by Emer McCourt), national and gendered aspects of identity, through their unrealisability as transformative forces, are seen as 'elsewhere', always somewhere other than the site of inquiry. This technique, which places questions of nation, class and gender within the interpretative frame of an individual adolescent, dramatically recontextualises both Goretti's place in the nation and her gendered identity and allows such concepts to be read as forms of excess that intrude on her own (stable) sense of self. In turn, as I have already argued, the depiction of Goretti's predicament, in itself, is excessive of the discourses within which she is trapped. In these terms the film can be seen, in part, as fulfilling *Cahiers'* criteria for militant film in that 'the pattern of the historical-social configuration of that moment' and the 'particularization of this general discourse in a series of exemplary scenes' are represented through the relation of Goretti's negotiations not only to her predicament but, through a focus on what *Cahiers* terms its 'effects of meaning',[52] to the recipient of the film. It is this latter imperative that provides the film with an explicit educational function and yet, simultaneously, entails that the film is caught in those very traps of identitarian politics it seeks to evade: a dilemma signalled by its ambiguous, almost weary, closure.

In many ways, such a description accords with the summary of the film by Rod Stoneman, one-time commissioning editor of Channel 4, who interprets *Hush-a-Bye Baby* as depicting 'some of the impossible sexual and political contradictions experienced by young people growing up in Derry'.[53] The story of Goretti, a fifteen-year-old Derry Catholic, and her friends Sinéad, Dinky and Majella, the film explores their attempts to understand their sexuality within a society of political and religious oppression. When Goretti's relationship with her boyfriend Ciaran McGuigan leads to pregnancy the constricting forces of her world close in suffocatingly around her. Relentlessly the humour and iconoclasm of the first half of the film give way to ultimate despair as the impossibility of her situation is gradually revealed. Ciaran is lifted by the British Army as part of its 'Supergrass' initiative while, across the border, the Gaeltacht of Donegal provides another unwelcome context for Goretti's suffering in its embodiment of restrictive Catholic/Gaelic Nationalism. Caught between competing ideologies, Goretti's situation is in all ways liminal: the space within a culture where violence occurs and voices go unheard.

Derry Film and Video Workshop, the company that made *Hush-a-Bye Baby*, was formed in June 1984 with the aim of creating 'an indigenous contribution to media representations of our lives'.[54] This conception of the 'indigenous' remained with the workshop through its short life and Margo Harkin, the major figure in the production, has since been explicit in her insistence that *Hush-a-Bye Baby* was made solely for an Irish audience and that any resonance it has beyond this formation is incidental to that primary aim. After gaining funding from Channel 4, the workshop produced its first work, the documentary *Mother Ireland* (1988), which was subsequently banned in the UK due to its inclusion of an interview with Mairead Farrell, an IRA volunteer shot dead by the SAS in Gibraltar. The film has yet to be broadcast. However, *Mother Ireland*'s focus on the contradictions and difficulties implicit in the relationship between gender liberation and national struggle re-emerges in *Hush-a-Bye Baby*, the company's first and only feature film. Shortly after its release Channel 4 withdrew its funding for independent workshops and the company ceased operations. However, despite its brief life and meagre output, it has remained an influential example of what can be achieved in community media within Northern Ireland.

Hush-a-Bye Baby was originally submitted to Ulster Television (UTV) who rejected it[55] – an early sign perhaps of the controversy that it would later cause – but it was eventually produced with funding from Channel 4, RTE, the Arts Council of Ireland and British Screen. As press releases indicate,[56] the film was conceived as early as 1984 and was developed through a process of drama workshops with local young people over a two-year period. Alongside this, the scriptwriters (Harkin and Stephanie English) conducted a number of anonymous interviews, mainly with women who had been through the experience of pregnancy outside marriage. It is significant that, despite the long production process, the workshop retained the film's original 1984 context as this provides the structures of feeling from which the film gains its ideological and structural momentum. In January 1984 Ann Lovett, a fifteen-year-old girl[57] from Granard in Co. Longford, was found dying under a statue of the Virgin in a remote part of the town. Having attempted to conceal her pregnancy from her friends, she died while giving birth; her baby was also found dead at the scene.[58] Only two months later, also in the Republic, the body of a baby was found in a plastic fertiliser bag washed up on the beach. It had been stabbed to death. A young single woman, Joanne Hayes, confessed to murdering her child but, in what became known as the 'Kerry Babies' case, she was eventually cleared when it was revealed that her own illegitimate baby, which had died at birth, was found buried at the bottom of her garden. In this latter instance, however, it was not simply the distressing facts of the case that provoked alarm but also the heavy-handed methods of the police and the lurid inquisitions of the media. As the details of the case became known the ordeal of Joanne Hayes proved a vivid illustration of the often covert structures of power through which women's bodies are brought within the remit of the Irish state – a process enacted not simply through legislation but through the full panoply of ideological state apparatuses.

However, while it is understandable that the film invokes what is an all-Ireland context in its analysis of Goretti's situation, more properly the film's Derry location places it centrally within the specific peculi-arities of Northern Irish abortion law – legislation that is similar but not identical to legislation in the Republic. A 1983 referendum in the Republic approved by a large majority a constitutional amendment specifically banning abortion, although this created anything but an unequivocal situation. Most notoriously, crisis point was reached in 1992 when a fourteen-year-old rape victim was prevented from travelling to England for an abortion by a High Court ruling. The ensuing public outcry threatened the status of the government itself and it took the Supreme Court of Ireland to overturn the ruling, thus permitting abortion in certain limited circumstances. While the change in public perception between 1983 and 1992 is indicative of other social transformations in what is now known as the 'New Ireland', it would be inappropriate to see the events of 1992 as any-thing other than a stopgap measure. Certainly such cases will continue to occur and the current legislation, already stretched beyond its limitations, will eventually fall apart entirely.

Abortion in the United Kingdom is permitted for social and medical reasons under the Medical Termination of Pregnancy Bill of 1967 but this was not extended to Northern Ireland, which is still covered by the Infant Life Preservation Act extended to the province in 1945. Due to a variety of amendments, this has led to an arcane situation in which abortion is permitted after 28 weeks but only when the life of the woman is threatened. Abortion at an earlier stage than 28 weeks is prohibited, although a degree of flexibility about this pertains. Since 1994 there have been five High Court judgments allowing termination before 28 weeks where there has been a proven risk to the life of the woman. As this suggests, such ambiguity in itself continues to create severe difficulties and the Standing Advisory Commission on Human Rights has stated that the abortion law in Northern Ireland is 'so uncertain that it violates the standards of international human rights law'.[59] Prior to its election victory of 1997, the Labour party accepted the case for extension of the 1967 Act to Northern Ireland, but, at the time of writing, there is no indication that it intends to act on this desire. Meanwhile it is estimated that each year seven per cent of pregnancies among Irish women (North and South) are terminated, with two thousand women travelling to Britain for abortions.[60]

Such confusion is reflected in the policy statements of the major Northern Irish political parties, which have resisted any change to the law despite three annual surveys displaying clear majorities in favour of legalising abortion when the physical or mental health of the woman is threatened or in cases of incest, rape and severe handicap.[61] In light of the issues raised in *Hush-a-Bye Baby*, the case of Sinn Féin is particularly illustrative. At the 1996 Ard-Fheis a motion was presented by the women prisoners at Maghaberry Prison arguing that 'individual women should have the right to control their own fertility and this includes having access to safe and legal abortions locally'. Speaking against the motion, it was argued that to adopt such a policy would be 'political suicide'[62] and eventually, after the longest debate at the Ard-Fheis, the motion was lost. However, it is clear that for Sinn Féin this issue is one that will continue to reappear for, as one correspondent to *An Phoblacht/Republican News* put it, 'when a conflict is unresolved, the conditions are still there for it to continue'.[63] The issue of abortion, then, is one that constitutes an excess within Republican discourses of national liberation in that it indicates precisely where the borders of individual free will are to be found. This is demonstrated in *Hush-a-Bye Baby* itself as a beleaguered Goretti is shown walking past the famous gable-end mural that pronounces 'You are now entering Free Derry'. In this way both the residual and dominant strands of Irish National- ism are implicated in an oppression that can encompass both Northern Irish Republicanism and the Nationalist sanctities of the Donegal Gaeltacht. Such matters have a wider resonance for the various Republican women's groups in Northern Ireland for, despite obvious common ground, it has tended to be the stubborn absolute of the border question that has most often led to division and disagreement between them.[64]

Despite the fact that *Hush-a-Bye Baby* is created out of these contexts, the film does not engage with the specificities of abortion law but rather ends at the point at which the dilemma faced by Ann Lovett has to be confronted. Indeed, as Luke Gibbons points out perceptively in relation to the number of recent Irish films that focus on childbirth, 'what is disturbing about many of the films is that they do not begin with birth but rather end with it'.[65] As this suggests, the narrative of *Hush-a-Bye Baby* is extremely sparse and becomes increasingly fore- closed. The narrowness of narrative possibility mirrors the narrowness of possibility within Goretti's predicament and with this the film's frame of reference inexorably closes in on Goretti and her conscious- ness. As such, she becomes enclosed within silence – the only people she feels able to communicate her situation to being the equally uncomprehending Ciaran and Dinky. The conclusion of the narrative at Christmas and the increasingly rapid flash cuts between Goretti and the Virgin Mary suggests the passivity of the Catholic icon but with the irony that it is the liminality of Goretti's position, rather than the centrality of faith, that has rendered her passive. The film concludes with a journey through one of Goretti's nightmares, possibly on Christmas Eve, from which she awakes screaming as her parents burst into the room. This connects the closing of the film to its opening – a bathroom scene in which Goretti's sister screams with mock horror when she discovers her daughter 'drowning' a doll in the bath (an event which prefigures the Seamus Heaney poem 'Limbo' that Goretti will later be seen studying at school[66]). In this way the repetitive nature of Goretti's fate is emphasised. The closure of the film at this point suggests a number of options. As her family intrudes upon the situation the claustrophobic focus of the film is widened and Goretti's predicament is placed back within the social realm. However, it is also possible to argue that this closure simply forecloses the irreconcilable ideological contradictions that the film has previously found itself trapped within. In this way the didactic element of the work identifiable at its closure – the manner in which it asks of the viewer 'What would you do now?' – is spurious insofar as the film itself has demonstrated that Goretti can make no such choice (although her previous attempt at abortion in the bath suggests a preference). Indeed what the film illustrates is the lack of alternatives open to Goretti rather than her response to the predicament, and it is in this way that the work gains narrative momentum; when Dinky asks her 'What are you going to do?' it is clear that no options suggest themselves.

Hush-a-Bye Baby's world premiere was to a packed and enthusiastic audience at the Rialto in Derry on 23 November 1989. Indeed, initial publicity in the *Derry Journal* (ironically, considering the views later expressed by some of its readers) was favourable and expectant. It then toured the European film festivals, winning awards at the Locarno Film Festival in Switzerland and the International Celtic Film festival, and was the Irish nomination for Young European Film of the Year Awards. The film's television premiere was on RTE on Thursday 20 September 1990 with a subsequent screening by Channel 4. Interestingly, the film gained the highest ratings for any film shown in that specific broadcasting slot.[67] As the film never received what can be considered a 'proper' cinematic release it is this date that can be understood as the moment of the film's reception, a moment that led to an intense and bitter (if brief) controversy.

Harkin's perception that the criticism the film received came initially from Republicans before spreading to the 'broader nationalist community'[68] is confirmed by the lively correspondence on the subject in the *Derry Journal*, and certainly it is striking that, despite the overall high profile granted to the film in this newspaper, the Unionist *Londonderry Sentinel* failed to bring it to the notice of its readers at all.[69] Indeed, some of the preoccupations of the letters page in the *Derry Journal* through 1990 prefigure the reception *Hush-a-Bye Baby* received from what was, admittedly, a tiny, if vociferous, band of regular correspondents. Prior to the film's broadcast, there was an agonised debate as to whether the (British) Comic Relief Appeal was funding abortion and contraception in Ethiopia, while more regular anger was vented towards the British tabloid press and their depiction and/or ignorance of Derry and its problems. However, by far the most common series of complaints related to RUC and British Army harassment and thus the film's inclusion of a complex encounter between Ciaran and a soldier was reserved for particular condemnation. As one correspondent insisted: 'As a 17-years-old boy, I have yet to meet the amiable Gaelic speaking British squaddies that appeared in this film. It was a farce.'[70]

The overall tone of much of the subsequent criticism *Hush-a-Bye Baby* received veered between mystification and denial and thus combined outraged Nationalist sentiment with moral condemnation in a manner reminiscent of the *Playboy* riots at the Abbey Theatre in 1907. Noting that 'the film makers had a golden opportunity to "get their message across"' (although what that message was remains uncertain), one correspondent was forced to conclude that 'the young people of Derry were presented in a manner which the British "gutter" tabloids would have been envious of'. Following this assertion it is unsurprising that the writer subsequently identified a covert Unionist agenda threaded through the work:

> Indeed the only thing I can think of that augurs in its favour is the film's recipe of blasphemy, foul language, attempted abortion and so forth. This may very well fit into the recently floated theory that the only 'Deadly Sin' left is the unwritten one – that which says 'you can do whatever you like so long as you don't oppose the British occupation of the Six Counties'.[71]

Similarly the next edition of the paper included a letter from 'Disgusted Viewer' criticising the portrayal of 'our' teenagers as 'gormless sex fiends' and wondering if the failed home abortion Goretti attempts might provide instruction for 'any young girl finding herself in the same situation'.[72]

This initial criticism prompted Derry Film and Video (which was now practically defunct anyway) to publish a clarification protecting bruised local sensibilities and insisting that the film 'is a fictional work and is not the story of any actual person or situation. Furthermore the school uniform used in the film is also a fictional one and does not belong to any school in Derry.'[73] By this point, however, the storm had been weathered and the *Derry Journal*, seemingly tiring of the controversy and generally well intentioned towards the film anyway, only published a few more vindications of the work before letting the matter rest. While these defences were mostly worthy but dull, there was the occasional entertaining intervention:

> Sir, Could I please offer my support to those criticising *Hush-a-Bye Baby*. I think they are right. There is no pre-marital sex, there is no teenager that swears, no-one in Derry has had an abortion, no-one gets alienated from their parents, every one goes to Mass on Sunday, listens to every morsel

from Bishop Daly and tops it off with a good bomb free match at the
Brandywell. And, last but not least, I visit them every Christmas,

Santa Claus.[74]

The criticism that *Hush-a-Bye Baby* received, then, was predictable
but at the same time not without valid grievance. In asserting that
Derry had previously been 'misrepresented' by 'traditional media
representations'[75] and in insisting on the value of 'indigenous' media
production, Derry Film and Video had conscientiously aligned itself
with a community that, not unreasonably, had expectations of
representation that the film had subsequently subverted. Much of the
criticism of the work was derived from a perception of the workshop
as a collective that sought to substitute (usually British) stereotypes
with the actualities of oppression. That *Hush-a-Bye Baby* ultimately
found oppression to be a more various matter reveals more about the
insubstantial nature of the company's original manifesto than it does
about the outrage the film provoked in the *Derry Journal*. In asserting
an implicit value to the indigenous and, in turn, orientating that
conception of the indigenous to mean the Catholic community of
Derry, the film was always likely to become entangled in the politics of
Partition and morality. In this, the struggle for self-definition in the
film, foregrounded through the close focus on Goretti's interior
consciousness, asserts a notional conception of the individual at odds
with a society in which the community and the family remain the
basic units. That this is one of the basic arguments of the film becomes
largely irrelevant when placed in the context of Derry Film and
Video's reluctance to interrogate the possible contradictions of its own
self-appointed role within its highly specific definition of what
community 'means'. Such considerations leave *Hush-a-Bye Baby* poised
fascinatingly between communal and individual conceptions of the
self and it is in the excess that this stance generates that the contradictions and possibilities inherent to cultural identitarian politics are
most clearly revealed through the narrative form of Goretti's progress.

The opening half of the film consists of a number of scenes located
in obviously contrasting cultural spaces. Goretti and Ciaran are the
constant figures within these contrasts and their movement through
them not only brings them together in a manner that is irresistibly
star-crossed, but also succeeds in suggesting the variety of possibilities
open to them as individuals. At the same time, while these early
juxtapositions are slightly heavy-handed, they establish the film's
resistance in terms of its identification of the key ideological and state

apparatuses that will subsequently threaten Goretti's fragile individuation. Reading the film through this Althusserian framework allows
both the complicities and the disjunctions of the various oppressions
to create a subtle weave of contexts and complicates Elizabeth Butler
Cullingford's sense that the film is merely a 'counter-hegemonic
narrative'[76] – an act of conflation that blunts the incisiveness of the
film's critique. To return to *Cahiers'* definition of militant cinema,
Goretti's and Ciaran's negotiations at this point instead constitute a
'particularization' of the general discourses with which the film is
engaged through 'a series of exemplary scenes'. It is in this way that
the univocal message of the film is brought into a relationship with
the self-conscious energies of 'the filmic process of production of
meaning'.[77]

Central to this is the interpellation of both Ciaran and Goretti as
gendered entities. Although fathers are peripheral throughout the film
(Goretti's is marginal within a matriarchal household while Ciaran's is
non-existent) and are supplanted by the role of the parish priest,
Goretti's family is dominated by women while Ciaran's is overwhelm-
ingly male. Similarly Ciaran's life is dominated by British soccer (not,
it is interesting to note, Gaelic football) while Goretti and her friends
are more motivated by dance. These initial contrasts are codified in a
scene set in a leisure centre at the beginning of the film. As Goretti,
Majella and Sinéad dance to the popular song 'Girls Just Wanna Have
Fun' (which suggests its own obvious resonances), Ciaran and his
friends play five-a-side football. While the leisure centre is a site of
modernity (and thus constitutes a contrast that will become increasingly important as the film develops), it is also a heavily segregated
space: men and women carry out their activities simultaneously but
are separated – most noticeably by a pane of glass on which one of
Ciaran's friends beats his hands as he vents his adolescent sexual
bravado. As the film cuts between the two respective changing rooms
the activity within each reflects the other: sexuality is transformed
into performance and Ciaran and Goretti ask about each other at
exactly the same time.

The scene concludes with Ciaran and Lennie discussing Goretti's
family and the fact that her uncle 'was stuffed by the Brits': the first
reference to the presence on the streets of British soldiers but one
clearly secondary to the more important matter of sexual activity.
While this location is typified by the extremes of sexual energy
displayed by all the characters (except for the devout Sinéad, played

by Sinéad O'Connor in an early role) a contrast is initially suggested between it and what follows: a rapid cut to a statue of the Virgin, which widens to reveal a classroom in which a priest discusses the sanctity of marriage with the girls and their classmates. However, this contrast is immediately subverted as the girls' predatory gaze fixes irresistibly on the priest's crotch. Through this, what will later be seen as the oppressive power of the Catholic Church is translated into another sexual opportunity, with the young priest rendered despite himself a sexual (though remote) icon. From this point onwards, locations are presented with increasing rapidity: Goretti's domestic life is revealed followed by Ciaran's, its mirror image. Here a catalyst for Ciaran's burgeoning Republican sympathies is suggested as his young brother is caught pretending to make petrol bombs using urine for petrol and a tie as the fuse. This cameo, along with Goretti's father's earlier statement that 'the place is crawling with Brits', reinforces the political subtext of the film, but this will mostly lie dormant until Ciaran's encounter with a British soldier and his subsequent arrest.

The simultaneity of Goretti's and Ciaran's activities continue through the day and conclude with a night at the disco – a segregated space, like the classroom, the home, and the leisure centre before it, where sexual desire is enacted within safe limits. In this location even Sinéad is allowed sexual agency as she is shown to be preoccupied with 'Clitoris Allsorts', a sexually brooding young man who gravitates, almost instinctively, towards the more confident Majella. This apart, the only contact between the sexes that is depicted in the film is that between Goretti and Ciaran – an encounter that ends, of course, in disaster. It is important to recognise, however, that these contrasting spaces and the distances between them are not, at this stage, presented as inherently oppressive. While it is tempting to construct an opposition between modernity and tradition that would place the leisure centre, the disco, football, sexual activity and the presence of British soldiers against the priest, the family, the Gaelic classes and the ceilidh (events that will decisively bring Ciaran and Goretti into the same orbit), in fact Goretti's easy movement from one to the other invites us to perceive her life as a dialectical unity forged through her own sense of identity. In this way Goretti is granted agency in that social forces are not given an objective status but are only depicted insofar as they have an effect upon her. Much of the film's power derives from the gradual reversal of this relationship. The early scenes of the film present the ideological and repressive state apparatuses of the society in systematic order: the family, the educational system, the church, and the military.[78] However, these forces will not become active until they begin to react with each other – a process that begins when Ciaran and Goretti are questioned by a soldier.

In this key scene, Ciaran responds to the soldier's routine enquiries with a nonsensical stream of Gaelic. While this is a piece of bravado for Goretti's benefit it is also, as Martin McLoone argues, 'an act of resistance – however incoherent, inarticulate and frustrated'.[79] However, in response to this challenge the soldier also responds in fluent Gaelic: 'Don't understand, mate. Can you repeat it, please? Well then, tell me what impact the "troubles" have had on Irish social, political and economic life.' McLoone's subsequent reading of this moment – that it represents the 'language of resistance [...] appropriated by the oppressor'[80] – considerably underplays the complexity and humour of the contradiction. As *Hush-a-Bye Baby* insists elsewhere, distinctions between oppressed and oppressor are by no means so clearly defined, and indeed the linguistic limitations of Gaelic will subsequently prove oppressive for Goretti as she searches in vain for an adequate translation of her condition. Instead, it can be argued that the soldier's transgression into a language that is presumably alien to him does not simply mark a boundary between oppression and resistance but rather suggests how the various ideological apparatuses present in the society will eventually coalesce as Goretti's own position becomes more desperate. Indeed, by the conclusion of the film all the cultural possibilities suggested in its opening are revealed to be forms of servitude. Even the sexual energy of the early encounters is circumscribed as a young woman in the same position as Goretti is denounced as a 'slut' by Majella. This sense of Goretti's dilemma as one being repeated around her is reinforced in a number of ways. Not only does the film refer directly to the Kerry Babies and the Lovett cases[81] but Goretti's sister is seen to have endured a similar ordeal. More to the point, towards the end of the film, it is reported that a baby has been abandoned in the Grotto at the Long Tower Chapel. The film then charts two contradictory movements. As Goretti becomes increasingly isolated, her predicament more specific to her own anguish, so her fate is seen as increasingly typical and one that is being repeated all around her.

It is possible, then, to see *Hush-a-Bye Baby* as a precarious text poised uneasily between conceptions of individual consciousness and social structure, old Nationalism and new Republicanism, the border question, cultural modernity and tradition, paternal and maternal structures of family, formal closure and indeterminate momentum. As each of these oppositions is self-sufficient so their intersection with other opposi- tions creates an excess that reveals the paucity of the competing discourses. It is through these moments that the film gains its extra- ordinary, if unsettling, power, for it is at such points of crisis that the repressive nature of ideological state apparatuses is starkly revealed. As a liminal figure within these negotiations, Goretti's silence articulates a deeper violence. While the film challenges the assumption that teenage girls are incapable of rational thought when confronted with a crisis pregnancy, it adds the less comforting caveat that rational thought is simultaneously not an option when one is trapped so securely within the mesh of competing, if ultimately complicit, discourses. It is in this way that the film asks far sterner questions of the relationship between gendered and national identity than Jordan's *The Crying Game* (1992), a work that, as I will discuss, is often con- sidered as undertaking the most thorough recent investigation of this intersection. In this later film, the ambiguities of sexual dissonance and its relationship to violence in Northern Ireland are reduced to an atavistic endgame enclosed within the parameters of a seamless thriller narrative. Questions of national identity, perceived monolithically as a moral dilemma concerning the use of violence, are evaded by the assertion of a conception of gender as representative of a more accept- able hybridised formation. *Hush-a-Bye Baby*, I would argue, denies such a comforting conclusion. By maintaining the creative tensions of the various cultural oppositions that afflict Goretti and acknowledging their symbiotic nature, the film forbids the possibility of such forma- tions proving redemptive. This is a bold strategy and one that inevitably imposes itself on the formal coherence of the film. However, as the careful juxtapositions of location and cultural space early in the film slowly give way to an increasing solipsism so we are able to glimpse the totalitarian nature of oppression as it becomes manifest within cultural legacies previously considered benign. In this way, as when Dinky barks at a statue of the Virgin Mary in Donegal: 'Don't you fucking move', *Hush-a-Bye Baby*'s ambiguous position articulates one of the modes that cultural resistance can take.

Conclusion: A Glance at *The Crying Game* (dir. Neil Jordan, 1992)

As I began this chapter by suggesting, one major difficulty in apprehending what remains a small number of Northern Irish films is that they appear over-extended – exhausted even – by a critical practice anxiously awaiting a more sensitive or realised cinematic practice. The critical act runs ahead of the existing corpus of texts, and laments, usually in only slightly different forms, the repeated manifestation in films of what appear to be the same simplifications and ellipses. It is in this context of assumed under-achievement that *Hush-a-Bye Baby* appeared anomalous. Indeed, a decade after its appearance it can be argued that the film has had little effect in encouraging film-makers to reimagine the perspectives that can be taken in relation to Northern Irish cultural politics. Perhaps it is for this reason that the imperative implicit in much criticism of Northern Irish film – which usually takes the form of an insistent demand for greater political and cultural explication – can often appear insatiable. This situation has arisen because of the slightly peculiar role that Irish film criticism has adopted in relation to the object of its study. While, at one level, such criticism is clearly anxious to see the emergence of an energetic – and hopefully indigenous – Northern Irish film industry and thus makes broadly encouraging noises towards that aspiration, at the same time, as I have discussed in relation to *Cinema and Ireland*, there has been a more pessimistic belief in the inherent complexity of the society usually travestied by Northern Irish films and a concomitant assumption that most (and certainly non-indigenous) celluloid perspectives on such complexity will succeed only in the creation of stereotypes. Despite the efforts of *Hush-a-Bye Baby*, then, a twofold question remains: firstly, what would a visual aesthetic capable of combining narrative development with what can be termed 'political responsibility' look like; and secondly, how could such an aesthetic, in its Northern Irish manifestation, reconcile itself to the previous traditions of film representations of Northern Ireland that, so far, have been found to be inadequate?

The one film that has been most often cited as providing a response to these issues is, of course, Neil Jordan's *The Crying Game*. The film's assertion of a matrix of gender, political identity and sexual affiliation as presented through the triangular relationship of the IRA terrorist Fergus (Stephen Rea), the black British soldier Jody (Forest Whitaker) and the black transvestite Dil (Jaye Davidson) appeared to propose a new way of thinking about the motivations and contradictions of violence in the North. For this reason the film has generated more critical activity than any other Irish film and, as such, has assumed a dominant position within the corpus that tends to distort, like a powerful magnet, the critical reception of those films that appeared before and after it. One way of recognising this dominance is in terms of *The Crying Game*'s symbiotic relationship with its secondary material. Because the film's examination of the relationship between violence, the state and gendered identity accords with contemporary preoccupations within critical discourse it has become difficult to separate the effect of the film as text from the theoretical analyses that it has generated. While it can be argued that such a comment tends towards blandness in that it may be said to be true of any work, in this instance its relevance resides in the manner in which the *totality* of the film's symbolic order has created similarly totalitarian critical responses. As an example of this it is worth noting the manner in which Harlan Kennedy's general survey of the historical significance of Irish cinema concludes with a reappraisal of Jordan's work:

> The obliquity of fable still seems the most telling and penetrating mode of discourse in modern Irish cinema. This is 'lying' as poetry, and poetry is art's best, guerrilla answer to the prose majeure of last-ditch colonial politics being played out by Britain in Ireland. *The Crying Game* – we begin and end with it – proposes a cinema about Ireland that rhymes a nation's Troubles with the troubles of all of us; that diffuses state politics into sexual and emotional politics; that explores identity and frontier not just in the map of nations but in the human psyche; that plants metaphors like landmines; and that discovers that Everything Is Not What It Seems.[82]

Read in these terms *The Crying Game* no longer 'represents' the process of national and gendered disorder but rather comes to stand in place of it, and it is for this reason that, for Kennedy, the film becomes an exemplary instance of a long-hoped-for ideal Irish cinema.[83] What has quietly collapsed in this utopian model is *Cinema and Ireland*'s distinction between the pre-existent 'economic, political and cultural complexity'[84] of Northern Irish society and its subsequent simplification in a film manifestation. Instead the unresolved contradictions of the film emerge organically from the conditions of its creation and ultimately stand as substitute for them: in planting 'metaphors like landmines', the film disrupts our complacent assumptions about our own identities just as the 'Troubles' are seen to disrupt identitarian perceptions at a national level.

Such a perspective chimes with Neve's view that the film is nothing less than 'a questioning of all our imagined communities and the identities on which they are based',[85] while for McIlroy the film's interrogation of essentialist identity formations asserts dramatically that 'all kinds of identities are fluid and equally legitimate' – a reading that entails that the IRA, 'with their theoretical underpinnings of Irish pureness (read Irish and Catholic), cannot be justified'. For this reason, as McIlroy develops his argument, '*The Crying Game* attempts to accept the barriers between and among people, and asks us to make the effort to imagine our relationships differently'.[86] This is similar to Kennedy's perception in that it finds in the film a dissolution of the formal oppositions by which Northern Irish cinema had previously sustained itself but it identifies with greater enthusiasm a kind of nihilistic liberal humanism that collapses *all* distinctions in the name of an identitarian relativism.

The most exhaustive commentary on *The Crying Game* has been provided by Patrick McGee in his book *Cinema, Theory and Political Responsibility in Contemporary Culture*,[87] a study built around, and dominated by, the analysis of this one text. For McGee, the significance of Jordan's film lies not with its communication of a univocal liberal humanist message, as in McIlroy's analysis, but rather precisely with its resistance to such coherence. *The Crying Game*, in these terms, 'is a profoundly political film not because it has a political message or expresses a political ideology but because it systematically fails to represent and resolve the historical contradiction that nevertheless negatively determines its aesthetic form'.[88] This perception of negative determination suggests that McGee's reading is in line with, but slightly more radical than, that of Lance Pettitt, who also identifies the film's 'contrariness' but sees this as a moment of *achieved* representation in that it expresses 'a moment of ideological contest between the dominant political/cultural blocs and subordinate groupings which have a specific location within an Irish context'.[89] What all these readings share is a sense of the film's transgression of previously assured oppositions; how they differ is in the extent to which they perceive the film as able, or willing, to create a new aesthetic unity out of this disparate material.

A powerfully realised statement of dissent from this orthodoxy has been provided by Joe Cleary,[90] who rejects *The Crying Game*'s mobilisation of oppositions and finds in the film's desire to transgress naturalised conceptions of identity a strategy of avoidance that prevents any consideration of the structures of power that have created such naturalising essences in the first instance. As he notes, the film 'can be considered a progressive narrative only if the interrogation of essentialist identities is considered a sufficient political end in itself'.[91] For this reason, 'the film must be considered superficial, if not reactionary, therefore, by any standard of the political that is still measured in terms of commitment to social change'. I have at this point wilfully collapsed any distinction between the film and its reception but the strident terms of Cleary's critique seem to take us, inevitably perhaps, back to *Cahiers*, and via *Cahiers*, back to *The Crying Game* itself as a discrete cultural moment. As we have seen, the film's reluctance to resolve formal and political contradictions energises critical readings ranging from the liberal humanist to the poststructuralist but, as Cleary recognises, one difficulty with such transgression is that, in itself, it can be seen as providing little more than a validation of the order that it consciously disrupts. In critiquing the fixed order through transgression of it, the power of that order has first to be acknowledged and its essential (rather than structural) force remains.

Cahiers' apprehension of this difficulty took the form of a critique of what it termed 'contemporary cinema'; a category that, in the words of Browne, 'inherits the classic Hollywood tradition, and stands in a critical relation to it'. In seeking to deconstruct the 'reality effect' of classical cinema, contemporary cinema draws attention to its own production through the moment of dramatic revelation but in so doing reinscribes another level of mystification. One common method by which contemporary cinema attempts this is through reimagining social and historical formations in terms of erotic relationships between characters. This, of course, is a trope of classical cinema but, as Browne notes, contemporary cinema 'reinscribes these narrative clichés in a mode of disclosure'. In this way, the fetishism of the transformation is recognised but the text

> reinscribes it, in a perverse mode, and thus designates the text's historical place in relation to these obsessions. The film in other words deconstructs this everyday knowledge of the cliché, by spelling it out. However, it leaves the cliché intact. The film adds nothing new as to the structural causality that governs the precise and exhaustive arrangement of formal elements – the cliché is embedded in an ideology maintained by contemporary social structures; the text acknowledges that it deconstructs without destroying.[92]

Such an awareness is well able to contextualise the seemingly confusing strategies of *The Crying Game* and its revaluation of the relationship between an IRA terrorist and a British soldier through the erotic possibilities of the mediating figure Dil. In fetishising the intense negotiations between these three characters through the precise deployment of a symbolic order, the film acknowledges a relationship to previous classic texts (in this instance Brendan Behan's *The Hostage* and Frank O'Connor's 'Guest of the Nation'[93]) and assumes a similar knowingness on the part of the viewer, whose role in the creation of the text is, therefore, one of *recognition*. The 'mode of disclosure' or the manner in which the film allows the viewer to recognise the cliché of the erotic symbol is, in this instance, Fergus's surprised discovery of Dil's penis at a point when he believes their relationship will be heterosexual. In Browne's terms, such a moment can be read as 'limited to the conscious rehearsal and criticism of bourgeois clichés'. Fergus's (and, by implication, the film's) subsequent readjustment of his experience in light of this revelation thus takes the form of a re-placing of Dil within the bourgeois conventions of a heterosexual relationship: she prepares his lunch and brings it to his work, he takes Dil for a meal, she gains revenge for Jody by killing the 'other woman' Jude (Miranda Richardson), and Fergus takes the rap for Dil's crime. The pleasure the viewer can find in this progression is based entirely on her or his recognition of its 'precise and exhaustive arrangement of formal elements' but, at the same time, the overdetermination of the conceit is constitutive of nothing more than play. As Jude exclaims in a knowingly referential moment, 'Jesus, Fergus, you're a walking cliché.'

This rehearsal of the clichés of bourgeois identity in the film is dependent on one further deployment of the attributes of contempor-ary cinema: what Browne refers to as 'the outsideness or disjuncture of its central figure to the world'. In building the narrative around three misfits – the British soldier who 'should have stayed at home', the transvestite who will 'fix on anyone that's nice to me' and, most importantly, the IRA terrorist whose kindness means that he is 'not a lot of use' – the film forces a distinction between the fantasy world they create and the real social conditions that they misunderstand. This technique, at one level, critiques classical cinema in that it attempts to draw attention to the 'apparency' of the image through forcing a disjunction between actual material circumstances and the viewer's apprehension of them. As Browne notes, 'the ideological effect produced by this conflation permits the spectator the illusion of uncovering a truth'.[94] However, as he insists:

in fact this is a strategy of masking the referent's real social determinations. Misunderstanding again hides the relation of the signifier to the subject. The impasse in such contemporary ('deficient') films, which link productive effects either to the designation of representation as sham, or to the images' artistic value as signature, is that such effects simply redouble the norms of the classical discourse. Such a writing practice simply reinscribes the same ideological effects without clarification or disclosure.[95]

It is then in the illusory revelation of truth – the recognition that, for instance, Fergus's kind nature is incompatible with terrorism – that the inverted world of the film is dependent upon the normative values it seeks to subvert. Similarly the revelation of Dil's penis prompts the awareness on the part of Fergus that Jody's sexuality in finding Dil attractive is not compatible with his status as a member of what Fergus perceives as a colonising military force. In this instance Jody's representation as a soldier is revealed to be a sham but the underlying material contradiction is evaded by the concentration on the artfulness of the conceit itself. As Dil notes at one point in relation to her own identity, such concealments are no more than 'details, baby, details'. Kennedy then is correct: in the world of *The Crying Game* 'Everything Is Not What It Seems' and yet it is the film's very investment in the supposedly disruptive power of 'seeming' itself that prevents it from finding a position outside the bourgeois codes of representation it wishes to critique.

As the central revelation scene in *The Crying Game* is indisputably the most famous moment in Northern Irish cinema it is perhaps appropriate to conclude at this point. Although this analysis has suggested that the majority of critical responses to *The Crying Game* have fundamentally overestimated the disruptive power of the film, it is possible to have sympathy with the instinct that wants to assert such significance if only because of the sense such a perception gives of a culture in progress. Similarly, an oppositional reading of the film should not concentrate on the film's silence about the material origins of Irish and British Nationalism – although the absences this creates are readily identifiable – but should recognise instead the power of the bourgeois ideology in the film to pose delusory questions about its own functioning. Neve's sense that 'Fergus does not so much escape from politics into private life as find a different kind of politics'[96] is only supportable if it is assumed that identitarianism is not the foundational frame within which *The Crying Game*'s negotiations are conducted. To come to such a conclusion is not to suggest that identitarianism is an inevitability within cultural practice in the North despite its current predominance. Instead it suggests an imperative on the part of Northern Irish film criticism to police more rigorously the extension of bourgeois presuppositions into its own practices. As Browne insists, the ultimate lesson of the *Cahiers* project is its awareness that film criticism 'must be ordered by a *politique*' in order to negotiate its way 'in a political arena where good and "proper" sense is regarded as readily accommodated by the dominant ideological venture'.[97]

3

Violence, History and Bourgeois Fiction

And now, as he watched television beside his wife-to-be (and son-to-be), Chuckie listened to a variety of people tell him that the Troubles were at an end. Peace had come at last. The war was over.

Then Chuckie lit on what he had been clumsily attempting to think: *What* war? No one he knew had been fighting.

Robert McLiam Wilson, *Eureka Street*[1]

Just as recent criticism about representations of Northern Ireland in cinema has often found itself caught between expectation and disappointment, between a weary recognition of what exists and a more optimistic awareness of the possibilities of what might be, so criticism of Northern Irish prose fiction has found itself similarly in limbo. Indeed, as with those readings of Northern Irish cinema that perceive it as a coherent object of study, the critical framework of response most commonly adhered to when considering Northern Irish fiction is one that identifies a previous surfeit of stereotypical (usually foreign) representations of the place and, as a consequence, calls for an indigenous tradition to assert itself, one capable of offering more authentic (or, as I shall discuss, 'realistic') narratives. For Eve Patten, in her survey 'Fiction in Conflict: The North's Prodigal Novelists',[2] the new novelists she identifies write against 'received images of Northern Irish society from British, Irish or American sources', while for Gerry Smyth, the kind of Northern Ireland previously imagined in the 'Troubles thriller' 'tends towards melodrama and a sort of voyeuristic violence in which stock characters and images are recycled in more or less disabling ways'.[3] In opposition to this his demands are clear: 'the novelistic imagination in Northern Ireland must surely be concerned with developing new languages and new perspectives, precisely to break out of the orthodoxies which have fed and sustained the conflict'.[4]

Whether recent fiction from Northern Ireland succeeds in meeting Smyth's strident demands is a moot point. Certainly, as this chapter will argue, the two Northern Irish novelists most often assumed to be asserting the 'new', Robert McLiam Wilson and Glenn Patterson, do so in a way that is, at best, highly sceptical about such urgency. Their writing is fascinated with – but also undeniably wary about – the assumption that the novel form can contribute to a wider dismantling of assumed sectarian polarities in Northern Irish society at large. Perhaps then it can be argued that this form of critical utopianism places excessive faith in the possibilities of what can be identified as 'indigenous knowledge' and its ability to sweep away what Smyth calls the 'stock character', what Patten terms 'sterile images',[5] and what Eamonn Hughes has referred to as 'the impasse of a closed form failing to gain a purchase on an apparently static but unresolved society'.[6] It is important to recognise that 'apparently' is the crucial qualification in this judgment. Hughes, like Smyth and Patten after him, asserts repeatedly the fact that the North is not, in his phrase, merely 'a tightly-enclosed province bounded by outworn loyalties and obscure allegiances',[7] but is, rather, 'a modern place with the pluralities, discontents, and linkages appropriate to a modern place'.[8] In these terms, much of Northern fiction becomes not a representation of social reality, but instead a formal mystification of a false representation of an underlying complexity.

Patten's engagement with the emergence of the 'new' in Northern Irish fiction presupposes a similar model and demands 'the overdue exploitation of literary strategies such as perspectivism, ambiguity and displacement which, though categorically postmodern, may also be perceived as attributes of a sustained constitutional and psychological identity crisis germane to any representations of a contemporary Northern Irish self-image'.[9] While this critique, in a manner similar to Smyth's and Hughes' analyses, relates fictional representation to social practice, it also asserts – through the assumptions implicit in the word 'overdue' – the presence of other normative developments in fiction alongside which Northern Irish writing appears anomalous. In this way, the malaise that afflicts Northern Irish fiction is understood as a dissociation of sensibility. As Northern Irish fiction has failed in its task to represent, as Hughes expresses it, 'what is, rather than what ought to be',[10] so it is perceived (again as with cinematic images of the North) as a form that lacks any organic connection with the under-lying elements of the cultural and social conflict – an embarrassing aberration revealed even more clearly if it is compared to what Patten identifies as 'poetry's monopoly on literary/political exchange in a series of landmark volumes'.[11] Understood in these terms, it is not that the supposed insularity of Northern Ireland has prevented the deployment of non-indigenous literary strategies (after all, the two forms most commonly associated with Northern Irish fiction, the thriller and the 'love across the barricades' romance, both have their roots elsewhere) but rather that those forms that have taken root in the North have proved so inappropriate. Where the ironies of postmodern perspectivism are desired, all that the bookshop can provide is Troubles trash.[12]

It can be seen, therefore, that for Patten, Smyth and Hughes the dominant tradition of Northern Irish fiction has failed to establish an adequate representation of Northern Irish society specifically because of its reluctance to engage with formal and aesthetic complexity and because of its concomitant reliance on a monolithic perception of the conflict. However, while Patten's careful analysis is ultimately reluctant to endorse the emergence of a 'regional voice' within a society that 'already relies too heavily on fixed perceptions and definitions',[13] another critical school is more definite in its demands. Bill Rolston's 'Escaping from Belfast: Class, Ideology and Literature in Northern Ireland' proposes itself as an anti-bourgeois critique of recent Belfast fiction and in this asserts the need for a working-class literature to emerge (or perhaps to be more fully recognised as 'literature'). As this suggests, underwriting *this* form of aspirational criticism is the assumption that bourgeois ideology is solely the product of (and confined to) middle-class society and that it is, for this reason, incapable of offering a 'realistic portrayal'[14] of working-class life in the North. The limitations of this opposition, and the failure it assumes on the part of middle-class writers to capture 'reality more truthfully',[15] lead in turn to critical assessments that blur distinctions between an actual social formation and its subsequent representation. As Rolston notes: 'The bourgeois novelists do not allow their working-class characters to speak for themselves. Were they to speak for themselves they would reveal many of the exact opposite characteristics from the bourgeois mannequins portrayed in the novels.'[16]

As one of the few analyses of Northern Irish culture to perceive bourgeois ideology as a significant factor, Rolston's argument is important and yet, despite this, more can be learnt from its theoretical limitations than from its moments of insight. Just as his analysis is underwritten by a certainty about the nature of working-class experience, so the strategies of bourgeois interpellation are deemed equally transparent. Moreover, in locating bourgeois ideology so securely within middle-class consciousness, the bourgeois project – which can be summarised as rendering normative middle-class values of non-engagement with sectarian and political formations – is always doomed to failure in that its inherent inappropriateness to working-class experience will always and necessarily be revealed. As Rolston notes, bourgeois novels 'are constantly and avidly read by Belfast working-class teenagers. Until these teenagers have literature of their own class to read (and, given the first point made here, that day is still a long way off), they are going to suffer the disjunction of being taught through the bourgeois novels about a world which does not correspond with the real world around them.'[17] This is an optimistic conclusion posing as pessimism: while middle-class values are being inculcated into working-class experience, the disjunction this is built upon will ultimately be recognised by the teenagers just as surely as Rolston too has recognised it. In this way bourgeois ideology is identified, its strategies laid bare, and its effects safely circumscribed. In these terms what Rolston's analysis cannot contemplate is any suggestion that bourgeois ideology does not just (mis)represent social conditions but rather establishes the framework through which the reality/representation opposition to which he subscribes is made possible. For this reason, the only weapon that can be deployed against bourgeois ideology's polite fictions is the non-negotiable, always objective, 'reality'. As Rolston notes: 'In the present real world there is anti-imperialist struggle, loyalism, emergency legislation, assassination, rioting, intimidation, and so on. This is the real world of Belfast teenagers, not the sterile, idealistic "world" portrayed in the bourgeois novels.'[18]

Rolston's critique is thus similar to the analyses of Patten, Smyth and Hughes in its utopian drive, its perception that the North has been badly served by an existing prose tradition, but it differs in that it prophesies the emergence of a literature of commitment rather than desiring a greater degree of formal complexity. Ronan Bennett, himself perhaps a novelist of the kind desired by Rolston's analysis, shares with Rolston a suspicion about the role of the middle class in impoverishing indigenous Northern Irish art:

> On the rare occasions the conflict penetrates the arts, its treatment tends to be apolitical, disengaged, sceptical. There is a striking paradox at work: most of the artists and writers who have explored the strongly held

political loyalties underpinning the Troubles have attempted to do so by disavowing strong political views of their own. The mainstream artistic mediators of the conflict have tended to opt, like the middle class audience they serve, for an apolitical vision. The work is marked by aloofness, by being above it all, by self-conscious distance from the two proletarian tribes fighting out their bloody, pointless, atavistic war.[19]

The oppositions that structure Bennett's argument here revisit the terms of Rolston's analysis in a markedly similar manner. Again middle-class consciousness is seen as a form of illusion imposing a false template on the reality of working-class political engagement and, as with Rolston's essay, Bennett's argument ultimately deploys what are considered the non-negotiable realities of political violence as a means of repudiating such myth-making. As he argues, Northern Irish writers 'did not speak when RUC men invaded the Bogside and beat to death a defenceless semi-invalid. They did not speak when Bogsiders rose up to defend their homes and their families.'[20] Despite the rhetorical momentum of Bennett's argument at this point, the difficulty with this assertion can just be glimpsed: Northern Irish writers *did* speak but, unfortunately, they did not say what Bennett wanted to hear.

This is not a glib point. While, in many ways it is difficult not to be sympathetic to Rolston's and Bennett's demands that Northern Irish writers should examine what Bennett terms their 'complacent conventions about the conflict',[21] such demands can only be effective if the criticism that makes these assertions is equally stringent in interrogating its own complacencies. This is of particular relevance when the cause of the malaise is, as in this case, attributed to bourgeois ideology. A materialist criticism that adopts such a magisterial tone, that is convinced of its own ability to identify what is understood as the creeping spread of bourgeois thinking while being assured of its own ability to remain uninfected, risks the danger of considerably under-playing the extent to which bourgeois ideology has, *in the first instance*, established the framework of engagement through which these demands can be made. This is recognisable in these instances through Rolston's and Bennett's reliance on an opposition between reality and artistic representation which assumes that it is the role of representation to comment *upon* this reality and that, similarly, representation is ultimately incapable of shifting the terms and apprehension of such reality. Because of this rigidity, the definition of what can be termed the 'political' is strictly circumscribed. It is forced into a series of unhelpful oppositions (politics/literature, politics/liberalism, politics/

middle-class disengagement) which entail that it becomes little more than a cipher for direct intervention, and in this way one of the key elements of bourgeois ideology, the assertion of the possibility of an apolitical space, is reinforced. That this adherence to binary thinking, particularly in the case of Bennett's analysis, leads to a casual sectarianism is a predictable symptom of this limitation rather than a significant factor in its own right.[22]

These inherent difficulties should not lead to the assumption that a criticism of Northern Irish fiction based upon an analysis of bourgeois ideology is an unfeasible project. Rather, such a criticism must conduct itself with a certain introspection, aware of the risks attendant on the notional act of making an 'intervention' and sensitive to the different manifestations such an ideology takes in different histories and different cultures. For the purposes of this analysis the characteristics of the bourgeois text can be sketched (albeit tentatively) by reference to Roland Barthes' codification of 'the general prospect of [the] *pseudophysis* which defines the dream of the contemporary bourgeois world'.[23] In this brilliant critique Barthes lists seven characteristics of perception through which bourgeois consciousness reconciles itself to material circumstances. While the general tendency of these characteristics indicates the typical bourgeois reliance on common sense, identity and experience as parameters of reason, as I will argue (and as Barthes recognises), the amorphous, essentially reactive, nature of the bourgeois text entails that its shape changes in order to encounter and/or assimilate disparate material – a process defined by Barthes as 'identification'. To perceive the bourgeois formation as a static or transhistorical phenomenon might well be said (paradoxically) to be, in itself, an example of bourgeois mystification.

One way of accounting for what I have termed the 'utopian' tendency in criticism of Northern Irish fiction and film is that such a strategy makes possible the act of criticism itself. It creates the terms of its engagement through its assumption of a pre-existent, if unsatisfactory, body of texts, and through the rhetorical momentum implicit in the act of rejecting this corpus can call for the dissolution of the old order while promising the ultimate emergence of new forms. This act of partition – readily identifiable in the critical frameworks of Rolston and Bennett but also present in Patten's and Smyth's – is obviously vulnerable to an accusation that it divides formal and historical continuities into formal epochs but, more seriously, it can also be understood as a form of criticism that seeks to place itself beyond history in its desire to occupy a space from which this division can be observed. An alternative mode of critical engagement – and one that this chapter will attempt – is one that resists the temptation to signal the obsolescence of certain fictional responses to Northern Irish society and seeks instead to observe the working-through of the formal internal contradictions of these responses and the manner in which this suggests an alternative implicit critique. As I have noted else-where, bourgeois ideology is, at best, a fleeting presence; it does not make itself known simply as a middle-class confidence trick (for if it did it would be singularly ineffective), but rather can be glimpsed through the ellipses, disjunctions and silences of an individual text's progression towards closure and the manner in which it makes itself amenable (or resistant) to theory. What follows is a discussion of a number of recent Northern Irish novels that, in differing ways, illustrate this awareness.

A Wreath Upon the Dead (Briege Duffaud, 1993)

By placing Rolston's and Bennett's demands for a more ideologically committed Northern fiction alongside Patten's and Smyth's awareness of the need for 'new' languages and forms to emerge capable of reimagining the orthodoxies of the conflict in terms of aesthetic models established elsewhere, it can be appreciated to what extent recent Northern Irish fiction has had to negotiate its way between the assump-tions of 'normative' and indigenous formal traditions. Briege Duffaud's agonised Northern Irish *Bildungsroman, A Wreath Upon the Dead*,[24] is an interesting text to consider in these terms in that it attempts to make a transition from what Terry Eagleton terms the 'typically recursive and diffuse'[25] strategies of Irish fiction to a bourgeois narrative realism he associates with the English tradition. The deployment of such an opposition is, of course, fraught with critical difficulties, not the least of which is that it risks the re-assertion of the fantasy identified by Smyth as 'the post-colonial fairy-tale which tells of the Big Bad Wolf of English realism versus the playful, subversive, anti-realist nature of Irish story-telling'.[26] Indeed as Eagleton himself warns: 'There is no assured metropolitan norm from which Irish literary culture is a systematic deviation.'[27] However, the terms of Eagleton's opposition remain useful in this instance in that they highlight the manner in which Duffaud's novel self-consciously mobilises these two formal traditions, and the two worlds of South Armagh and London they depict, as a means of proposing an ineluctable *national* difference: the irremovable dash that exists between 'Anglo' and 'Irish'. Ostensibly the story of two women from the small Armagh town of Claghan – Maureen Murphy, a writer of romance fiction, and Kathleen O'Flaherty – *A Wreath Upon the Dead* is a sprawling, multi-layered and multi-voiced historical romance describing not only the two female protagonists' lives but with this Maureen's attempts to write a novel about Cormac O'Flaherty, a nineteenth-century Catholic folk-hero and ancestor of Kathleen's, and his romance with Marianne McLeod, the daughter of a Protestant landlord. In this way the novel charts two trajectories: the attempts and ultimate failure of Maureen and Kathleen to assimilate themselves, and by extension their Irishness, within modern bourgeois conventions as symbolised by 1960s and 1970s London, but also Maureen's inability to reconcile the historical debris of Irish National-ism with the demands of the classic realist text. For this reason the active self-reflexive element of the book takes the form of its growing realisation that it cannot be the novel of Cormac and Marianne that Maureen initially wishes it to be:

> So what am I to do now, she wondered, am I to give up the whole idea of writing this book? You can't write a romantic novel without romance. She could have got over Marianne being neither beautiful nor aristocratic but she couldn't get over her not being loved. Not very well. Not if what she was writing was supposed to be a love story. And there was hardly much point having Cormac as a hero if he wasn't even heroic. If he wasn't a rebel or a poet or a romantic lover, if he was just a poor galoot ready to grab at anything to hoist himself up in the world.[28]

Such anxieties suggest why the novel takes its title from Patrick Kavanagh's 'A Wreath for Tom Moore's Statue',[29] a sour poem that notes that 'the dead will wear the cap of any racket' and one that, interestingly in light of Duffaud's own criticism of Ireland's desire to fly too close to the flame of bourgeois ideology, condemns such an existence as 'the tedious narrative of a mediocrity's passion' – a phrase that well defines the lives of most of the novel's major characters. However, despite the fact that the actual material of history remains so stubbornly beyond Maureen's imaginative powers, it finds its own manifestation as the unhappy union of Cormac and Marianne revisits subsequent generations as a kind of genetic trait. Kathleen falls in love with Eric McLeod, a Protestant bourgeois descendant of Marianne's family, and a child, Sarah, is born of the coupling. Despite being raised in London, Sarah's embodiment of these two parallel histories indicates that she carries within her a potentially lethal mix of incompatible historical and religious elements, and her destruction is assured when she kidnaps Eric, holds him hostage in the house that once belonged to Cormac and Marianne (and that Eric had been instrumental in preserving), and finally kills them both as she unwittingly brings the decayed building crashing down on top of them. The ambiguity of this event ensures that the novel concludes on a note of irresolvable despair: Kathleen and Maureen seek refuge in the bourgeois sterility of middle-class France and Claghan is left to continue its unhappy imprisonment in history. As Maureen notes in a bitter conclusion:

> Everyone in Claghan will be dead and buried before the true story gets told. There *is* no true story, it's just a mess of ambiguities and lies and more or less guesses. And it doesn't matter, it doesn't change a thing. Claghan will make up whatever truth suits it. Don't we all?[30]

It is in this way that *A Wreath Upon the Dead* can be seen as an exemplary instance of the persistence of an opposition within Northern Irish fiction between realism and an impulse towards the recursive. The text's unresolvable struggle with history is symbolised by the gradual concealment of its recursive elements by the contingent demands of its formal realism and it is this transition that makes the experience of reading the novel oddly bifurcated. The carefully developed narrative of Cormac and Marianne, constructed through the use of multiple perspectives, ends abruptly as the novel turns its attention more fully to the failure of Kathleen and Maureen to reconcile their own historical experience with bourgeois consciousness, and as such the encroachments of both bourgeois ideology and formal realism are seen as unwelcome inevitabilities. This bitter awareness is made manifest most obviously in the novel's satiric representation through free indirect discourse of Eric as a middle-class Protestant whose classically bourgeois mindset prevents any form of political awareness from developing:

> *He* [Eric] knew by experience how narrow-minded and selfish middle-class values were, and he intended to encourage, or even *force*, his own students to question and reject them. The problem was that there was going to be one hell of row when he told his parents he wanted to go to teacher training college with Dave. *They* thought he was going to do law, at Queen's. So far he hadn't done anything to disillusion them because Dad could be a bastard if you caught him in the wrong mood. He thought it would be far simpler to belong to a family like Dave's who looked on teaching as a great step up the social ladder. Or like Maureen's, for whom

teaching was the only hope of getting out of the bog if you wanted to stay in Northern Ireland. When he thought of it like that, he supposed Roman Catholics *must* be a bit oppressed. They didn't seem to have quite as many choices as ordinary people.[31]

The failures and hypocrisies of Eric's muddled political activism are returned to throughout the novel and symbolise what is seen as the desperate provincialism of Northern Irish Protestantism. In this way, Eric's heartless abandonment of Kathleen indicates a more profound abdication of responsibility: an intimate betrayal between factions and classes. While this demonstrates something of the novel's larger theme of the impossibility of reconciliation, its identification of such impossibility in terms of formal and linguistic tensions suggest the novel's similarity to the Field Day Theatre Company's early analyses of Northern Ireland as a site of conflicting languages. This can be most clearly identified by a comparison of Duffaud's text with the colonial 'mapping' of Irish history enacted by Field Day's first production, Brian Friel's *Translations* (1980). In both these texts the larger, essentially colonial, antagonism between the two cultures is imagined in terms of a precise moment of betrayal: in *Translations* this moment is located in 1833 as the troubled Gaelic-speaking community of Baile Beag encounters British troops engaged in an ordnance survey of the area, in *A Wreath Upon the Dead* the fall occurs in 1842 – a similar moment of interaction as Irish Catholic Cormac and Scottish Protestant Marianne elope and marry. What is significant about both these distillations of historical anguish is that they derive not from a normative oppressor/oppression opposition but rather from a failed attempt to be a 'good' colonial. In *Translations* it is the activities of the well-meaning Lieutenant Yolland rather than those of the brutal Captain Lancey that create the conditions for violence, while in Duffaud's novel it is the responsible landlordism of the McLeods as compared to the previous owners, the absentee Wattersons, that creates chaos. In these terms both texts propose the existence of an equilibrium of injustice and suggest that it is the disruption of this eternal equilibrium that leads to specific historical anguish. Yolland's tentative question, 'Do you think I could live here?'[32] mirrors Marianne's perception that 'it is hard that I should be so excluded, who feel such sympathy for their way of living',[33] and both these misrecognitions generate a romantic attachment to a figure who embodies cultural difference (Cormac in *A Wreath Upon the Dead*, Maire in *Translations*) and, from this point onwards, assured disaster.

Such a structure suggests not only the usual message of the 'love across the barricades' genre – that personal affection or emotional contact will always be subservient to the ceaseless momentum of a community's sectarian affiliation – but also that even those moments of tentative cultural exchange are nothing more than instances of particularly appalling false consciousness. Just as the hesitant attempts to 'understand' the other that drive the plot of *Translations* are contextualised by our knowledge that the famine is lurking offstage, soon to destroy whatever fragile alliances may have survived the activities of the brutal British military presence, so in Duffaud's novel the final collapse of Cormac and Marianne's house through Sarah's ill-advised actions forecloses the ambiguous personal and historical motivations that the novel has left unanswered. Interestingly, this deployment of the collapsing cottage as a symbol of a decayed and anachronistic Irish history is a plot device that mirrors the closure of Field Day's 1982 production, Friel's *The Communication Cord*, a farce that, according to Edna Longley, 'comfortably fails in its intention to subvert the pieties of *Translations*'.[34] In these terms, each specific disaster must be allowed its own reverberations while contributing to a more general denudation of a betraying and betrayed history.

This structural complexity suggests something of *A Wreath Upon the Dead*'s monumental ambition and in this way it is appropriate to see the novel as a form of South Armagh epic. This epic status, however, is generated solely through the strategic historicisation of the 'love across the barricades' genre – in other words, it takes the discrete moment of potential and inevitable tragedy that is the normative role of this trope (the micro-narrative that flares briefly and then burns itself out against the background of the macro-narrative of historical and political stalemate) and reads it as a genetic trait that can recur on any given occasion. This is innovative insofar as it appropriates a device most obviously used as a means of providing momentum and ultimately closure to a plot and transforms it instead into a narrative structure suggestive only of an endless circularity. History, or what can pass for history in such a brutal landscape, therefore informs the reader only of an absolute failure of communication and of the ultimate futility of any subsequent attempt. As a consequence of this structure, the circlings, repetitions and visitations that then dominate the novel place it within the territory of Northern Irish Gothic, and certainly those elements of the text that accord with such a reading make themselves immediately apparent: the narrative is constructed out of letters, testimonies, diaries and memoirs; the themes of physical and emotional entrapment are all-pervading; buildings become the repositories of memory, fear and retribution. The inevitability of this formal logic entails that in *A Wreath Upon the Dead* the dead must continually exert a retroactive force. The Cormac/Marianne union repeatedly finds new manifestations through family histories and just as this suggests a close assimilation of the structure of *Wuthering Heights*, so we ask of Cormac the same 'hermeneutical riddle' that Eagleton identifies 'the Lockwoods and Deans of the present' asking of Heathcliff: 'What is he? What does he want?'[35]

The Nationalism of *A Wreath Upon the Dead*, then, is a nationalism of despair. In a novel so preoccupied with making explicit the tangled motivations of its major protagonists (an element that, on Eagleton's reading, indicates most obviously its debt to the 'story-shaped'[36] world of classical realism), Cormac represents an irreducible element within Irishness, all that remains unknowable and unassailable. It is the inevitability of the misery that this brings, rather than any prospect of resolution, that generates the novel's insistent demands for reparation:

> We did suffer, that's true enough. We were forced to live on potatoes, and they failed, and a good many of us died. It took generations for us to recover from it. Maybe we've never recovered. Maybe it explains Bobby Sands and the rest, explains our neuroses, our shame of birth, our easy acceptance of death? That's why I have to keep apologising for being objective. Martin McCormack thought it was disloyal of me to want to be objective. Given, he said, the continuing circumstances. Anyone in Claghan would say the same. Because we *did* suffer and that does, surely, set us apart. Justify us. Does it?
> Could it?[37]

It is the tension between this obsessive circling and the contingent pressures of 'continuing circumstances' that leads to *A Wreath Upon the Dead*'s undeniable complexity. However, ultimately this complexity is achieved through the accumulation of biographical and historical detail rather than through formal transgression or the subversion of normative reading strategies. As it remains in the first and last instance a bourgeois text approaching and attempting to assimilate reluctant material, it is encountered as a jigsaw puzzle of a thousand pieces rather than of a hundred: the terms of engagement remain the same, all that differs is the number of clues to be solved. If nothing else such an awareness serves as a reminder that a novel that attacks bourgeois ideology is not necessarily an anti-bourgeois text, just as a text that appears to promote classically bourgeois values can also be subversive in the method through which it communicates such ideologies.

Resurrection Man (Eoin McNamee, 1994)

Eoin McNamee's *Resurrection Man* serves perhaps as a good example of this latter possibility and is a text that, in its own right, occupies a peculiar space within the critical narratives of Northern Irish fiction I began this chapter by detailing. A fictionalised account of the activities of a Loyalist murder gang, the Shankill Butchers, during the mid-1970s, for Ronan Bennett its significance lies with the fact that it is one of only a small number of novels concerned with the activities of Loyalist paramilitaries. However, as Bennett notes, McNamee

> is not interested in the ideology of the murder gangs or the political ends they serve: his preoccupation is with the inner life, and his portrait of the interior landscape of Ulster loyalism – prefiguring Thaddeus O'Sullivan's 1996 film *Nothing Personal* – is unremittingly bleak psychopathologies shaped by neurosis, inadequacy and sexual fear.[38]

This is, in isolation, a relatively neutral judgment and it is curious that Bennett chooses not to condemn what appears to be another example of the tendency to portray Northern Irish working-class politics as 'irrational and bloody slaughter', a tendency that he identifies and attacks so fiercely throughout the rest of his analysis. Gerry Smyth, however, is more definite in his appraisal and perceives the novel as an exemplary instance of the failure of Northern Irish fiction to develop 'new perspectives'. Finding in the narrative 'a sort of existential longing for non-being and a postmodern scepticism towards any kind [of] personal or political identity', he identifies passivity as the dominating attribute of the work's major characters, who are unable to develop or respond to any situation except through violence. For this reason, *Resurrection Man*

> reveals itself as another reactionary response to the 'Troubles', interested not in sectarianism (nor indeed in the more significant agendas of state sovereignty which underpin sectarianism in Northern Ireland) but in some inscrutable darkness at the heart of the self. The local matters only in so far as it can be incorporated into a larger existential overview, as some sort of evidence for the human condition.[39]

Understood in these terms, McNamee's novel revisits the tired concept of a Northern Irish 'identity crisis' but rather than searching for the social and economic factors that create such insecurity, seeks instead to allow the ambiguities and ambivalences it engenders to infect the formal strategies of the narrative itself. Smyth also recognises this aim but the conditional nature of his recognition ('the novel resists any straightforward reading, attempting to insinuate at a formal level the problem of alienation which would appear to be the text's major theme'[40]) implies that it is not properly realised. Like Bennett after him, Smyth seems willing to acknowledge the extraordinarily unsettling power of the novel but is unable to endorse the ethical foundations on which it is built.

How then can *Resurrection Man*'s refusal to engage with social and political motivations be accounted for? If it does deny the concept of human agency and with that suggest an inevitable longing for violence within the Northern Irish psyche, as Smyth argues, the terms of this abdication cannot be allied with the traditional Northern Irish thriller's reliance on those stereotyped characters and scenarios we have already observed Patten, Smyth and Hughes rejecting. Perhaps, though, a way into the novel can be suggested through the veiled terms of Smyth's critique itself. In identifying the novel's preoccupation with 'some inscrutable darkness at the heart of the self', the possibility of reading the novel through the frame of Joseph Conrad's colonial adventure *Heart of Darkness* (1902) is strongly alluded to (even though it is an interpretation Smyth himself does not undertake). Such a comparison is illuminating. Most obviously, the two texts feature parallel quests: as Marlow is employed to find Kurtz in *Heart of Darkness*, so in *Resurrection Man* Ryan, a journalist, must discover who is carrying out a series of savage murders and mutilations in Belfast, a search that leads him inexorably to Victor Kelly, the leader of the Loyalist gang.[41] Alongside these primary quests (which structure the plot and its drive towards resolution in both texts), Kurtz and Victor are also presented as engaged in their own quests to discover the private and public limits of 'civilisation' – a project that involves accentuating the hypocrisies of the political framework within which they exist by forcing such contradictions to their extremes. In this way, both figures are enmeshed within the political codes of the society while having the ability to transcend them through sheer force of charisma. Just as Marlow says of Kurtz's world-view, 'it had candour, it had conviction, it had a vibrating note of revolt in its whisper, it had the appalling face of a glimpsed truth – the strange commingling of desire and hate',[42] so in *Resurrection Man* Heather is similarly entranced by Victor:

She said it wasn't hard to guess from the way she talked that she was smitten straight off which was the God's honest truth not something she ever wished to hide. She was mad for him like no other man. He could make her cream herself just by looking. [...] Before they got in bed he took out this big gun he had stuck in his belt and spun it around in his hand all the time watching himself in the mirror on the wardrobe with an expression of being somewhere else completely, until she said to him come here, please, hurry up. I can't bear it.[43]

As this suggests, another shared aspect of the novels is that in each the charismatic anti-hero is adored by an uncomprehending female figure who ultimately refuses to acknowledge anything of his fallen status. At the point of closure in both *Resurrection Man* and *Heart of Darkness*, not only has the anti-hero been betrayed and then destroyed by the political forces that shaped him but his legacy has, as a result, entered the realm of the mythic; a process that leaves the Marlow/Ryan figures uncomfortably aware that their own actions and motivations have begun to resemble the actions of the Kurtz/Victor figures with whom they are obsessed. Marlow 'had peeped over the edge'[44] in his final meeting with Kurtz and acknowledged the possibility of succeeding Kurtz as a demi-god, while the violence the increasingly fragmented and unstable Ryan perpetrates on his wife Margaret is seen as simply a further manifestation of the totality of violence Victor has established across Belfast. It is in this way, of course, that both quest narratives revisit the myth of the Fire King and his uncertain reign in the sacred wood – the location where power is not absolute but rather can only exist alongside the awareness of its inevitable usurpation. Understood as such, it can be argued that the primary purpose of both works is to reveal the structures through which corrupt and decaying institutions create mythologised individuals and moments – instances that serve as symbols of the institution's contradictory greater purpose.

As there are similarities of plot, character and structure between *Resurrection Man* and *Heart of Darkness*, so the works share a preoccupation with the struggle to find a language adequate to the experience being described. F.R. Leavis in *The Great Tradition* famously criticised Conrad for the imprecision of his adjectives, his refusal of lucidity, and asked, 'Is anything added to the oppressive mysteriousness of the Congo by such sentences as "It was the stillness of an implacable force brooding over an inscrutable intention"?'[45] The role of Leavis in the critique of *Resurrection Man* is taken by Smyth, who identifies in McNamee's novel a futile attempt to locate 'the possibility of a language that can communicate the reality of politically motivated, savagely executed violence'.[46] This is an awareness that Ryan and his fellow journalist Coppinger encounter when contemplating the first of Victor's murders:

> There was someone out there operating in a new context. They were being lifted into unknown areas, deep pathologies. Was the cortex severed? They both felt a silence beginning to spread from this one. They would have to rethink procedures. The root of the tongue had been severed. New languages would have to be invented.[47]

If *Resurrection Man* fails to invent these new languages, it does at least establish the preconditions for their emergence through its rejection of what it terms the 'language of denial',[48] its obsessive circlings around 'ambiguous statements of condemnation', and Ryan's uneasy perception that his own reports of the killings were 'covert, unexplained, dissatisfying'.[49] The only conditional comfort that the novel can offer in the face of this semantic failure comes with the novel's very first word, 'Afterwards'; an indication perhaps that language will ultimately regain its ability to encounter those subjects and events that at the moment of occurrence appear to have defeated it.[50] As with *Heart of Darkness*, the novel's past tense forecloses, if not entirely, some of the instabilities its narrative asserts.

The formal similarities of the two texts are clear, then, but it is the manner in which this comparison allows for a reconsideration of *Resurrection Man*'s ethical critique of Northern Irish violence that is, perhaps, of greater significance. While *Heart of Darkness* explores the horrors of the colonial project in the Congo as a means of expressing an existential crisis within human identity, crucially it does not ultimately move beyond colonialism or use colonial history as a plot catalyst to enable its subsequent preoccupations. Instead, colonialism in Conrad's novella is expressed as an absolute totality, the inescapable frame within which all the mediations between individuals take place and within which the European psyche is both constituted and destroyed. As Edward Said observes in his reading of the novella: 'By accentuating the discrepancy between the official "idea" of empire and the remarkably disorientating actuality of Africa, Marlow unsettles the reader's sense not only of the very idea of empire but of something more basic, reality itself.'[51] The disturbance of reality in *Resurrection Man*, it can be argued, derives from a similar instinct. The narrative voice's imprecision about cause and effect, its refusal of objectivity, does not evade socio-historical context but assumes and demands the recognition of a sectarian totality beyond which it is unable to venture. In these terms the silences of the novel are not denials of what Smyth terms the 'agendas of state sovereignty which underpin sectarianism', but constitute a recognition of their effects. It is in this context that the novel's preoccupation with complicity needs to be assessed. The banality of the 'everybody's guilty' scenario often found within cultural representations of Northern Irish violence[52] derives not from its assumption of equal complicity but, more precisely, from its usual reluctance to extend that complicity to its fullest extent. In other words, what remains unimplicated in such a judgment is the very position from which it is uttered. Understood in these terms, *Resurrection Man*'s awareness and complication of this paradox is of central significance to its ethical critique:

> Coppinger was saying about the courts here, the way they are. No juries, evidence being given behind screens by unidentified witnesses – soldier A, soldier B, that kind of thing. The strange charges they come up with. Conspiracy with persons unknown to murder persons unknown. I was arguing it was a denial of justice. Coppinger says it's all just a mechanism for dealing with different forms of complicity. He says this town has invented new ways of getting involved, like it's all just one big experiment in human guilt.[53]

Just as ambivalence is central to the effect of *Heart of Darkness* in that it invests possibilities in the cultural fantasy of extermination offered by Kurtz and draws our attention to the inadequacies of Marlow's 'solution' to the contradictions Kurtz embodies, so the ultimate conclusion of *Resurrection Man* suggests that the violence of Victor and his followers is neither particular to a mutant strain within Loyalism,[54] nor a specific embodiment of a general evil, but is rather a violence that exceeds the possibilities of the novel form itself. *Resurrection Man* refuses to clear a critical space for the disinterested reader and in so doing proposes that any disinterested judgment 'about' the violence it depicts is merely another form of cultural utopianism, another form of bourgeois inoculation.

The trajectory of this comparison suggests that *Resurrection Man* is not a text of 'postmodern scepticism' as Smyth defines it, and nor does it invest in the postmodern categories of 'perspectivism, ambiguity and displacement' that Patten calls for. Instead, it can best be understood as a text of modernism itself, as a belated attempt to read Belfast through the tropes and images implicit in the modernist vision of the city. Rather than presenting spatial and temporal fragmentation and the juxtaposition of disparate forms of cultural community, the Belfast found in the novel is one of internal coherence and uniform preoccupations. In these terms it is a city that 'has withdrawn into its placenames'[55] and that 'holds commerce with itself',[56] as the seemingly random acts of violence that take place connect with each other like beads of mercury. This symbolic order suggests why Victor's descent into violence is understood as a descent into modernism itself:

> Victor sat at the wheel of the car until dusk most nights. He preferred it when it began to get dark. By day the city seemed ancient and ambiguous. Its power was dissipated by exposure to daylight. It looked derelict and colonial. There was a sense of curfew, produce rotting in the market-place. At night it described itself by its lights, defining streets like a code of destinations.[57]

As with *Heart of Darkness*, the onset of nightfall allows for a transformation of perception to take place: the relics of colonialism provide the preconditions for modernism, the gathering together of disparate historical and physical symptoms, and the subsequent rereading of these traces as an expressive totality. In *Heart of Darkness* the gathering gloom allows Marlow to make a connection between the Roman conquest of Britain and nineteenth-century colonialism in Africa, while in *Resurrection Man* the darkness allows Victor to reconcile the 'sense of curfew' with the unsold commodities in the market. This early moment of transformation indicates something of the interpretative strategies both texts will employ in the construction of meaning, but more significantly it also provides the narrative impulse in the texts (what *Resurrection Man* terms 'a code of destinations'), aligning the resolution of the quest with the protagonist's resolution of the various contradictory elements he encounters. It is in this way that the symbolic order of both works embodies most obviously the centripetal energies of modernism rather than centrifugal energies of postmodernism. Both quests, of course, must necessarily fail. The 'code of destinations' that modernism offers is, at the same time, predicated on the awareness of its own lack. The search for symptoms leads only to the identification of further symptoms and so *Resurrection Man*'s conclusion is only half-realised and dependent upon the unfinished business of personal alienation:

> When he had told Heather this Ryan turned and walked away. She watched him until he reached the corner of the street. He was part of the city now,

part of its rank, allusive narrative, but she felt like a character in a strange tale. An outlandish woman. He was going, he had said, to the morgue in the City Hospital to see what the autopsy revealed, although they both knew what he would find. Bodies laid out as if for a journey. That they would carry news of the city and its environs. The Pound. Sailortown. The Bone. That their news would be awaited. That they would test their quality against the dark and take their places among the lonely and vigilant dead.[58]

As Ryan is trapped in the city, forced (like Victor before him) to become the symptom of a sickness he cannot understand, so Heather is trapped in an alien narrative with no possibility of resolution. This final paragraph acknowledges the novel's debt to *Heart of Darkness* in that it pits the small significances of the tale that has been related against the forces of an inscrutable darkness but, more pointedly, it juxtaposes this debt with a precise gesture towards James Joyce's *Dubliners* through the concluding word 'dead'.[59] Such an analogy further complicates the dissection of implication and complicity with which the novel has engaged itself. As Heather is forced to acknowledge the futility of her role as Victor's emotional support (just as Gabriel Conroy perceives his own limited role in the emotional life of Gretta in 'The Dead'), so, as in *Dubliners*, death finally emerges not as a tawdry symptom of an underlying sickness, but as the final binary opposition that must be encountered. Such a parallel encourages a retrospective interpretation of *Resurrection Man* to emerge. *Dubliners* presents a city so traumatised by colonialism that the possibilities of human agency are denied. As a location it has internalised its own possibilities to such an extent that even a recognition of the colonial context, and the analogous mindset it demands, is not possible. In this way, colonialism in Joyce's collection makes itself known through its lack of a signifying practice, through its frustrated attempts to break into modernism. A similar self-referentiality can be identified in *Resurrection Man* through the meaningless nature of its violence and Victor's gradual awareness that the more significance he attempts to graft onto an event the less meaning it has. In this way, the modernism of the novel recognises its own anachronism and, through its hollow silences, calls for the dissolution of the very conditions that created it.

Cycle of Violence (Colin Bateman, 1995), Kissing the Frog (Annie Dunlop, 1996)

As the title of Colin Bateman's second novel, Cycle of Violence,[60] suggests, it shares Resurrection Man's preoccupation with the modes through which violence is replicated and sustained. Here, though, the similarities end. The novel tells the story of Miller, a journalist with a Belfast newspaper, who is sent in disgrace to 'Crossmaheart'[61] – a fictional version of Crosmaglen in County Armagh – following a drink-induced altercation after the funeral of his father. Soon after his arrival, Miller falls in love with Marie Young, the girlfriend of the disappeared journalist, Jamie Milburn, Miller has been sent to replace. When the discovery of Milburn's body on the town dump leads the already emotionally insecure Marie to something close to mental breakdown, Miller feels impelled to discover the root cause of her unhappiness and uncovers evidence of a sex crime committed by four men in Marie's childhood. Miller systematically tracks down her abusers (although, as it is revealed at the conclusion of the novel, they actually assaulted Marie's sister) and, unwittingly in each instance, causes their death. Ultimately Miller and Marie consummate their relationship, Marie leaves Miller a note acknowledging the 'absolute perfection' of his lovemaking and, as a consequence of this realisation and the inevitable disappointment that will ensue, commits suicide, while Miller himself is finally killed following a farcical argument in a local shop about a loaf of mouldy bread. The best intentions of those who wish to change Crossmaheart for the better are, in this way, seen as futile; any possibility of reconciliation between either individuals or communities is an impossibility and sectarian violence will continue – in this frontier outpost at least – because too many of the population seem to enjoy it.

Such a bald summary does not do damage to the intricacies of Cycle of Violence in that it indicates most obviously the intensely plotted nature of the novel, a formula with which Bateman has found startling international success.[62] The cyclical nature of the violence that afflicts Crossmaheart is imagined not just as sectarian hatred but also in familial and sexual terms and, indeed, it is the achievement of the novel to suggest something of how these different forms of aggression are interrelated. Sexual violence leads to sectarian violence (with one exception the abusers of Marie's sister eventually become prominent – and bigoted – members of both communities), the beatings Marie received from her father as a child continue to exert an emotional force in the present, and the conflict itself has seemingly lost track of any original motivation and become nothing more than a series of revenge killings. With this awareness, one preoccupation of the novel is exploring how this cycle can be broken. Miller's act of historical retrieval in tracing the men he believes to have abused Marie offers one such possibility, although his best intentions in only wanting to 'talk' to the men are thwarted insofar as each meets his death (usually in a slightly grotesque way) immediately after the interview. The apparent failure of Miller's revenge quest impacts upon the novel's engagement with the thriller form itself and the vacuum that is left by this failure is filled by Marie's suicide – another method of breaking the cycle of abuse. However, by this stage of the novel the narrative seems to have given up on any idea that agency on the part of the individual can lead to constitutive action beyond forming fragile and momentary intimate personal connections.

Understood in these terms, the despair that *Cycle of Violence* discovers is the despair of a classic Arnoldian liberal humanism. In the wreckage of a society so alienated against itself, a society in which personal motivation is not even reducible to self-interest, the novel abandons such wider hopes of redemption and promotes instead the idea of a retreat into a personal emotional enclave, a life in which Miller can hope that he and Marie will 'turn the cycle of violence into a tandem and we'll ride through the South of France. She will be my Paris Bun. It will be the Cycle of Romance. We will get married on the top of the Eiffel Tower. Then we'll bungy jump off.'[63] What thinking about the novel in this way reveals is the manner in which it impels a reconsideration of the social sickness from which the couple are trying to escape. While it is normative in the Northern Irish novel to consider social and sectarian violence as an archaic, pre-modern relic and concomitantly to imagine escape from that society as a break into the modern (as in *A Wreath Upon the Dead*), Crossmaheart in *Cycle of Violence* betrays instead all the symptoms of the modern which, in an English context, Matthew Arnold, and after him E.M Forster,[64] found so repellent:

> Once a quaint picture postcard village, it had been swamped in a couple of years by the dregs of the city, guinea pigs in a scheme to alleviate the urban decay and religious mayhem of Belfast by shifting it to an idyllic existence in the country, with its own industries, its modern leisure facilities and enlightened infrastructure. The planners had taken everything into account,

except human nature. They transferred scum from slums into scum with immersion heaters. They had hoped Crossmaheart would reflect all of life's rich tapestry, and perhaps for one bright shining moment it had; but then someone had stolen it. The factories soon fell prey to the gangs and the symbols of war, and the onset of recession finally closed them down. The leisure centre was bombed, the shopping mall fell vacant.[65]

Of course, the obvious and significant way in which Bateman's vision of the modern departs from the classic liberal humanist line in this instance is that in Crossmaheart it is not modernity that crushes humanity through the remorseless workings of capital but rather 'human nature' that imposes itself on the modern and corrupts it. This sense of the town as a self-inflicted wound is significant to the wider procedures of the novel not just because it repeats Bateman's perception that an enlightened Unionist administration is, at the very least, well-meaning if naive, but also because it gives ethical force to the overall theme of the novel, which can be summarised as the inability of rational thought to impose itself on the random chaos of human experience – a preoccupation that, as I will discuss, also obsesses Wilson's *Eureka Street*. In these terms, the cycle of violence in which Miller, Marie and all the other significant characters are trapped is the blind, mutually assured destruction of the 'scum'. In turn, this realisation substantially reduces the significance of Miller's investigations and the remit of the novel of the whole. As Craig, a local RUC officer, glosses it: 'There is a lot of scum about in this town, Miller. If you're doing a little bit to get rid of some of that scum, I won't get in your way.'[66]

As these considerations suggest, *Cycle of Violence* is both an engagement with the thriller genre and a troubled subversion of it. In a perceptive discussion of Bateman's first novel *Divorcing Jack*, Gerry Smyth identifies a similar nihilism underwriting that text and suggests that the combination of 'intimacy with the routines of life in a sectarian society' with a 'simplicity of structure' and 'a frequently surreal plot' leads to an 'engagement with a strand of "postmodern thriller"'.[67] In these terms, the novel is compared to the early films of Quentin Tarantino in that 'the pleasure of the text is organized in the first instance around the shock of the violence and the intermingling of genres'. In *Cycle of Violence* such intermingling can be located not just in the violence itself (at one point Miller is about to be killed by a hairdresser terrorist who insists on perming his hair before carrying out the act) but, more pointedly, in the frustrated terms of the quest structure that constitutes the main part of the novel.[68] The haphazard nature of Miller's progress, his failed desire to 'understand' why abuse happens and the fact that this project leads only to more deaths, leaves the novel uneasily contemplating the possibility of a world in which the idea of sequential narrative is an impossibility. In this way one of *Cycle of Violence*'s obvious antecedents is Neil Jordan's *Angel* from 1982. As I have previously discussed, in this film the protagonist, Danny, is similarly engaged on a quest to 'understand' and it is this journey that transforms him inevitably into a retributive angel of death. The comparison is useful. Just as the horror of *Angel* lies in its recognition that in its vision of Armagh society it is not possible to feel the appropriate amount of revulsion for the killings that take place, so underwriting *Cycle of Violence*'s Tarantinoesque parade of violence is a similar nostalgia for the possibility of a world in which an individual act (even of violence) creates a meaningful reaction.

This nostalgia is most clearly identifiable in what seems to be the key moment of nihilistic despair itself – the suicide of Marie. In a society in which alcohol is presented as the drug of choice, the only method through which the inhabitants of Crossmaheart can begin to make sense of their world, Marie's decision to stop taking her anti-depressant medication is highlighted as a rare moment of decisive individual action:

> 'Aren't I okay?'
> 'You seem...'
> 'Aren't I okay?'
> 'Okay, you're fine... but you have them for a reason Marie, they're not just sweeties...'
> 'But I've been taking them like sweeties... little rewards to keep me on the ground... but I don't need rewards any more, Miller. I need to be myself whatever that is, not whatever I become when I take pills...'
> 'But the pills keep you yourself...'
> 'Do they?'
> Miller shook his head. 'I don't know.'
> 'Do I seem any different?'
> 'No.'
> 'So no pills, and the same old me.'[69]

Having taken the decision to stop taking her medication, Marie is perceived as having regained a state of full individuation and from this point can recognise that suicide is the only reasoned response to the situation in which she finds herself. In this way, despair gives way to affirmation in that her suicide becomes the one rational moment in a chaotic society and an act quite beyond the understanding of all the other characters in the novel, including Miller. The redemption that the novel finds, then, is one based upon a rejection of what is seen as false consciousness, a nostalgic assertion that it is still possible to 'be myself whatever that is', and in this, as I will discuss, *Cycle of Violence* is markedly similar to Wilson's *Eureka Street*. The bourgeois origins of this technique are obvious but in the case of Bateman's novel its presence oddly recontextualises other aspects of the novel that may also seem typically bourgeois. *Cycle of Violence* delights in the arcane and the coincidental: at one point Marie's landlady begins quoting Oscar Wilde in ignorance, at another moment Miller responds to a blind man's question with a nod of his head. Similarly, the novel is preoccupied with the desperate assertion of precise facts, so that, for instance, we are informed with great certainty but with no obvious purpose that Miller eats 'a bacon and coleslaw sandwich'. Such moments are not just symptomatic of bourgeois fiction's obsession with detail (although that is part of their purpose) but also constitute a recognition that in the deracinated world of Crossmaheart such detail is as meaningful as any other. It is in this way that bourgeois realism expresses its own mode of dissent.

At this point *Cycle of Violence* can be usefully compared to Annie Dunlop's *Kissing the Frog* in that both can be understood as Northern Irish Protestant popular fictions concerned with the extension of bourgeois ideology into hostile territory. Crucial to the narrative strategy of *Cycle of Violence* is the emphatic distinction between Miller's previous life of bourgeois family tedium with which the novel begins and the subsequent realisation, following his exile, of the atavistic horrors of sectarian violence in Crossmaheart. Such a distinction allows Bateman to place Miller in the role of the uninitiated (asking naïve questions such as 'Is it, like, a religious thing?'[70]), and, perhaps more importantly, to preserve a fragile sense of Northern Irish liberal modernity, symbolised (unusually for the genre) by Belfast – the city in which Miller dreams of building a new life with Marie. In these terms Miller is recognisably a product of the culture – and thus can conduct himself with a certain knowingness – while appearing entirely out of place in Crossmaheart itself. This is most obviously signalled in Miller's perception of the two bars in the town: Riley's (Catholic) and the Ulster Arms (Protestant). Despite Miller's previous recognition that Protestant culture is 'his own',[71] he encounters the Ulster Arms as an alien and strange territory:

Miller could hardly tell the difference between it and Riley's, the same aura of barely suppressed violence, the same whiff of desperation brought on by poverty laced with alcoholism. Where Riley's was decorated with Gaelic insignia, hurling pennants, Glasgow Celtic team photos and throbbed to the beat of a Rebel Rebel juke box, the Ulster Arms had its Glasgow Rangers Supporters Club flags, its Loyalist Prisoners of War banner and a juke box full of Protestant out-of-work ethic interpretations of country classics. Nobody smiled very much in either bar, save the staff, who smiled because it was the done thing, but resignation dulled their eyes.[72]

The novel's exoticisation of the sectarian binaries of Crossmaheart at this point is dependent, crucially, not on a general rejection of the terms of the sectarian opposition itself but rather on a rejection of what are perceived as the particularly ugly and pointless manifestations of such oppositions found in working-class culture. This distinction allows the novel to maintain its delicate position as both a Baedeker and an exploration of the unknown. The novel forms connections with the non-Northern Irish reader purely through its assertion of a shared set of bourgeois conventions, which, in the instance cited above, accords with what Barthes terms 'Neither-Norism' – the moment at which 'both parties are dismissed because it is embarrassing to choose between them'. In this way the novel 'flees from an intolerable reality, reducing it to two opposites which balance each other only inasmuch as they are purely formal, relieved of all their specific weight'.[73]

In the case of Dunlop's novel the movement of the bourgeois into hostile territory is not understood as a confrontation with the world of working-class violence, as in *Cycle of Violence*, but is rather posited as a coming to terms with all that lies beyond the hermetically sealed world of Protestant Magherafelt (described as 'the most claustrophobic town on earth'[74]). The terms through which the book sells itself on its back cover are interesting in light of this:

Two women grow up in a small Protestant Northern Irish town, and dream of turning their frogs into handsome (and generous) princes. But life isn't like that. Paddy (Fenian) Butler is Catholic, unfaithful and terminally careless. Sonia cannot redeem him. Nor can Marian transform her fiancé, Jonathan, into the sort of man you'd want to marry. He's too mean, for a start.

Sonia is glamorous and has love-bites on her bottom. Marian is plain and has a Christian Conscience. But both women discover that kissing the frog isn't the way to do it. They have to find ways of being women – not princesses – in their own right.

And they do.

Described as such, *Kissing the Frog* would initially appear to offer itself as a form of *Bildungsroman*, and yet the narrative momentum that such a term suggests is rarely present in the text. Instead the progress of Sonia and Marian is marked by a series of epiphanic moments, which, in turn, are not of sufficient force to disrupt significantly the soon established and subsequently fixed patterns of interaction between the major characters. The world of the novel is one drained of signification, and despite the back cover's promise that the girls will 'find ways of being women', resolution is only reached when their respective partners force such resolution upon them through their own less than honourable actions. In its circlings and repetitions, its inability to enter narrative, the novel presents a world before history and, as such, appears to establish only the preconditions for another novel yet unwritten. In this way, *Kissing the Frog* is a novel engaged in a lengthy (and ultimately, perhaps, futile) wait for something to happen.

For these reasons alone *Kissing the Frog* is a peculiar example of the teenage romance genre in that the triumph of narrative momentum over provincial boredom that this genre usually rehearses is here a battle that is conclusively lost. Although *Kissing the Frog*'s vision of Protestant bourgeois tedium can be seen as similar to that which we have already found in *A Wreath Upon the Dead*, Dunlop's novel is more intriguing in its refusal to contrast such quietude with the social violence to be found elsewhere in the North. The Protestant Magherafelt that is presented here is not imagined as an essentially hypocritical location denying the realities of the civil war that rages all around it (as in *A Wreath Upon the Dead*) but in fact is contrasted only with the cosmopolitan opportunities of London – possibilities encapsulated by Marian's glamorous Aunt Angela, the voice of the urbane escapee, another figure frequently found in teenage romance narratives. It is then the achievement of *Kissing the Frog* as teenage romance to render the world of Protestant mid-Ulster entirely normative within the terms of the genre, as Magherafelt becomes the location of bourgeois entrapment from which the girls must escape. Again, as is coherent with the genre, such escape is effected through the gaining of qualifications. As Marian observes: 'To be fair to her, my mother tried very hard to be normal during my A levels. Maybe she'd also heard of the Omagh O level suicide. Or maybe she was as terrified as me that I might fail all ahead of me and be forced to remain in Magherafelt with her.'[75]

This precise focus on the limitations of the bourgeois provincial suggests why *Kissing the Frog* barely acknowledges the clichés of socio-sectarian violence often found in the Northern Irish manifestation of this genre. The novel observes in a disapproving manner the background level of sectarianism of the society (encapsulated most obviously by Marian's boyfriend, Jonathan, and the fundamentalist Reverend Sims, 'a hardline stick-in-the-mud who wouldn't eat an egg a hen had laid on a Sunday'[76]) but resists developing the relationship between Sonia and Paddy in terms of a love-across-the-barricades romance despite, at numerous points, gesturing towards this direction. Throughout the course of Marian's and Sonia's progress, social and cultural violence is acknowledged as a shadowy presence at the edges of consciousness, but it never directly impinges on their lives in any significant way and is certainly of much less importance than the primary concern of sexual and emotional fulfilment. Even at moments when sectarianism is voiced more directly, its status in the text is only indicative of other unresolved issues, which exist within the realm of the family:

> When Sonia married Paddy Butler it was a sad sordid ten-minute affair in a grubby registry office.
> Mrs Anderson was very miffed about it. 'This is very selfish of you, Sonia,' she said the morning of the wedding, 'You could have converted and had an arch of hockey sticks at the chapel door. I may never get the chance again to see the inside of a Catholic church. You're no fun any more.'
> 'If you were any sort of mother at all,' said Sonia irritably, 'you'd have disowned me for marrying a Catholic. Like Marian's mother would have done.'
> One of my mother's most famous statements was: 'If you marry a Catholic, Marian, I'll say "Marian? I have no daughter called Marian."'[77]

The overall effect of this strategy – which both acknowledges socio-sectarianism and yet resists finding in it anything of interest – is significant. At one point, casual reference is made to a local restaurant that has been damaged by a bomb, but there is no indication as to who planted it or why they did so and the incident plays no further part in the narrative. In a similar way, the implicit Unionism of the text is understated: at one point in her childhood Marian hears 'Land of Hope and Glory' playing on the radio and feels 'something, I don't know what it is'.[78] One way of interpreting this avoidance is within the terms established by Bennett that I have discussed previously: that *Kissing the Frog* is another manifestation of middle-class culture 'marked by aloofness, by being above it all, by self-conscious distance from the two proletarian tribes fighting out their bloody, pointless, atavistic war'. The resolute refusal of the novel to extend beyond the parameters of its own middle-class society would certainly seem to lend validity to this accusation. However, what this interpretation cannot account for is the effect that this apparent abdication has on our own reading practices. By alluding to wider socio-sectarian issues in the North and yet refusing to elaborate upon them or to make them a motor for the subsequent narrative, the text actually demands a reading of greater, not less, contextual sensitivity. For instance, Sonia's family, the Andersons, are initially described as having 'a huge dairy farm outside Magherafelt' and for this reason 'Sonia was a superb hockey player because she practised in a cleaned-out slurry pit',[79] while Marian's mother desires to prevent her daughter 'gallivanting round the country associating with riff-raff at band parades'.[80] In each instance what is identified and demanded here is a precise knowledge of, respectively, the symbols of the rural Protestant bourgeoisie and those of working-class Loyalist culture. The demands of such knowledge upon a specific reading practice are subversive of the genre within which *Kissing the Frog* operates in that this avoidance of context as unimportant demands a simultaneous commitment to it. This can most obviously be contrasted to what Smyth identifies as Bateman's tendency to 'hector [...] the reader'[81] about the implications of the conflict in the North. While Bateman assumes that his reader will have knowledge of the North only through stereotype and prejudice, Dunlop assumes a more knowing, sly form of engagement.

It is not possible, of course, to identify with any great confidence general tendencies in Northern Irish Protestant popular fiction from a consideration of just these two examples and yet certain similarities between the two are of interest. In both novels Protestant bourgeois society is typified by a crisis of narrative: in both worlds very little happens and what does happen is insignificant. In *Cycle of Violence* such quietude is compared with the Northern Ireland that surrounds such oases – an 'elsewhere' in which the occurrence of 'happenings' is so frequent and meaningless as to overburden any attempt on the part of the individual protagonist to find structure or significance. This all-or-nothing scenario can be compared to *Kissing the Frog*'s vision of a bourgeois tedium so all-encompassing that the totality of its structures prevents any extension beyond itself. For this reason, escape is not understood as constituting a rejection of the bourgeois world-view but is rather imagined in terms of a movement from the bourgeois provincial (Magherafelt) to the bourgeois cosmopolitan (London).

Finally, any consideration of these two novels would be incomplete without noting the pronounced narcissism on the part of the authors that is implicit in their narrative structures. The local newspaper columns that *Cycle of Violence*'s bicycling journalist Miller writes 'made a lot of people laugh and a lot of people cry and it made him quite well known, if not across the city at least across the newsroom',[82] and in this he is a version of Bateman himself.[83] Similarly, in *Kissing the Frog* Marian's ultimate mode of escape in becoming a flight attendant appears to echo the profession of the author, who, it is noted on the inside cover of the novel, is an air stewardess for Gulf Air. Although such a parallel may be little more than a coincidence, at the same time it does draw attention to the uncomfortable negotiations in both these novels between generic expectation and the assumed knowledge of specific experience. For Bateman, particularly, this perception of experience is highly significant in that it is deployed in all his novels against what he assumes are his readers' complacent assumptions about the conflict in the North. As a result, the spiky iconoclasm of Miller's perceptions of sectarianism in Northern Ireland serves as a means of illustrating the ways in which the enlightened Protestant bourgeoisie also disrupts the fixed templates of oppressor and oppressed in the North as they are asserted by the ill-informed. This strategy is by no means straightforward. Miller is the representation of enlightened Protestantism in the text but he represents this formation only insofar as he refuses to acknowledge any economic or cultural allegiances. At the same time, this representation through the refusal to represent is legitimised by reference to the actual experience of Bateman himself. This doubled technique gives momentum to the text's disruption of both genre and political ideology, which, through this process, are forced into an uneasy alliance. Understood as such, it is the amorphous nature of the Northern Protestant bourgeoisie that transgresses both the teleology of the thriller form and the cause-and-effect symmetry of the sectarian cycle of violence itself.[84] However, although such a manoeuvre is complex, at the same time it accords with the more familiar bourgeois perception that personal experience will inevitably reveal ideology as false consciousness; a belief that is, as I will discuss, similarly crucial to the strategies of Wilson's *Eureka Street*.

Fat Lad (Glenn Patterson,1992), *Eureka Street* (Robert McLiam Wilson, 1996)

The novel is an urban form; a bourgeois, urban form.
                                                    Robert McLiam Wilson[85]

I began this chapter with a consideration of the various ways in which literary critics have assessed the state of fiction in the North and concluded their surveys with either a demand for, or the recognition of, a new mode of expression. While such constructions ultimately reveal more about the act of criticism itself, it is appropriate to conclude with a consideration of the two novelists who have most regularly been cited as providing a template for what the 'new' might look like: Robert McLiam Wilson and Glenn Patterson. However, such an analysis can only be of relevance if it recognises both the debt that the 'new' owes to the 'old' and, more significantly, just what contingent pressures are placed upon the 'new' text through such an identification. In *Literature and Revolution* Leon Trotsky identified how the 'new' emerges through the relationship of literary form to ideology:

> New artistic needs or demands for new literary and artistic points of view are stimulated by economics, through the development of a new class, and minor stimuli are supplied by changes in the position of the class, under the influence of the growth of its wealth and cultural power. Artistic creation is always a complicated turning inside out of old forms, under the influence of new stimuli which originate outside of art. In this large sense of the word, art is a handmaiden.[86]

While this intervention is perhaps best seen as a series of primary speculations intended to nudge the form/ideology opposition beyond simplified notions of reflection or embodiment, Trotsky's model nevertheless remains useful in that it allows form to be envisaged as occupying an intersection of three interrelated elements: the ideological stimuli resulting from a new or developing class, the pre-existent 'old forms' available to the writer for transformation or development and, finally, the transformative effect of the form on those ideologies, which it simultaneously expresses. In this way, as Trotsky develops his argument, literary form is inherently dualistic as it is implicated in 'heightening (or lowering) the general level of craftsmanship' while 'in its concrete historic form, it expresses definite demands which, in the final analysis, have a class character'.[87] For this reason, then, literature takes its place as part of the superstructural relations of production just as, concomitantly, it functions in the context of these relations.

Indeed, to take the argument one step further, while it can be seen that these relations produce the ideological formations that legitimate the values of the class in power, because these superstructural legitimations of the productive forces of society operate ideologically they are always riven with tensions and contradictions. Considering the symptoms of such tensions as they are manifest in Patterson's *Fat Lad*[88] and Wilson's *Eureka Street* allows both texts to be considered as representing a new mode of expression in Northern Irish fiction related to a specific socio-historical change close to that envisaged by Trotsky.[89] Moreover, the 'definite demands which [...] have a class character' that Trotsky directs us towards as a defining aspect of literary form can be seen as reorienting the traditional concerns of the Northern Irish novel and revealing new lineages.

Fat Lad depicts the return to Belfast of an exile, Drew Linden, a young Protestant working for a national chain of bookshops. As his life is an embodiment of the effects of the social and family violence endemic in his childhood so he becomes the 'fat lad' of the title: a referential mnemonic for the six counties of Northern Ireland.[90] In this way Drew

> blamed himself for his father beating him up (becoming, in effect, an accessory to his own abuse), blamed himself, moreover, for the deaths of upwards of one thousand people in indiscriminate bombings and random shootings in all corners of the country, few of which, needless to say, he had ever visited; and all because, long ago, he had learnt to blame himself for having been born in the first place.[91]

The focus of the novel, then, is on the negotiations and reconciliations necessary for Drew both to assimilate his past and to move beyond it, and this process is enacted through the three relationships he conducts focused respectively on London, Belfast and Dublin.[92] The structure of the novel that results is complex, drawing on historical resources from the construction of the *Titanic*, through the foundation and consolidation of the Northern Irish state, the beginning of the current period of social violence, and the Anglo-Irish Agreement. This historical breadth is conveyed through a form that ensures that, as Patten remarks, 'appeals to an epic or romanticised heritage are [...] underwritten by prosaic commentary, shattering the conceit of ingrained tragedy with fresh and ambiguous perspectives'.[93] Such 'fresh' perspectives, it can be argued, derive mainly from the novel's juxtaposition of traditional socio-sectarian identity with the modern façades and ambivalences of a Belfast redeveloped in line with the fetishes of most late-capitalist European cities. It is in the articulation of the tension between these two modes that *Fat Lad* is at its most striking and yet, as I shall be discussing, it is also at these points that the bourgeois origins of its experimental technique are most clearly revealed.

Wilson's *Eureka Street* is perhaps even more ambitious than *Fat Lad* in its desire to capture the totality of Belfast as a site of flux and incongruity. In the novel, Wilson maintains a more consistent polemic edge that develops the fierce critique of Northern Irish society established by his earlier *tour de force*, *Ripley Bogle*.[94] The novel also shares with *Fat Lad* a perception of Belfast as in transition between 'old' sectarian certainties and 'new' redevelopment, and reserves much of its most aggressive satire for the ease with which commodifications of local violence are seen to attract huge amounts of capital on the global market. There is an unevenness about these attacks, although the structure of the novel is impeccably balanced between the parallel narratives of two friends: Catholic Jake and Protestant Chuckie. As Jake, a cynical, grief-laden drifter, is the ideological heart of the book, the point from which most of the satire against Republican activists and sympathisers stems, so Chuckie's narrative, which concentrates on his almost mystical ability to manipulate the mysteries of reified capitalism, allows for a wider perspective. As I shall discuss, *Eureka Street* owes its greatest structural debt to the novels of Charles Dickens, and Wilson's fantastical, carnivalesque and sentimental vision of Belfast enables a breadth of perspective that at many points appears to be aspiring to the condition of epic. With this it is appropriate that the novel ends happily: Jake is reconciled (on his own terms) both to Aoirghe, the embodiment of Republicanism, and his own fate, while Chuckie finds love and fatherhood by looking beyond the parameters of Northern Ireland itself. The novel, then, is one of redemption and, like *Fat Lad*, ends at a point at which the future can at least be encountered if not predicted. In this way the novel's opening line, 'All stories are love stories', gestures to the destinies of Chuckie and Jake but also, perhaps more importantly, to the many extended descriptions of Belfast and its inhabitants.

Both these novels, then, envisage a narrative of Belfast, a coherent story that can be recounted, and in turn locate themselves at a point of tension within this journey. In many ways such an approach can be seen as inherently iconoclastic: the recognition of the new recontextualises that which is perceived as old sectarian piety and the result of this tension is to undercut the monolithic certainties of both narratives.

It is through such terms that these two novelists, considered as a pair, have been perceived previously.[95] However, while this approach enables a certain structural energy it also raises other questions about the resultant trajectories of the works. Just as both novels can be seen as explorations of the formal representation of community, so the resultant ideological contradictions of the texts should only be perceived in terms of their formal coherence. Indeed, while these novels can be seen as embodying such contradictions the temptation to read these as reflective of the social divisions and discontinuities implicit in Northern Ireland itself should be resisted. Rather, one can say that the contradictions of *Fat Lad* and *Eureka Street* do not represent a more general socially derived contradiction but rather are produced by the novels themselves through their necessary *relationship* to the ideologies they dissect. Pierre Macherey describes this process by way of a metaphor:

> For Marx and Engels, the study of an ideological phenomenon – that is to say, a conflict at the level of an ideology – cannot be isolated from the movement at the economic level: not because it is a different conflict, a different form of the conflict, but because it is the conflict of this conflict. The composition of an ideology implies the relation of the ideological to the economic.[96]

In this way it is the contradictions themselves that allow the novels to enable meaning, as it is through those contradictions – through that which is not said – that the relationship of the works to Northern Ireland is mediated. This in turn necessitates a focus on the formal properties of the novels, as it is through the formalisation of ideology in its relationship with the literary work that contradictions that are ordinarily imperceptible are revealed. Any account of both *Eureka Street* and *Fat Lad* as specifically bourgeois texts must begin at this point.

Such considerations are salutary, for they suggest that the role of criticism in relation to these novels should not be that of substitution or, as Macherey states, 'a pursuit of its discourse',[97] but rather should be to place itself at that point of contradiction, 'the *relation* between the implicit and the explicit',[98] and account for the necessity of that contradiction's existence. For this reason, while one can contend that these novels are inherently bourgeois in their form, such bourgeois ideology is not simply a reflection of the many different and amorphous practices that constitute the general bourgeois ideology but rather is a result of the formalisation of these practices through the relationship between the text and that which Macherey considers implicit. This, in turn, suggests other qualifications about the categories of analysis. To define *Eureka Street* and *Fat Lad* as 'bourgeois fiction' is not to imply a unity of discourse in their modes of expression but rather to posit, in Eagleton's phrase, 'a network of over-lapping features'.[99] Indeed formal unity is not the necessary or usual condition of the bourgeois novel; instead the self-consciousness of the form leads to an interrogative expressive technique that offers a liberal iconoclasm while concomitantly forbidding the discussion of certain key prerequisites. As we shall see in consideration of *Eureka Street*, bourgeois fiction often constructs a site of ideology – understood strictly as false consciousness – against which the formal structures of the work rebel. Placing itself in opposition to this monolithic formation, the typical characteristic of the bourgeois novel's narrative voice is a diffuseness, a quicksilver quality that attempts to anticipate potential criticism not least through an apparent critique of its own practices. However, it is in this desire to control potentially dissident readings that the limitations of the bourgeois novel are simultaneously revealed. Unable to theorise (or extend beyond) its own practices to a position from which the formation of society as a whole can be grasped, the typical tricksiness of the formal technique gestures also to a solipsism that is both seductive and yet also expressive of the bourgeois world-view.

This is germane to *Eureka Street* and *Fat Lad* in a number of central ways. If the novel form has reason to claim for itself the status of the epic of the bourgeois era then this is precisely because of its tendency to group itself around 'narrations of the socialisation of the individual', as David Lloyd puts it in his analysis of nineteenth-century Irish novels.[100] In this, as he further states, 'The anomalous individual learns to be reconciled with society and its projects, whether, as mostly for men, through labour or, as mostly for women, through love and marriage. The verisimilitude of realism resides in its capacity to make such narratives of self-formation normative.'[101] Although Lloyd's analysis here is beholden to Georg Lukács's conception of the pre-1848 bourgeois novel and is centred on the crisis of representation in Irish fiction of this period, his delineation of the bourgeois form describes well the strategies of representation also found in *Eureka Street* and *Fat Lad*. This, it can be argued, is more than mere coincidence. Just as those novels that engage Lloyd take part in a wider civilising process, 'the passage from savagery to civility'[102] as he puts it, so the satiric purpose of both *Fat Lad* and *Eureka Street* is predicated on a similar state of nativist violence out of which the individual develops

and is humanised. In this way, the progression from sectarian affiliation to fully individuated subject that can be found in these novels
involves the recognition of the effects of capital on previously assured
anachronistic divisions *and* the transformation of these divisions in a
new order. 'The production of ethical subjects',[103] in terms of both
modernity in general and the text itself, which Lloyd perceives as the
ultimate result of this process, serves equally well as a summary of the
bourgeois novel's project in modern Northern Ireland.

At this point it is worth looking in more detail at the strategies
implicit in this progression. In *Eureka Street* the core values of humanist individuation that ultimately (must) triumph are presented as
marginal, easily threatened, and attainable only through a process of
testing; a quest structure leading to ultimate redemption. This is realised
in both metaphorical and literal ways, as when Jake finds himself
caught in a riot:

> At each end of the dark lamp-lit street, masses of people had started
> charging towards me. On one side, I had the helmeted and shielded Royal
> Ulster Constabulary, and on the other, the forces and supporters of
> national liberation. I sat like a prick in the middle, pebbles and bottles
> failing to bounce all around me.[104]

Despite this danger, the confident ironic tone of the narrative voice
remains in place, as indeed it has to if it is to avoid being aligned with
the oppressive concept of ideology that is everywhere else evident in
the society. As Jake notes in conversation with Aoirghe: 'Politics are
basically antibiotic, i.e., an agent capable of killing or injuring living
organisms.'[105] In this context *Eureka Street*'s technique of presenting as
marginal those positions it simultaneously strives to advance is
characteristically bourgeois in that bourgeois ideology is typified by a
refusal to see its own position as complicit with (or an embodiment of)
power.[106] Similarly the isolated individualism of the book's hero not
only invigorates the centre ground – which is his sole preserve – but
facilitates an intimacy with the reader that provides the novel with its
ethical drive. By isolating the liberal voice and placing it between two
warring factions (factions that are, by definition, indistinguishable, as
when Loyalist bigots are described as identical to Republican Aoirghe
'bar the tits and the university education'[107]) the relationship formed
between the narrative voice and the reader is therefore central to the
novel's ideological structure. This, in many ways, is reminiscent of
Charles Dickens' narrative technique in which the hidden secrets of

British society are revealed to the reader through the intimacy of assumed knowledge and the subsequent exoticisation of everything that lies beyond that world-view. For this reason, it is appropriate that *Eureka Street* enters into a creative communion with both Dickens and, later in the novel, Leo Tolstoy:

> In 1869, Mortimer Lurgan, a shabby copying clerk at the Ulster bank in Donegall Place, spent eighteen cold hours on a pavement outside the Chandler's building in College Street. A reading was to be given by the famous English novelist Charles Dickens. It was his first visit to Belfast and probably his last. Mortimer Lurgan wanted to be in the front row for such an event. [...]
>
> After the reading one of the organizers introduced Mortimer to the exhausted novelist. When Dickens was told that Mortimer had slept on the street in his eagerness to attend, his old, lined face flickered with brief interest. 'Well Mr Logan,' he said, 'it is pleasant to meet such a true aficionado.' Smiling kindly, Dickens was bundled into a curtained carriage.[108]

While one of the functions of this passage is to emphasise the love of fame that Chuckie inherits from his ancestors, it also provides an important indication of the reading strategy the novel will insist upon. Just as Dickens is seen to be exhausted from his efforts to communicate his art, so the struggle of the novelist to convey meaning is valorised as honourable labour and compared favourably to the laziness and hypocrisy of the indigenous Northern Irish artist. As Jake comments in relation to Tolstoy: 'at least old Leo had done some actual work' – an achievement very much unlike the local 'subsidised galleries stocked full of the efforts of middle-class shitheads too stupid to do anything else'.[109] Such an opposition internationalises the perspective of *Eureka Street* as fiction and simultaneously marginalises the presence of the novel as an unwelcome interloper within the codes of Northern Irish art. For this reason, the novel reserves particular condemnation for poetry and particularly 'Shague Ghinthoss', a Nationalist poet described as 'a hypocritical Janus-faced tosspot'.[110] In this attack Wilson is continuing a particular vendetta against the form he has voiced previously in his career,[111] associating poetry not just with Nationalist thinking but also with an outmoded, predominantly rural, vision unable to countenance the changing picture of the new Ireland. Again, as with all that is condemned in *Eureka Street*, poetry is seen to be clouded by ideology and thus unable to see events as clearly as fiction.[112]

It is in these ways that Wilson unites the form of the labour in which he is engaged with the marginalisation of the ideology central to *Eureka Street*'s purposes and in so doing implicates the reader in an intimacy created by an accumulation of detail. This technique, which convinces through the flattery of assumed knowledge,[113] is close to the naturalism that Lukács perceived as a result of the failure of the 1848 European revolutions; the point at which liberalism became merely 'the ideology of the narrow and limited class interests of the bourgeoisie'.[114] The symptoms of this transformation include the reproduction and naturalisation of capital and, perhaps more importantly for our purposes, a predetermined view of the social whole. Fredric Jameson's reading of Zola in these terms is illustrative of my point:

> Zola already *knows* what the basic structure of society is, and this is his weakness. For him the basic raw material, the professions, the socially determined character types are already established in advance: this is to say that he has succumbed to the temptation of abstract thought, to the mirage of some static, objective knowledge of society.[115]

This static view of society negates the possibility of a dialectical transformation of its different elements and in turn relegates significance to the realm of the private individual and his or her relationship to capital. As such, specifically realised character dominates over typicality and what Eagleton terms 'meticulously observed detail'[116] becomes the favoured technique for realising this vision. In *Eureka Street* the character of Chuckie becomes less a typical representative of Belfast working-class Protestantism and more a richly idiosyncratic figure (although bourgeois criticism would not recognise such a distinction) created through statistics:

On my thirtieth birthday

I had been alive for:	360 months
	1560 weeks
	10,950 days
	262,800 hours
	15,768,000 minutes
	94,608,000 seconds
I had	
urinated approx:	74,460 times
ejaculated approx:	10,500 times
been asleep for approx:	98,550 hours (11 years, 3 months)
smoked approx:	11,750 cigarettes
consumed approx:	32,000 meals
drunk approx:	17,520 litres of liquid (approx: 8,000 of which contained alcohol)
walked approx:	20,440 miles

sustained an erection for approx:	186,150 mins, 3,102.5 hrs, 129.27 days
grown approx:	5.40 metres of hair
had sex approx:	175 times
earned approx:	no fucking money[117]

Paradoxically perhaps, it is precisely because of this accumulation that the narrative voice must become ever more *lisible*, ever more insistent, while any risks attendant to this strategy are minimised: through naturalism in *Eureka Street* and through a hesitant formalism in *Fat Lad*. In the former, the narrative voice often assumes the status of a deity bestowing favours ('Belfast was only half awake and its citizens were mild and lovable as children'[118]), although more usually the novel's characters (including Jake and Chuckie) are redeemed through relationships with women who provide both scrutiny of motive and ultimate reward ('Sarah had come and ironed me smooth, pressed the tough stuff right out of me'[119]). *Fat Lad* also uses women to delineate the progress of its hero although, as is appropriate to its formalist leanings, they have a far greater symbolic role in the narrative. As Drew moves from his relationship with Melanie in London, through Kay in Belfast, and ultimately on to Kay's half-sister, the Dublin-based Anna, so the symbolic structure of the work becomes more crucial to Drew's ultimate redemption. In this structure Drew is always presented as in relationships – at no point is he single – and the natural analogy with the strained connections and alliances formed by Ulster Protestantism creates its own symbolic order. This is first established early in the novel as Melanie considers a gift given to her by Drew:

> A pair of tailor's dummies stood back to back in the corner by the window. Two mud-brown velveteen lollies licked into approximate human shapes (the prototypes on which her occasional creations were modelled), locked in a struggle they were powerless to resolve.[120]

This image of the dummies, unable to overcome whatever mute force of resistance divides them, immediately suggests both the lack of communication between Drew and Melanie and the strained relationship between Northern Irish Protestantism and Britain, an implication reinforced by Drew's sporadic disloyalty and unfaithfulness.[121] Leaving London for Belfast to take up a post as assistant manager at 'Bookstore', Drew soon enters into another relationship, this time with Kay Morris, a Belfast Protestant who embodies the commercial energies of the city's industrial (and largely Protestant) past. In this union, the desire is that of self-recognition and their kissing is described as 'ancient turtles rubbing necks';[122] an appropriate image for an activity that is given the overtones of a tribal rite. As the possibilities of this relationship (as an internal settlement based on a shared cultural inheritance) are rejected so Drew is ultimately drawn to Anna – the other to Kay's indivisible self – and the novel's symbolism gains in momentum. After their first parting the portents become ominous:

> A dog, it is said, passing that spot three hours later sat down on the footpath and howled its bafflement. Howled and howled until its owner whipped it, kicked it, and finally dragged it, whining and yelping, out from under the ghostly X of their clasped hands.[123]

By this stage of the work the narrative style maintains an uneasy mix of formalist procedures and naturalist inevitabilities which are not resolved until Drew and Anna finally consummate their relationship. As this is the ideological heart of the book so the symbolic structure that has gained in momentum up to this point allows for its own closure in the reconciliation of partitioned geographies and political sensibilities:

> Vast movements of peoples were communicated in the silence of a single kiss. Borders were crossed, identities blurred. Land masses rose and fell with their bodies.
> Not surprisingly, their lovemaking was long and intricate and when it was over they felt the movement ebb away into the future.[124]

This culmination can be read in Lukács's terms as genuinely historicist insofar as it portrays 'the conception of history as the destiny of the people'.[125] In this way the climactic union between Drew and Anna 'stand[s] at the meeting point of great social-historical collisions',[126] unifying the personal and the historical through the emphasis on 'typicality'. For this reason the formal tensions that typify *Fat Lad* can be reread as representing a collision between historical realism and symptoms of historical privation, the milieu 'against which supposedly private histories are unfolded'[127] or, to return to Lloyd's analysis, another version of 'the passage from savagery to civility'.

Lukács's more general reservations about the symbolic mode are of relevance at this point, for while the symbol has the potential to convey immanent meaning it can also (and simultaneously) signify the defeat of the novel at the hands of reified capitalist society. As Jameson, in his account of Lukács, puts it: 'by having recourse to [symbolism] the writer implies that some original, objective meaning in objects is henceforth inaccessible'.[128] This, in turn, represents a classic feature of the bourgeois formalism that *Fat Lad* tends towards: its inability to give voice to the mysterious connections and meanings that constitute modern society. In place of this voice social phenomena are instead marked by silence; they appear to lead an entirely independent existence that is both self-fulfilling and foreclosed. *Fat Lad*'s two major symbols, the goldfish ('its nose and tail so close together in the bowl it was almost able to eat its own shit'[129]) and the *Titanic*, are both illustrative of this condition. In the case of the latter, the status of the ship (and with this its relationship to the conditions of Drew's ancestors) is reduced to the repeated refrain '*Irishglug and Irishgurgle*' and 'a single, incontrovertible fact: *the fucking thing sank*'.[130] In this way the *Titanic* as symbol is drained of immanent meaning and instead merely takes the place of a historical process (the relationship of Ulster Protestantism to the Union and to Home Rule) which it is beyond the parameters of the novel to articulate in any other way. The symbol of the goldfish is more complex in that it is, in itself, representative of an exhausted and circular mode of existence. Released into a bath by Drew's sister Ellen it still 'describe[d] a perfect circle, the exact circumference of its bowl':[131]

> – That's disgusting!
> She slapped the water with the flat of her hand.
> – Swim straight can't you. Look, like this.
> And without another thought she had plunged her hands – wrists – forearms – elbows – into the water, floundering in the goldfish's curved wake. It couldn't elude her for long, though. She realised that she need only keep her hand poised in one place and the goldfish was bound to come round, time and again.

As an image of pointless habitual life the goldfish symbol is resonant but its full implications can only be grasped if it is recognised that the presence of the symbol in itself is symptomatic of deeper silences. To return to Macherey's formulation, the goldfish does not reflect the condition of Northern Irish life but rather the formalisation of these practices through the relationship between that which is amorphous and voiceless (actual historical conditions) and the possibilities of the bourgeois text. As a symbol it seeks to extend beyond the parameters of the novel itself just as it is testament to the self-contained status of the work and, therefore, the impossibility of such a desire.

This tendency towards exhausted symbolism mirrors the mystifications of capital that are endemic in both novels. While both *Fat Lad* and *Eureka Street* catalogue in great detail the sectarian framework of Belfast, perceiving it in both cases as representative of a residual mode of thought, the imposition of explicit capital on this framework is fetishised in its unknowability. In Wilson's novel capital is built upon an alienated notion of identity, which, although satirised, is ultimately seen as preferable to that which it supplants. Its appearance in the text occurs mostly within Chuckie's narrative and it is perhaps significant that it occupies a much more marginal role in Jake's story – the figure who represents the dominant liberal ideology of the novel taken as a whole. For Chuckie, however, it is the realisation that commodifications of Irishness attract capital that provides its own rewards:

> John Maynard Keynes was wrong. Malthus had no idea. Chuckie had simply made it up as he went along. He had dished out a whole series of off-the-cuff pipe-dreams and improbabilities, inventing non-existent projects and ideas never intended or likely to exist. After three hours of bullshit, lies and fantasies, some of which he couldn't even understand himself, they had agreed to grant him eight hundred thousand pounds over the first eight months of his operation.[132]

The satirical purpose of this passage is self-evident but it is important to note that, unlike other characters in the novel, Chuckie's access to wealth does not lead to alienation but rather is simultaneous with his general development into a fully realised individual. In Chuckie's fantasies this leads to the possibility of raising enough money to be able to buy Ireland completely ('FINE OLD COUNTRY, RECENTLY PARTITIONED, IN NEED OF MINOR POLITICAL REPAIR. PRICED FOR QUICK SALE'[133]) and, as such, completely supersede the old with the new. The opposition this suggests entails that at few points does *Eureka Street* attempt to recognise the interconnectedness of the two poles or to implicate capital within that which the novel signifies as residual. Instead capital is positioned as always outside the borders of Ireland itself, or, as the novel puts it, 'the money that flooded in from the European Community, the international fund for Ireland and all the other pass-the-hat agencies the Irish loved so'.[134] In this way capital is associated with change and non-nativist perspectives and so, despite the satirical attacks on the ease with which Chuckie gains his fortune, the novel's closure leaves open the possibilities inherent in its influx.

Fat Lad is similarly ambivalent about the status of capital-as-change, but capital occupies a more complex position in the novel, gesturing towards greater formal realignments. The bookshop Drew works in, Bookstore, is part of an entire 'recasting'[135] of the city that replaces the military by the commercial: 'The army had long since departed from the Grand Central Hotel, on whose levelled remains an even grander shopping complex was now nearing completion.'[136] The significance of this information in the novel's opening chapter not only introduces the opposition between the old and the new but also asserts the novel's development from Patterson's previous *Bildungsroman, Burning Your Own*,[137] a work located more confidently within the perspective of the old. Bookstore itself, the company that necessitates Drew's return to Belfast and thus the motor of the plot, also negotiates its way between past and present in the act of creating a seamless continuity:

> Many people in many different towns took them for a local firm; some were even prepared to swear (market research had proved it) that their family had always bought books there, though the first shop was opened as recently as 1977 and the majority had appeared within the last five years.[138]

Owned by three Cambridge graduates and effortlessly bourgeois in the denial of its status as a multinational, Bookstore serves as an analogy for the transgressive bourgeois form embodied by *Fat Lad*, for, like the shop recently rooted in Belfast, it is a characteristic of bourgeois form that it can take on local colour, appeal to cultural and historical specificity, and yet still engage itself with essentially the same process.

As the new slowly gains dominance over the old in *Fat Lad*, so conceptions of the past, both social and personal, are perceived as increasingly arbitrary and open to appropriation. This has been considered as representative of an embryonic Northern Irish postmodernism[139] in a manner similar to the recent poetry of Ciaran Carson,[140] but in both cases such an appellation more fully reveals the covert debt that postmodernism owes to formal bourgeois improvisation. Towards the end of *Fat Lad* the sterilities that govern Drew's childhood have almost entirely given way to Belfast as multi-cultural event:

> The street filled with music. Fifties pop, acid house, a shriek of jazz trumpet from somewhere, a crash of metal from a jukebox somewhere else, Indian restaurant music from an Indian restaurant. Discrete yet oddly harmonious; a symphony for any city, summer 1990.[141]

The recognition that Belfast can finally become 'any city' and is therefore able to move beyond the opposition that sustained the novel to this point is immediately shattered by 'a single discordant note' of gunfire as the old reasserts itself in the midst of the possible. This uneasy balance – which, as in *Eureka Street*, never quite recognises the connections between the two poles – will remain for the rest of the novel and, in this way (again like *Eureka Street*), the possibly redemptive mysteries of capital remain.

If these considerations suggest that *Fat Lad* and *Eureka Street* embody too thoroughly the shifting perspectives of bourgeois fiction it is important to recognise that both works envisage a concomitant reality in the physical fabric of the city itself. Both novels can be mapped (although Wilson trades in allegory by including locations such as 'Poetry Street' and 'Democracy Street' within this) and the recognition of the authentic this provides counterpoints with the symbolic and the fantastic found elsewhere in the works. This is a persistent strategy of the liberal novel:[142] the physical is written on by the shifting allegiances of the characters and thus provides both stability and concrete symptoms of the inevitability of change. The opposition thereby constructed becomes one envisaged as between setting and character (a divorce which for Lukács typifies the post-1848 bourgeois novel). Just as location is stable (even if, as in the case of *Fat Lad*, it signifies the new), so character is allowed to be internally divided; a process semi-satirised in *Fat Lad* through Drew's pompous notebook assertion that 'Duplicity is the Northern Irish vice. We are always (at least) two people and always false to (at least) one of them.'[143] The liberal novel, then, becomes both an elegy for the passing of the old and an embodiment of the inevitability of change. One's attention is immediately drawn to this aspect in *Eureka Street* by the front cover publicity, which promises 'A novel of Ireland like no other'. It is around that 'of' (rather than 'about') that this strategy is made apparent – a rhetorical trope efficiently destroyed by the novel itself when Jake is approached in Lavery's bar by a potential paramour:

> At one horrible and confiding point she told me that she had a theory of life (it couldn't be a theory *about* life, it had to be a theory *of* life, it had to be an eighteenth-century disquisition, it had to be the fucking *Origin of Species*).[144]

In the same manner, the shift from 'about' to 'of' on the front cover creates its own insistent reading strategy which again gestures towards the status of epic – another *Origin of Species*.

It is in these ways that *Eureka Street* and *Fat Lad* construct a field of possibilities that both texts will fulfil and supersede by their conclusions. Oppositions between the old and the new, between sectarianism and capital, between character and location, are negotiated and ultimately resolved through the process of redemption for the major figures in the narrative as they transcend the inherited detritus of their upbringing and attain a state of full individuation. It is in this area that both novels are most typically bourgeois. Transformation is not just a possibility but rather a necessity, for, as Jake tells Aoirghe in *Eureka Street*, 'An opinion that remains unchanged quickly becomes a prejudice.'[145] For this reason, and in contrast to the greater formal complexity of *Fat Lad*, closure in *Eureka Street* has a linear simplicity. Although Althusser's famous maxim that 'ideology never says, "I am ideological"'[146] overplays the totalising and unitary nature of ideological interpellation, in Wilson's novel the implications of a similar conception of ideology drive the narrative through the relationship of Jake with Aoirghe. This is illustrated through the novel's preoccupation with the perceived rigidities of ideological structures as a disabling feature of life in Northern Ireland, and the perception of these structures is rarely presented as anything other than a matter of false consciousness. It is for this reason that *Eureka Street* soon establishes an important structural opposition between ideology and sight. Eyes are considered as 'those democratic unideological things [...] giving witness, testimony',[147] while the possibility of the gaze enabling a moment of revelation is central to the harrowing account of the bomb blast in chapter 11. It is in the resolution of this opposition that the novel formulates its closure. Unable to transform the conditions of the society with which it is concerned, *Eureka Street* instead circles obsessively around the possibilities inherent in the idea of character as revelation. Aoirghe, who functions throughout the novel as a cipher of Republicanism, is redeemed through her witnessing the marks of violence left on the body of the child-victim Roche. As she is remade as a compassionate figure she is simultaneously transformed in terms of her relationship to the dominant ideology of the novel and Jake's narrative voice. In these terms the final line of the novel, 'She smiles and she looks at me with clear eyes', signals both the triumph of sight over discourse and the awakening, both literally and metaphorically, from false consciousness. It is in this way that the decency (embodied by Jake as both a rational *and* humanist alternative) that the novel had previously constructed as a marginal site of peripheral values in opposition to the perceived dominant social ideology of atavism and rhetoric (represented by Aoirghe's earlier Republicanism) is allowed a partial victory. This is necessarily circumscribed within the realm of character not only because any other transformation would be beyond the bourgeois parameters of the novel's form but also because such a transformation would compromise the satirical framework central to the novel's purpose.

Fat Lad's closure is more conclusive and makes a greater attempt at transformation of the social whole. Drew is relocated to Paris, his father apologises for his previous abuse and, through this, Drew acknowledges the hurt that was done to him as a child. For this reason, 'leaving was hard – much harder than he'd remembered. Perhaps because there was more *to* leave this time.'[148] In turn, his father, who functions in the novel as an embodiment of both the disabilities and the sensitivities of Ulster Protestantism, suffers a stroke and is reduced to a child-like status:

> Jack smiled awry, seeming to bow a little under the weight of the pendulous daisy-chains as he rose from his black and gold chair, stiff but dignified, lavender straw cradled in the crook of his arm, buttercup yellow beanie perched, brim up, on his head.
> – Yes, he said. Yes.[149]

This echo of the conclusion of *Ulysses* not only acknowledges a formalist debt but also attempts to broaden the redemption of Drew to encapsulate the community of which he is now an assimilated part. Such a transformation lies outside of the scope of the novel but it hints at the possibility of a form that can mobilise symbolism with an immanent function.

In some ways charting these novels' creation of a full individuation out of social fracture can tell nothing but the same old story; the bourgeois paradigm refigured in Belfast is only slightly different to its manifestation elsewhere. Despite this, there is little point in criticising the works for what they do not achieve. As *Eureka Street* and *Fat Lad* synthesise a form that is expressive of the conditions out of which they come they do not just reflect a changing order but also change the terms of that order. *Fat Lad* can be seen as a combination of the realist and the bourgeois text. It is a realist text insofar as it sees the history of Ulster Protestantism as, to use Lukács's phrase, 'the pre-history of the present', striving to present through Drew Linden the 'typical' aspects of that society. However, it is simultaneously a bourgeois text in that such negotiations are played out against the backdrop of naturalised and consolidated capital, which the novel can address only in an oblique manner. *Eureka Street*'s satiric purpose ensures that its aims are more direct but its opposition of ideology to what it insists upon as 'truth' ensures other equivocations. Such alliances and silences should not be surprising, for the tensions and uncertainties of both these novels ultimately owe little to a postmodern sensibility but rather more to the shifting perspectives and elisions of the post-1848 bourgeois novel tradition. For this reason perhaps the final word on these novels should be left to Lukács, writing about Flaubert and Meyer:

> True, the weapon of satire, the passionate romantic contrast between past and present prevents these writers from becoming apologists of the liberal bourgeoisie, gives their work significance and interest; but it does not help them to escape the curse of alienation from the people. However much they may repudiate or criticize the ideological consequences of this historical situation – and so they do – the socio-historical facts themselves, whose ideological consequences they combat, are inevitably reflected in the content and form of their works.[150]

Conclusion

Ultimately *Fat Lad, Eureka Street, Cycle of Violence, Kissing the Frog* and *A Wreath Upon the Dead* come to similar conclusions. While each novel charts a form of resistance it is possible for the individual to take when faced with the perceived constrictions of Nationalist and/or Unionist ideology, at the same time they all acknowledge (although to varying degrees) the futility of attempting to resist the onward march of postmodern capitalism. In this way, the limits of personal action are circumscribed within identity politics, or rather, the classic opposition between personal responsibility and communal affiliation which it has been the role of Northern Irish literature to mediate is recontextualised by the looming presence of a new mode of being that will render both alternatives redundant. It is for this reason that the necessary response to this inevitable reordering is ambiguous: at one level the violent dissolution of the old polarities is longed for and the presence of its initial symptoms welcomed, at another level the inability of these novels to predict what shape this future may take leaves them poised uneasily between the known and the unknown. As *A Wreath Upon the Dead* most obviously indicates, all that can be done in the face of this confusion is simply to list the diversity of the antagonistic symptoms:

> The recent Irish fiction Maureen read might be about cool Trinity graduates discussing Chekhov over a feed of escargots with lean liberated blondes who knew all about birth-control, but the parish priest, the Pope and the Provos were still the stuff of her mother's weekly letter. Those lean liberated blondes did after all share an Ireland with frightened teenagers shamefully obliged to give birth at the back of a ditch in the snow, an Ireland where new-born babies were dumped into bogholes on top of the corpses of those martyred millions who died long ago precisely to keep their land holy and pure and sinless. The country of John McGahern's poised heroines certainly, the elite dinner-party world of Terence de Vere White, of John Broderick, of Julia O'Faolain, the country of Grafton Street chic, of drugs in Ballymun, of U2, of centrally-heated bungalows, video rentals in every street – but also the country of Bobby Sands starving to death naked in a prison cell whose walls were smeared with the excrement of eight centuries' hate [...][151]

It is tempting when faced with such contradictions to suggest that the Northern Irish novel is itself merely a reflection of a historical moment of economic and political indeterminacy and that a subsequent reordering of that structure will herald a new stability in the form. However, this crude version of base and superstructure does not adequately account for the various negotiations between indigenous and non-indigenous literary forms that are already implicit in the Northern Irish novel, and risks merely reasserting the utopian critical oppositions that I began this chapter by discussing. Instead it can be argued that what is most clearly revealed when surveying recent Northern Irish fiction is not a putative crisis of the subject in the face of historical flux but rather the extent to which that flux has been used to give shape to the underlying stability of bourgeois characters who become typical in their atypicality. The rapacious nature of bourgeois ideology, its instinctive urge to assimilate, ensures, at one level, the success of this procedure, but it also demands a price. Because of the obsessive interest in the precise moment of interaction between cultural identity and the individual subject found in Northern Irish culture it is inevitable that ultimately this opposition will fossilise into irredeemable self-consciousness. It is as a result of this fetishisation that the bourgeois humanist project, built as it is around an assumed unity of identity and self, collapses into itself and becomes instead a form of identitarian camp. The manifestations such camp can take and the possibility of reading them as an immanent critique of bourgeois ideology in Northern Ireland is the subject of the final chapter.

4

Three Forms of Camp

Again we find the Marxist classics agreed on attributing to the petty bourgeois a maudlin sentimentality. The sentimental Eugène Sue, who is pilloried in *The Holy Family*, and the sentimental Proudhon, appear as the archetypal French petty bourgeois. In Germany, the petty bourgeoisie is offered that brand of socialism which the *Manifesto* ironically dubs 'true'. The pretentious garb in which its 'eternal truths' were presented was put together from 'speculative cobwebs, embroidered with flowers of rhetoric, steeped in the dew of sickly sentiment'. Even the idealist Hegel made fun of Schiller's unattainable ideals.

Maria Ossowska defining 'bourgeois sentimentalism'[1]

As this study has been suggesting, there are limits to the identitarian project and borders that it cannot cross. As identity formations in Northern Ireland have their genesis not in the need to encounter opposition but rather in the contemplation of an absence within the subject itself, so much of what can be understood as the discourse of Northern Irish identity politics takes the form of a cultural *possibility*; a strategy intended to find a voice from within (and give shape to) a contradictory ideology. It is for this reason that identity, despite the prerequisite that it should appear as a self-sufficient, achieved entity, is at the same time a construct that is forever reinventing itself. Identity's call for recognition, the manner in which it demands acknowledgment of itself, contradicts that which is, simultaneously, its most crucial appeal: the self-evident, totalitarian, nature of its demands. As identity makes itself known through spectacle, as self-conscious declaration, so it offers itself as something to be consumed: its message no more than a declaration of existence. In turn, the insistent cries for acknowledgment that such a declaration demands become insatiable: as it always wants more than it receives, the identitarian imperative is both foreclosed by the bourgeois codes through which it makes itself known and yet also always seeking to be in excess of itself. As the presence of these negotiations indicates, the play of identity in Northern Ireland has, to adapt Judith Butler, 'cultural survival as its end'.[2] Indeed, although she develops this perception in terms of gender performance, the 'clearly punitive consequences' Butler identifies as the possible risk of such performance (a result of its urge to articulate itself 'within compulsory systems') are similarly manifest within the frameworks of Northern Irish society. As this chapter will discuss, identity formations in Northern Ireland die, or rather become parodic, when the competing demands of contingent politics and tradition overwhelm their delicate structures.

There are possibilities and limits implicit in this awareness. As cultural identity remains preoccupied with a demand for ever greater acknowledgment of the integrity of its cause so its failure ever quite to explicate the full complexities, incoherence and contradictions of the subject lead it to a series of increasingly excessive proclamations. It is at this point that the self/utterance paradigm that it is nominally the role of identity to unify begins to fall apart and the contingent roots of the project become visible. Butler's perspective on this transformation in terms of gendered identity is again highly relevant here:

> Gender ought not to be constructed as a stable identity or locus of agency from which various acts follow; rather, gender is an identity tenuously constituted in time, instituted in an exterior space through a *stylized repetition of acts*. The effect of gender is produced through a stylization of the body and, hence, must be understood as the mundane way in which bodily gestures, movements, and styles of various kinds constitute the illusion of an abiding gendered self. This formulation moves the conception of gender off the ground of a substantial model of identity to one that requires a conception of gender as a constituted *social temporality*. Significantly, if gender is instituted through acts which are internally discontinuous, then the *appearance of substance*, is precisely that, a constructed identity, a performative accomplishment which the mundane social audience, including the actors themselves, come to believe and to perform in the mode of belief.[3]

In insisting on the status of gender as a temporal phenomenon, Butler is able to assert its strategic function, the manner in which its constant readjustments and manifestations in response to threats and challenges to its essence begin to erode the perception of permanence that is its most obvious appeal. In this way, the maintenance of identity becomes an act in its own right. Rather than functioning as the location from which a social constituency begins to press its claims for redress, identity itself begins to make ever more pressing demands for its own continuation. It is for this reason that, for Butler, gender identity 'is also a norm that can never fully be internalized', it becomes 'phantasmatic, impossible to embody'[4] and, as such, can be seen as little more than a rehearsal of its own empty forms.

This is not to suggest that there is in the first instance an originary moment of 'pure' identity well able to articulate the claims of a social group and bespeaking a unity of self and utterance, but rather to observe that it is around such fantasies, and their impossibility, that identity organises itself. The 'maudlin sentimentality' that Ossowska identifies as a central symptom of 'petty bourgeois' ideology is a result of the inevitable failure on the part of that formation to reconcile its 'eternal truths' to contingent historical demands. Of course, this does not mean that the bourgeoisie would be well advised to abandon this quest, for it is through the repeated failure of the present social configuration to fulfil the demands of the equally contingent 'eternal truths' that bourgeois ideology presses its own economic claims. 'Sentimentality' in these terms is not a moment of luxury beyond the terms of the economic nexus but is instead a central imperative through which demands for redress are negotiated. It can be argued, however, that such acts can never be entirely successful. Implicit in the concept of sentimentality is an awareness of loss, the inevitability of what Butler terms 'the failure to repeat'. Just as that which is lost cannot be regained in its original state, so within the identitarian spectacle is 'a de-formity, or a parodic repetition that exposes the phantasmatic effect of abiding identity as a politically tenuous construction'.[5]

One way of defining this performative process – what Butler terms a *'stylized repetition of acts'* – is, of course, as a form of camp, and it is through this mode that the maudlin sentimentality of Northern Ireland's own identitarian preoccupations makes itself known. As claims for social redress are based around the acknowledgment of loss, the fact that the supposed integrity of a cause is compromised by the violence being done to it in the present, so the repetition of the original claim becomes parodic, an increasingly desperate assertion of something irredeemably lost. Understood in these terms camp becomes indicative of an overdetermined identity formation, a form of fossilised identitarian excess lamenting the loss of a unified subject position but also aware of the impossibility of such a synthesis. The danger inherent in this parade of identity is the ever-present possibility that its parodic nature will ultimately take on a life of its own;

that the performance of socio-sectarian affiliation will eventually become so self-delighting that the symbols of its fetishisation will become dissociated from its ostensible cause. It is at such moments that the vulnerability of the identitarian project is revealed, as the elaborate edifice of the construction becomes top-heavy with accumulated detritus.

Some care needs to be exercised at this point. While in these terms camp can be described as a fetishisation of the subject, a form of immanent critique arising out of bourgeois ideology, camp is more usually perceived as a highly conscious – and often highly radical – misreading deployed against dominant ideological forms through its mobilisation of externality. In these terms, its status parodies bourgeois consciousness's insistence on the distinction between surface and depth. The title of Richard Dyer's codification of the importance of campness within gay culture, 'It's being so camp as keeps us going',[6] indicates well the importance of camp as a strategy of cultural survival. For Dyer, camp can be understood in these terms as a form of 'self-defence'. As he notes: 'Particularly in the past, the fact that gay men could so sharply and brightly make fun of themselves meant that the real awfulness of their situation could be kept at bay – they need not take things too seriously, need not let it get them down. Camp kept, and keeps, a lot of gay men going.'[7] Dyer's reading of camp is heavily indebted to Susan Sontag's 'Notes on "Camp"',[8] an essay that, despite its age, remains one of its most vivid engagements with the concept. For Sontag, camp is 'a sensibility (as distinct from an idea)' and as such is almost impossible to track down, for 'to talk about Camp is therefore to betray it'. It is for this reason that, like Dyer (and, as I will discuss, Tom Paulin), Sontag believes camp is best recognised by identification of its presence through the listing of various camp icons.[9] This form has to take the place of analysis because of camp's own 'particular fugitive sensibility'.[10]

How, then, can one find a position from which camp can be talked about without running, in Sontag's words, 'the risk of having, oneself, produced a very inferior piece of Camp'?[11] One crucial aspect of her model of camp as sensibility is its insistence on camp's intimacy with what is being parodied or transformed. In this way, camp is not merely parasitic on the dominant culture from which it draws its inspiration but, more significantly, depends upon a degree of affection. Throughout 'Notes on "Camp"' the concept is discussed with a gentle under-standing: 'Old-fashioned, out-of-date, *démodé* objects, Sontag writes, are to be cherished for in their 'necessary detachment' they arouse 'a necessary sympathy'. For this reason, 'time liberates the work of art from moral relevance'.[12] The subversive potential of camp in these terms does not lie in an exclusivist impulse, nor does it gain its force through the creation of aesthetic hierarchies. Instead, camp re-evaluates and re-encounters historical objects through a deliberate stripping away of their historical essence. Once they have been reduced to a surface form they are integrated into camp sensibility, modifying that sensibility in turn. It is in the course of this process that camp's subversive potential to (in the words of Sontag) 'dethrone the serious'[13] is revealed. Camp's rejection of sincerity in the face of a overdetermined cultural practice not only proposes its own radical cultural history but also establishes a space outside modern bourgeois society's 'hyperinvolvement'.[14]

Reading camp in these terms suggests something of the particular form of historical engagement it demands. At one level it prizes the artefacts created by history, on another, the commitment it makes to these objects is conditional, based upon a fundamental belief in their malleability. This perception can also be extended to the realm of human consciousness. Sontag again:

> What Camp taste responds to is 'instant character' (this is, of course, very 18th century); and, conversely, what it is not stirred by is the sense of the development of character. Character is understood as a state of continual incandescence – a person being one, very intense thing. This attitude towards character is a key element of the theatricalization of experience embodied in the Camp sensibility. And it helps account for the fact that opera and ballet are experienced as such rich treasures of Camp, for neither of these forms can easily do justice to the complexity of human nature.[15]

The terms of such a transformation suggest why camp is so closely related to conceptions of character as viewed through the lens of identitarian politics. In both, character becomes a finite, foreclosed entity – an achieved state of being that can only be assimilated or rejected. As I discussed when considering recent fiction from Northern Ireland, a crisis sporadically occurs in bourgeois ideology when this sense of a cultural identity as an 'achieved state' is juxtaposed with the bourgeois commitment to a reading of the human subject as developmental, the idea that there is a narrative of wisdom gained through the accumulation of experience. When faced with these mutually exclusive imperatives, the solution usually proposed (as in Robert McLiam Wilson's *Eureka Street* or Colin Bateman's *Cycle of Violence*) is to sacrifice the expedient claims of identity to the presentation of a further awakening that reveals such affiliations as false consciousness (hence *Eureka Street*'s conclusion 'She smiles and she looks at me with clear eyes'[16]). Camp's rejection of such possibilities not only constitutes an implicit questioning of the value of this mode of emergence but also – and more contentiously – seems to invite an actual commitment to identity's formal structures. In this way camp becomes an unlikely ally, if not of identity itself, then at least to the symmetries and oppositions on which it is dependent.

Camp, then, fulfils a number of important roles within bourgeois society. In exposing the shallowness of identitarian constructions of the self through a determined focus on the surfaces of their manifestation, it is a celebration of those identities while at the same time containing a more dangerous awareness of their ultimate interchangeability. Its intimacy with those codes, the profound knowledge of the society it demands, similarly allows for a demarcation of a culture while, as Dyer reminds us, providing a mode of cultural survival in the face of real or imagined violence. Camp is thus transgressive of the limits by which identity normally offers itself. As an overdetermined spectacle, identitarian camp represents the dissociation of the symbol of community affiliation from the community itself, but just as it can bring about this rupture, it can also function as a means of creating new communities. It is for these reasons that Northern Ireland is fertile ground for the development of camp consciousness. In a society built around a series of delicate personal and communal negotiations, camp provides a means of asserting a knowing distance from the intimacies of the conflict while allowing an affiliation to an identity position to be both committed and yet sceptical. Camp's role as a mode of shibboleth, the manner in which it creates communities through the exclusionary powers of knowledge, is well suited to a society built upon a constant series of negotiations between competing interests. Similarly, the version of camp deployed as a means of cultural survival is ubiquitous in the North, as with, to take an obvious example, the fetishised use of the phrase 'the Troubles' to describe social and sectarian violence. Because 'Troubles' suggests both familial and social intimacies, its sentimentality is a mode of disengagement from the reality of the violence while still containing within it a mode of commitment. As this substitution suggests, it is not too fanciful to observe that it's being so camp as keeps Northern Ireland going.

I wish to argue then that there are three predominant, and often competing, forms of Northern Irish camp. The first two modes can be identified, straightforwardly enough, as varieties of camp consciousness arising out of Unionist and Nationalist culture. The third is slightly more complex but can be understood as 'non-aligned' or 'dissenting' camp: a camp sensibility that foregrounds a *shared* cultural inheritance through the attempt to look beyond what are assumed to be inflexible sectarian polarities or one that asserts a position of uncompromising independence in a self-conscious opposition to them. Of course, these three modes are not mutually exclusive. In actuality, they feature inter-changeable elements, codes, phrases and methods of engagement. More pointedly, they are all predicated on knowledge of each other for their continued efficacy.

Perhaps it is necessary to note at this point that such a codification does not suggest that Northern Irish camp can be placed in opposition to a form of sophisticated internationalism found elsewhere. While it may appear a banal assertion, it is nevertheless important to stress that all bourgeois societies develop their own forms of camp culture. Similarly, camp is not merely the preserve of a knowing cultural elite able to observe its sheer awfulness in a manner not available to wider society. While, as Sontag recognises, one important feature of camp can be its unknowingness of itself as such (which is why, for instance, Dyer can identify the Queen Mother as a British camp icon), the fact that it is simultaneously (and more importantly) based upon what Dyer terms 'a question of how you respond to things'[17] opens up its radical – almost, one might argue, democratic – potential. Just as, for Roland Barthes, 'there is no law, whether natural or not, which forbids talking about things',[18] so a commitment to camp does not demand the accumulation of any substantial cultural capital.

It is at this point that some consideration of the relationship between camp sensibility and kitsch becomes necessary. In a perceptive account of the significance of kitsch for cultural theory, David Lloyd identifies the importance of 'standardization and circulation' to the nationalist project:

> Cultural nationalism requires a certain homogenization of affect, a require-ment served not so much by selection as by proliferation, the dissemination of countless ballads, newspaper articles, symbols and images that are virtually indistinguishable. Indeed, a considerable degree of stylistic uniformity, a simulacrum of the anonymity of 'folk' artifacts, is indispensable to the project: stylistic idiosyncrasy would be counterproductive, stylization is of the essence.[19]

As I will discuss in relation to the poetry of the Ulster Defence Association during the 1980s it is through a process markedly similar to this (the generic repetition of the ballad form and its distribution through cheaply produced desk-top-published magazines) that a coherent ideological position was fleetingly established. For Lloyd the reason cultural nationalism produces – and identifies itself with – kitsch lies with their similarly homogenising effect. As kitsch homogenises economic production so cultural nationalism's appeal is built upon the establishment of a political homogeneity – its need to assert itself as the one and only answer to the question of oppression. In these terms kitsch and camp offer themselves as critiques of bourgeois modernity. While camp selects, kitsch proliferates. Camp empties the bourgeois artefact of its quasi-moral significance and celebrates merely its form, while kitsch renders the moral currency of the artefact itself worthless through the hyper-inflation of infinite reduplication. Kitsch then reinvests content into artefacts that bourgeois culture would ostensibly despise. As Lloyd notes, 'kitsch is mannerism, sentiment congealed into attitude. Its relation to commodity fetishism in general lies in its mass-produced standardization of affects and its apparent displacement of social relations.'[20]

This is not to suggest that a kitsch artefact cannot also be camp although it may mean that a camp artefact is not necessarily kitsch. In what Lloyd terms 'the resistance of kitsch to aesthetic judgement',[21] it becomes an allegory of a historical dislocation on the part of oppressed communities, at once 'the desire for and the impossibility of restoring and maintaining connection'. In this way, its negation of meaning simultaneously 'gesture[s] towards a trauma that will not and cannot be fully acknowledged'. Kitsch, in these terms, cannot be a sensibility in the terms in which camp is a sensibility. Indeed, it can be argued that kitsch is the antithesis of a sensibility, its very investment in the artefact gesturing towards the impossibility of an attitude based around 'how you respond to things'. By comparison, it is precisely camp's appropriative instincts that enable it to recognise and consume kitsch icons but, as this act suggests, it is dependent on a greater degree of self-confidence – an encounter with bourgeois modernity on one's own terms.

Lloyd's identification of the function of kitsch artefacts within a resistance culture suggests a way of approaching Tom Paulin's much-anthologised poem 'Off the Back of a Lorry',[22] a text that in its own right also undertakes an exploration of the interconnections between camp and kitsch in Northern culture:

> A zippo lighter
> and a quilted jacket,
> two rednecks troughing
> in a gleamy diner,
> the flinty chipmarks
> on a white enamel pail,
> Paisley putting pen to paper
> in Crumlin jail,
> a jumbo double
> fried peanut butter
> sandwich Elvis scoffed
> during the last
> diapered days –
> they're more than tacky,
> these pured fictions,
> and like the small ads
> in a country paper
> they build a gritty
> sort of prod baroque
> I must return to
> like my own boke.

Here the creation of a 'prod baroque' through the fleeting presence of camp images and kitsch icons acknowledges, to return to Lloyd, 'the desire for and the impossibility of restoring and maintaining connection'. Paulin's perception that Northern Protestant culture has failed to establish a constitutive political practice is seen to create a vacuum of signification that is filled by the accumulation of artefacts and reified images. As these objects are saturated with immanent meaning so the text as a whole becomes a cargo cult of historical residues. Perhaps in this technique one can identify the tendency also found in Sontag's and Dyer's analyses to define camp primarily through recognition; its 'fugitive sensibility'[23] demanding that anything more than a respectful contemplation of its symptoms as they are manifest in diverse forms will damage it irreparably. Moreover, 'Off the Back of a Lorry' shares with those accounts of camp the necessary intimacy with the artefacts listed. Rather than puritan disgust with such 'pured fictions' (although this can be identified in the poem as well), as Eamonn Hughes has observed, 'its "tune" is that of "These Foolish Things" – which alters its apparent disgust to exasperated affection'.[24] Such a connection is revealing not just in its reorientation of the poem towards the affection Hughes identifies but also because it indicates something of the poem's desire to reconstitute that which is lost through a scrutiny of the few traces of its presence that remain – a project that the equally camp strategy of 'These Foolish Things' also attempts.

The poem then is a camp text not simply because it lists camp icons but because it extends to those artefacts its own camp sensibility. Camp's ability to assert a *conditional* form of commitment to a dominant culture, the manner in which it demands a profound knowledge of that culture while finding within it a subversive enclave, is here utilised to the full as the Ulster-Scots vernacular word 'boke' acts as a shibboleth demarcating the community while indicating the poem's own presence within it. In this way the final two lines of the poem signal the emergence of the lyric 'I' as some form of controlling authority able to organise the necessary response to the disparate nature of the material encountered previously and yet at the same time the parodic, wilfully portentous, nature of this declaration becomes its own form of high camp. To express this differently, the poem 'performs' its function to the same degree of agonised self-consciousness as that found in Ian Paisley's 1966 prison journal to which the poem refers.[25] This is a camp moment in the same way that, for Dyer, the Queen Mother is a camp British icon: both are particularly overdetermined symbols of an identity position that have become unknowingly parodic through repetition. These camp moments shoulder spaces for themselves in the poem alongside more distinctively kitsch artefacts; objects that more purposefully 'speak for' – through allegory – the processes of loss, threat and decay. In these terms, the slightly sinister configuration of 'a zippo lighter and a quilted jacket' describes well Lloyd's perception of kitsch as 'sentiment congealed into attitude'. In the poem's resurrection of despised objects and moments there is a celebration of the 'tacky' and the 'baroque' and a more painful identification of loss. Similarly, the poem's recognition of the ways in which Northern Irish Protestant culture has been reconfigured in American popular culture is both playfully camp and, simultaneously, an acknowledgment of the dislocations and fractures of emigrant experience.

Reading 'Off the Back of a Lorry' in this context provides the imperative and the momentum for the analyses that follow. As the poem indicates, the act of writing *about* camp must inevitably involve the doubled gesture implicit in camp itself. At one level such writing must acknowledge its place within the codes of the society from which camp arises, its intimacy; at another it must recognise that camp is an indication of a more troubled relationship between self and identity and thus assert its own knowing distance. As Sontag notes by way of a justification for her own intervention: 'I am strongly drawn to Camp, and almost as strongly offended by it. That is why I want to talk about it, and why I can. For no one who wholeheartedly shares in a given sensibility can analyze it; he can only, whatever his intention, exhibit it. To name a sensibility, to draw its contours and to recount its history, requires a deep sympathy modified by revulsion.'[26] Camp implicates as it liberates, it identifies symptoms of cultural sickness but it is unable to suggest anything of what might exist beyond such sickness. Like Marxism itself, its implicit critique arises out of – and will ultimately disappear along with – the established order of capitalist modernity. In the examples of identitarian camp this chapter will identify this process is re-enacted at a microcosmic level, for in each instance identity formations have fossilised and become little more than the juxtaposition of empty formal oppositions. While such moments map the general modes through which self and identity dissociate and therefore indicate the limits of the bourgeois identitarian project itself, they are also all unique insofar as the manifestations of this dissociation (the moment of camp) are highly individual – often idiosyncratic – gestures in the face of a potential defeat.

Dissenting Camp

It is hard to think of any Northern Irish writer whose approach to his or her material has been more consistently camp over such an extended period than the Belfast poet and art historian John Hewitt. Camp in these terms can be defined as the camp of the overdetermined identitarian spectacle – the camp of Paisley in the Crumlin Road Jail or the camp that Dyer identifies in Nelson Eddy and Jeanette MacDonald musicals. In this configuration, the performance of an identity position – Paisley as Protestant martyr, Eddy and MacDonald as the paradigm of bourgeois romantic lovers, Hewitt as dogged man of the Left in a sectarian society – is conducted with a high seriousness, an unknowingness about itself, which eventually arrives at a position whereby it becomes a spectacular critique (a critique *through* spectacle) of the earnest values it wishes to promote. It is the fetishisation of an idea through repetition.

As this suggests, one can find evidence of this version of camp in any Hewitt text insofar as it is in the consistency of his ideological position that the force of the inevitable parody makes itself known. Indeed, in these terms, it is Hewitt's achievement as a whole that constitutes the camp moment. His was a careful and methodical poetry typified by a patient, understated manner and yet the fetishisation of the act of thinking itself that this led to created an irredeemably self-conscious writing practice. As he noted in the 1949 poem 'Because I Paced My Thought':

> Because I paced my thought by the natural world,
> the earth organic, renewed with the palpable seasons
> rather than the city falling ruinous, slowly
> by weather and use, swiftly by bomb and argument,
>
> I found myself alone who had hoped for attention.[27]

Just as Hewitt's writing career was typified by this act of *pacing* his poetry so the isolation that he perceived resulted from it was also carefully cultivated: a way of codifying disparate elements into an overall identity. Indeed, by an odd series of coincidences that derived largely from the fact that his father disliked the local Methodist minister, Hewitt was never baptised and this became an important symbol for his own view of himself, as he observed in 'Planter's Gothic: An Essay in Discursive Autobiography':

> This has given me a sense of liberation; spiritually I have felt myself to be my own man, the ultimate Protestant. And when to this I add the fact that since our family doctor, a friendly old man in a frock coat, and with a pointed beard, had no great belief in vaccination, and going through the secular ritual with me, deliberately used an innocuous concoction, which left no scar, I have often felt myself doubly free from the twin disciplines of organised religion and science. In argument this has been advantageous, as I can quite honestly cry plague on both their houses, and, unimplicated, set up my own magic and mythology in opposition to either, for, like Blake, 'I must create my own system or be enslaved by that of another man'.[28]

As this suggests, Hewitt's perception of his own life was one in which the chance or random event would always became part of an overall symbolic structure; material for the creation of a coherent identity. This is not so much a repetition of the 'perfection of the man or of the work' aesthetic paradigm (although the subordinate position of chaos in relation to order accords with this principle) as an attempt to establish a disengaged position from which the self could be seen as imbued with potential meaning; in other words, classic identitarianism. The totality of the life as symbol is such that every event or impression must be found a place within it and in these terms the individual becomes a form of deity able to order disparate experience – the reason why Blake is the necessary inspiration. The hubris of this strategy is undeniable: Hewitt's perception of himself as the 'ultimate Protestant' allowed the construction of a position for himself outside what he perceived as the socio-sectarian monolith and in turn enabled him to cast a cold eye on the violent excesses of those who remained locked in that futile struggle. Central to the efficacy of this project is its high seriousness and yet it is this seriousness that inevitably becomes parodic. The impossibility of remaining 'unimplicated' demands constant repetition and these repetitions must adopt an elevated tone ('In argument this has been advantageous') in order to reconfirm one of identitarianism's central assumptions: that the self is a finished article, complete in all particulars, and able to account for any subsequent event. In this way, the work of Hewitt was the creation and maintenance of 'John Hewitt' as spectacle.

'Planter's Gothic' is, then, a good example of what I have termed previously 'non-aligned' or 'dissenting' camp: a tradition distinguished not so much by its relation to dominant state structures but by its identification – or rather construction – of a model of Northern Irish society that perceives Unionist and Nationalist identities as forms of servitude that have to be transcended. The forms this transcendence can take are, in turn, various. Whether the response to sectarian totality is Hewitt's socialism, a belief in regionalism and the concomitant investment in the territory as a shared space that this demands,[29] a sense that capitalist modernity will somehow render such oppositions redundant, or the kind of liberal humanism we have encountered in the novels of Bateman, what they share – and what gives the category its distinguishing characteristic – is a repeated fetishisation of individual identity as the means of achieving personal and communal liberation. The seductive power of this ideology derives from its coherence, its assertion of a third way beyond the binary oppositions of Northern Irish life; and yet it is, at the same time, entirely dependent on – and therefore must continually reassert – this vision of eternal atavism it simultaneously wishes to dismiss in order to justify its own position. In this way, Hewitt's 'I can quite honestly cry plague on both their houses' serves as its ultimate manifesto, for it is solely through the repetition of this call that non-aligned identitarianism makes itself known. As this suggests, such a position is quite unable to examine inequalities of power across the sectarian matrix it describes, for to do so would be to render problematic the symmetry of the opposition from which it draws its momentum. Instead, the ideology of non-alignment draws its optimism from the belief in its ultimate triumph as its evangelical zeal, based on personal testimony, persuades others to make the same transcendent leap. Robert McLiam Wilson's response in interview to the subject of 'the twin ideologies of Unionism and Nationalism' illustrates well this certainty:

> Yes, but I think it is clumsy. Yes, because I think they are increasingly meaningless. You see it in particular with the whole kind of rave thing. You see it with people who are under twenty-five. Their philosophies are entirely piecemeal. This heterogeneous inheritance makes monoliths very difficult to deal with. People of that age have grown up with normality as the Berlin wall was coming down – the kind of developments that seem to us absolutely fantastic. So they have the expectation that that is the currency: the political and moral currency of the world. I think that people think that this place is involved in a conflict, heated and kept on the simmer by irresponsible political leaders.[30]

In this version of the model Hewitt's 'houses' have become Wilson's 'monoliths'. The wider cultural perspective he invokes dismisses the indigenous socio-sectarian institutions while hope is placed in cultural and political exchange across international boundaries. Non-alignment in these terms is envisaged as capitalist postmodernity – not so much a shift in the economic nexus as a more profound trans-formation of consciousness that will render adherence to a monologic certainty an epistemological impossibility. Understood as such the relentlessness of the narrative, its sheer inevitability, not only locates the monolithic as residual but also provokes a discreet nostalgia about the nature of the loss incurred. This is because that which will trans-form the socio-sectarian bloc can only be welcomed conditionally: the identification of an 'entirely piecemeal' philosophy gestures towards the absences and betrayals implicit in the capitalist future. Such a stance, in its doublings and contradictions, is indicative ultimately of a particularly intense form of liberal humanist despair: not only does it recognise that the present is dreadful, it is also assured of the fact that it will soon be obliterated by something worse. Moreover, this desolation is intensified by the loneliness inherent in the awareness that only a select few can maintain a position of disinterestedness capable of observing the transformation. In this way, certainty mingles with doubt, nostalgia for the old order with a desire to witness its dissolution.

Wilson's vision then is ultimately dependent on a distinction between illusion and reality, or rather on the conviction that the privileged liberal humanist stance can adjudicate between competing realities. In this way, it can be argued that the actual aim of this manoeuvre is not to identify symptoms but rather to reconfirm the identity position from which the perception comes. As I have previously observed, the determinedly objective status of this stance entails that it is reluctant – or unable – to examine the actual constitution of power within the two monoliths it seeks to dismiss and, for this reason, it is a position that can be appropriated by the state itself in its manifestation as bourgeois liberal democracy. A booklet produced by the Northern Ireland Office in 1989, *The Day of the Men and Women of Peace Must Surely Come...*,[31] is an example of such a desire and, as its title suggests, also constitutes a distinctly camp moment in its own right. Basically a revision of the dominant myths of the conflict that have arisen since 1968 through a comparison of the 'media image of the masked terrorist' with 'the true face of Northern Ireland',[32] it concludes:

> Most people, dependent on the media for their information, see Northern Ireland as a community in turmoil – wracked by violence, bitterly divided, socially regressive. That perception is wrong.
> In reality, the community, together with Government and the forces of law, order and justice, is determined to succeed. It resists the small band of terrorists with a resilience which is impressive. It is coming to grips with its historic legacies, resolved to break their stranglehold. The economic and sectarian chains which have bound it for too long are slowly but inexorably being loosened. [...] Mutual respect and a willingness to appreciate the other's point of view are rendering bigotry irrelevant.
> Faith in the future is stronger than ever.[33]

Here the limits of the illusion/reality opposition to which non-aligned identitarianism clings are pushed to their full extent. As with Wilson's analysis, the monolith (imagined in this instance as 'chains') has to be both powerful in its ability to beguile so many and yet inherently weak insofar as it is a form of false consciousness above which the individual can rise. This entails that the strategy of the booklet is one that must simultaneously magnify the threat to social stability in order to justify its intervention on behalf of liberal values and yet belittle that same threat as, ultimately, a residual and fading moment within the larger narrative towards communal and economic freedom. For this reason, *The Day of the Men and Women of Peace...* is constitutive of more than simply an abdication of political responsibility on behalf of the British government. Rather, through its imagining of the conflict as an awakening from sectarian imprisonment, it constitutes just one example[34] of the dilemma faced by any liberal bourgeois state when forced to account for the presence of communal violence within its borders. Social liberation must begin with individual liberation, the state must reimagine itself as the apparatus with which the individual can achieve emancipation, and the gradual shifts in social consciousness (which are seen, of course, as inevitable) must be represented as a sudden and dramatic conversion.

It can be argued then that it is in the negotiation between social and individual interests that the strategy of non-alignment appears most troubled and it is at such moments that the parodic gesture, the performative function of identitarianism, is most vulnerable to reinterpretation as camp. 'As You Like It', a poem by Hewitt from 1975,[35] illustrates these dangers well and in its encounter with another quite alien form of camp consciousness also suggests something of the sensibility's appropriative strategies. The poem begins – in the patient, 'paced' manner I have already identified as central to Hewitt's work – by describing what can be considered a classically non-aligned gathering, a meeting calling for law reform. As such, it is a 'decent aim' inevitably condemned to attract only a small number of agitators. When 'half a dozen dribbled in' Hewitt is able to examine more closely the constitution of the group:

> We studied our associates, strange till now;
> the tall man like a burly front-row forward,
> the quiet workingman with collar and tie,
> that fat lad whose brave jokes gave light and air,
> the whispering friends who share some private gossip,
> those silent by the window... It could have been
> some sports committee, a debating club...

> Then two slim girls in slacks came clomping in
> on those high hooves they love now, with bare arms,
> and little golden chains about their throats.

This gradual, almost Larkinesque, accumulation of detail typifies the Hewitt style. Those he encounters at the meeting are isolated from each other, just as the meeting itself represents an isolated formation of decency within the sectarian divisions of Belfast. There is a wariness to the tone, a hope that a fleeting connection can be made, but also a scepticism about this possibility, underwritten by the wisdom of the narrator who 'in my long days' has 'learned the stereotypes'. However, just as every Hewitt poem must describe a process of learning, some new revelation that can be codified as experience, so in 'As You Like It' the tedium of constitutive social action is momentarily disturbed by what can be described as an 'act' of identity. This takes place as the narrator contemplates further his failure to place the girls who enter the room within any of the 'stereotypes/for civil rights, for workers' unity,/for the free mind against the book shut mind,/for rage against oppression somewhere else'. Suddenly a moment of realisation dawns:

> which of these urges I could not decide
> impelled these youngsters, till, at last, they spoke
> with rough-rasped workshop voices – they were lads
> linking with us against our laggard law
> which leaves them unpermitted, out of step.

It is this revelation that gives the poem its momentum in that it has to dedicate the rest of its procedures to the assimilation of this new information within a rational order. Just as the boys can be envisaged as a symptom of modernity operating within traditional structures, so the poem cannot conclude until a new equilibrium has been achieved. This takes the form of a resolution of the narrator's instinctive doubt 'that they posed an image/not to our serious purpose', that

> Here was no protest powered by indignation.
> This was play-acting; this was dressing up,
> hardly amusing, childish, dissonant.

Unwilling – or unable – to recognise that the dissonance of such 'dressing up' constitutes its own form of implicit critique, the narrator is thrown back upon the only resource that can be trusted in Hewitt's poetry, that of experience. In these terms, as the narrator's 'thought swerved', so an image of 'the great boy-actors of the Bankside Globe' is recalled and the Belfast transvestites' lonely hope of achieving common cause with other isolated individuals is compared with the 'sparkling ambiguities' of gender performance as play. The pathos of this comparison, and the stern realities of sectarian Belfast it juxtaposes against the brilliance of the Renaissance stage, finally allows sympathy to transmute into empathy:

> And if it seems like farce, I am unfair;
> their brittle miming primes my resolution
> to pin my stubborn pledge to principle.
> They have their quaint quirks – that is one of mine.

It is through this conclusion that Hewitt's experience is reborn in a new pattern. The final subject of the poem becomes not the activity of the meeting and its members but the manner in which Hewitt's thought can incorporate dissident material. This conclusion, however, cannot be entirely circumscribed by this process. The categorisation of the activities of the boys as 'quaint quirks' and the poem's presentation of their activities as indicative only of desperation seeks to limit the dangerous tensions that their presence indicates – the manner in which their self-interested desire to see more liberal legislation relating to homosexuality contrasts with what should be the less self-serving energy of 'indignation'. Understood as such the narrator's recognition that such 'quaint quirks' mirror quirks of his own is only allowable insofar as the poem can assume that the reader will see the hollowness of the comparison.

Describing the poem in these terms would suggest perhaps that it is the very presence of the transvestites themselves that lends the poem its camp sensibility. After all, 'the pathos of the homosexual' that Hewitt recognises here is the condition that, for Sontag, 'constitute[s] the vanguard – and the most articulate audience – of Camp'. For this reason, as she elaborates, 'homosexual aestheticism' becomes one of the 'two pioneering forces of modern sensibility'.[36] Similarly, we can recall Dyer's perception that camp can be a means through which the 'real awfulness' of gay isolation in a straight society 'could be kept at bay'[37] – a version of camp that seems well able to account for the difficult circumstances of the working-class 'lads' in 'As You Like It'. This reading, however, does not quite account for the more peculiar aspects of Hewitt's encounter. The poem *is*, I would argue, an example of bourgeois camp: this, however, is not due to the presence of transvestism within the procedures of an earnest, slightly self-important, meeting but rather resides in the poem's mannered response to the transvestites' presence as it moves from exoticisation to a uneasy form of assimilation. Indeed, in these terms, it can be argued that ultimately the boys are the least camp aspects of the poem in that the narrator deliberately avoids reading them as 'surface'. While, for Dyer, camp 'is a way of prising the form of something away from its content, of revelling in the style while dismissing the content as trivial',[38] 'As You Like It' attempts the opposite manoeuvre and resists the 'style' of the boys' initial appearance through a determined attempt to fill this form with 'meaning'. This is the necessary response of the poem as it is the only way to address the threat posed by their 'play-acting', their 'dressing up'. The poem's ultimate resolution in finding such dissidence to be another form of 'quirk' allows Hewitt to codify them as one of the many 'stereotypes' he has encountered and so the position of dissident commentator his writing more generally seeks to confirm is retained. It is a mode of authority born of powerlessness.

The camp of 'As You Like It', then, resides in Butler's perception of identity performance as a *'stylized repetition of acts'*, a way of granting 'internally discontinuous' acts 'the *appearance of substance'*.[39] The poem is significant because it tests the procedures of Hewitt's determinedly rational poetics, or rather, it is an arch pseudo-test whose outcome is assured from the first instance. This is essentially the means through which all modes of identity performance in Northern Ireland can attain the status of camp regardless of whether they come from non-aligned, Unionist or Nationalist perspectives. In response to a perceived external threat, the logic of identitarianism can only repeat – in increasingly extreme forms – its own presence. The triumph that inevitably ensues from these encounters reconfirms the historical legitimacy of that identity's constitution and enacts at a microcosmic level the larger progression of the social grouping the identity constitutes. This is necessarily parodic in that the form of the encounter must be seen to vary as little as possible and must retain as much of its intrinsic essence as it can. The value of identitarianism conceived as such is that it allows historical defeat to be read as victory. Despite the vicissitudes of changing circumstance, the persistence of the identity formation itself – its capacity continually to declare its presence whatever else may happen – becomes its ultimate goal. Camp, in these terms, is the narcissism of eternal self-recognition.

Unionist Camp

If, as I have argued, non-aligned – or 'dissident' – identity formations in Northern Ireland assert a perception of Nationalist and Unionist identity positions as univocal monoliths in order to justify their own intervention, so from within these latter positions other, equally strategic, constructions are necessary. Most obviously, if the objective of non-aligned identitarianism is the construction and maintenance of the autonomous 'I' – the subject who can, in Hewitt's terms, 'quite honestly cry plague on both their houses' – so the identity formations of Unionism and Nationalism must encounter and negotiate the more difficult terrain of 'we'. While non-aligned identity can withdraw into itself and grimly predict the dissolution of the old order upon which it is also reliant for its own efficacy, identitarianism that claims for itself a communal position must constantly reinvent the terms of its engagement so as to maintain its narrative coherence.

Such considerations are particularly apposite when considering the various realignments and metamorphoses of Loyalism during the early 1980s. In the long and indeterminate period of sectarian violence in Northern Ireland that resulted from the hunger strikes, those moments of constitutive political development that existed were spasmodic, usually incoherent and invariably frustrated. The preconditions for dialogue across the now securely factionalised communities were not in place and would not become evident until the close of the decade. It was because of this vacuum that expressions of cultural identity gained both a new vocabulary and a currency that would increase in intellectual momentum. Within popular Loyalism this took the form of a reliance on a series of increasingly strained analogies and hopeful parallels that sought to offer a revision of the relationship between itself and the state. While such expressions in themselves were indicative of the political stalemate that existed, they also articulated a frustration with the inheritance of cultural detritus out of which 'Protestant' identity was felt to be constructed.[40] It was in response to this perceived inadequacy that popular Loyalism began to explore analogies of dispossession: comparisons with historical moments from other cultures that required an objectification of the circumstances within which Loyalist identity located itself. In these terms this moment serves as an example of the tendency I have already suggested to be implicit in identitarianism in its most general definition: its ability to reimagine a historical defeat in terms of the danger it poses to the symptoms of the identity formation itself. This is a camp moment insofar as the objectification that it requires – its focus on the manifestation of the identity rather than its meaning – demands a repetition of its own terms with the full knowledge that the context out of which such manifestations arose is irrevocably altered. For this reason, the performance of this identity is simultaneously a viewing of it. As it constantly assesses its own relevance so its anachronism implies an insistent threat and demands a resolution of the contradiction it displays.

It is in this context that the poem 'Our Way' enters the culture:

> We marched in orderly lines
> thousands of us
> Our stars of David sewn on

to our bright new rags
We clutched our possessions
as we marched along
They said our war was over

We sang quietly whilst on the move
songs that our forefathers sung
and we were proud in the knowledge
that we were Jews
They said the meek would inherit the earth

As they herded us in we saw
the overhead pipes
They said it was to provide heat
but the odour of gas overwhelms us
When we were marching
we should have been fighting

'Our Way' was written in Belfast in 1983 by Sam Duddy, Public Relations Officer (and poet) for the (at that stage still legal) Ulster Defence Association. It was published in his collection *Concrete Whirl-pools of the Mind*[41] and appeared alongside much more openly militant and sectarian material. After approaching various publishing houses with no success, Duddy had raised the funds for the publication of the collection through the sale of his motorbike[42] and it appeared under the imprint of the Ulidia Press. 'Our Way', then, is the rather uncomfortable culmination of the whole collection. Preceded by marching songs proclaiming the heroism of the UDA, drinking songs condemning the cowardice of the Irish Republican Army, and general pieces recalling with affection the minutiae of Northern Irish life, the poem dramatises a historical moment, a monad, and locates in the systematic attempt by the Nazis during the Second World War to exterminate the Jewish race an analogy with the fate of the Protestant population of Northern Ireland. In this, the poem reimagines the idea of violence as a logical response to oppression and finds in the comparison a similar ancestral justification. Through a jumble of Old and New Testament references the poem concocts a structure of suffering and redemption based on the key line 'They said the meek would inherit the earth' and it is around the 'they' of this statement that the poem gains its violent momentum. While in the first instance this is taken, of course, from the Sermon on the Mount, in terms of the poem this sentiment is also – and simultaneously – voiced by the Nazis in order to encourage a passive acceptance of death on the part of the oppressed Jews. And yet, thirdly, in terms of the analogy, the 'they' referred to here is the British government, urging the Protestant population of Northern Ireland to turn the other cheek in the face of repeated attacks on their community by the IRA. Rather than accept meekly the inevitable destruction offered by a narrative of victimhood the poem, through the manipulation of a taboo analogy, urges a gesture of resistance.

This resistance is, however, decidedly muted and it could be argued that 'Our Way', in fact, suggests little more than uncertainty. While its use of this analogy articulates a specific frustration with the political deadlock in the North during this period it should be recognised that such a deployment also has its own lineage. In establishing a parallel with the suffering of the Jewish population of Europe during the Second World War, Duddy's poem reconstructs and revisits an analogy outlined in a press statement released in July 1973 by the Ulster Freedom Fighters (the cover name used by the UDA when engaged in paramilitary activity). Again, this statement was designed to justify (or at least impute a rationality to) its actions:

> We have more in common with the State of Israel, the Star of David on our flag. These brave people fought and won their battle for survival. We intend to win ours. And like the Jewish people, each time an act of aggression is committed against our people, we shall retaliate in a way that only the animals in the IRA can understand.[43]

The manner in which these two analogies interpret recent Jewish history in terms of both passive suffering and violent reprisal constitutes a useful illustration of the particular contradictions implicit in the UDA's activities over the past twenty years. Indeed, it is in this context of strategic political necessity, rather than as an atavistic recollection of previous wrongs, that this material should be viewed. Certainly, however one views the symmetry of Duddy's parallel in 'Our Way', it is an analogy contradicted by the military activities of the UFF through the same period.[44] As such the mobilisation of the comparison can account for contrasting impulses, or rather, the recognition of such contrasts constitutes a position of danger, the implied threat of the strained analogy.

It is in these ways that the contradictory impulses of the poem lend it an ephemeral quality that gestures to an uncertainty about the authority of its discourse. However, it is precisely this marginality, or perhaps its *dual marginality*, that reveals other, more telling, resonances and that ultimately questions the interpretative frames through which it may be read. Firstly, the poem is marginal in relation to the violence it urges. The revelation in the final line that 'we should have been fighting' constructs the text as a catalyst for action rather than an action in itself. In this, the analogy is intended to be self-evident as the recognition of the point of the parallel entails that the logical result of that parallel is remorseless. As John McGarry and Brendan O'Leary point out in *Explaining Northern Ireland*,[45] it is precisely because para-military violence is *instrumental* rather than expressive that it continually requires such justification. In turn, these justifications seek to close off possible dissident readings of the original act. Understood in this way, the poem's relationship to the violence it depicts mirrors the relationship of the UDA to the UFF itself. Just as the UDA is the political and cultural wing of the UFF (or indeed the UFF is the military wing of the UDA) so the symbiotic relationship between the two is made clear by the poem's exhortations. The existence of the UFF did, in fact, allow the UDA to maintain a constitutional stance, just as this poem, as a UDA text that was vetted by Andy Tyrie (the then commander of the organisation), provides a rationale for the continued violence.[46] The contradictions of this stance are thus similar to the contradictions implicit in the relationship between the two organisations themselves and indeed their nominal differences would finally collapse when the British government proscribed the UDA as an illegal organisation in 1992.

While this constitutes one marginality, the poem is also marginal in its relationship to the dominant matrices of Northern Irish poetry that had been established during the 1970s. To condense what is inevitably a very complex argument, for the poet Derek Mahon[47] the activity of the Northern Irish poet and his or her relationship to social violence could be perceived as dependent upon a 'wretched rage for order'.[48] In this the individual poem encounters social violence through a framework of personal responsibility and mobilises the conflict between those responsibilities and the demands of a social affiliation. In turn, these negotiations are concentrated specifically on the ambiguities and possibilities inherent in the individual poetic word itself.[49] The outcome of this practice, as is revealed by a consideration of Frank Ormsby's 1992 anthology of 'Troubles' poetry also called *A Rage for Order*,[50] is a continued emphasis on the development of the self as paradigmatic while simultaneously forcing any material consideration of the reasons *for* violence into a hypothetical domain. Duddy's poem certainly constitutes an interesting inversion of this stance, although it is worth emphasising that there is nothing unusual in the poem's use of analogy in itself. Indeed such usage accords with a more general interpretation of Northern Irish poetry that suggests that the formation of a distinct poetic aesthetic during the period of social violence from the early 1970s onwards entailed just this kind of search for historical parallels and discourses appropriate to the particular anomalies of the conflict. As a strategy this was naturally appropriative and it is perhaps of no surprise to find that the Holocaust was re-figured in this new context. However, 'Our Way' does differ from this paradigm in other, more marked, ways. Most noticeably, its interventionist position does not turn on or conclude with the poetic persona but rather is subsumed within the machinations of the overall analogy. Similarly, this is a poem resistant to the ambivalence of diction that marks out other Northern Irish poetic negotiations with violence. In its commitment to a communal position, the persona in 'Our Way' floats through the poem at once voiced (as it speaks) and yet voiceless (as it is annihilated). The crisis that makes itself present in this poem is a crisis in the status of this voice: a doubt as to who is authorising the utterance.

While these are the kinds of preoccupation that impose themselves on a certain reading of the text, ultimately their provenance as part of a literary-critical practice focused on the way the poem accords with and dissents from literary poetic traditions can only betray insecurities. They allow the work to be placed within a specific discursive practice, but they close off a sense of the text as constitutive of the identitarian moment itself. Instead, it is possible to propose that there is another subtext surrounding 'Our Way'. Although the poem may be seen as deploying analogy as a result of there being no other contemporary way to imagine the cultural dilemma of Ulster Loyalism, its status as a crisis text should only be countenanced if we in turn perceive that moment of crisis as an issue of self-representation – a conscious deployment of the inappropriate as a means of gesturing towards a greater separation. The sense of dispossession that the poem foregrounds – its reading of the politics of the UDA as sundered from all forms of institutional power – can be said to mirror the movement of working-class Loyalism away from the political interests of an established Unionism that had sought to subsume class interests prior to this period under a broad Northern Protestant hegemony.[51] While the fall of the Stormont regime in March 1972 and the imposition by the British government of Direct Rule had rendered any such broad cross-class or sectarian alliance unfeasible, its residual traces continued to linger within Loyalism for at least the next decade. 'Our Way' finally marks a recognition of this rupture through its creation of an analogy built upon an idea of dispossession. In asserting a distinction between a recognition of the residual and the emergent, the former is understood as the sentimental connection between the different sociosectarian interests of traditional Unionism,[52] while the latter is literally written out of Duddy's poem by the assumed death of its narrator.

This transition had many repercussions and constitutes part of the effect of a greater dissociation from 1972 onwards in the debates over 'Ulster Nationalism' inaugurated by Glenn Barr – another leading member of the UDA and subsequently to be a major ideologue in the organisation of the Ulster Workers' Council Strike of 1974. The early traces of this are present in a speech Barr delivered to the assembly at Stormont in October 1973 in which he insisted: 'I have no intention of remaining a British citizen at any price', and went on to suggest that 'Ulstermen have got more pride than to accept a white paper that has been thrown across the Irish sea at them. [...] An Ulsterman's first allegiance must be to the state of Ulster.'[53] In this can be identified what would later be recognised as both the progressive and reactive elements of Ulster Loyalist thinking. While changes in the constitutional position of Northern Ireland engender an expedient shift away from the residual or sentimental connection with Britain, this is achieved through the reactivation of supposedly indigenous qualities of stubbornness and pride also identified by Hewitt during this period as a central component of the Ulster regionalist sensibility. This is significant if only because, as Deniz Kandiyoti has observed,[54] such manoeuvres, which portray the 'modern' as the more authentic through the revitalisation of an underlying ethnic trait, allow for the presentation of discontinuity as continuity in the face of a shift in the dominant hegemony. This becomes an often-repeated pattern in the majority/minority politics of Northern Ireland. A similar instinct was at work in 1978 with the formation of the New Ulster Political Research Group by Tyrie, Barr, and another prominent UDA leader of the time, Harry Chicken. The NUPRG experiment arose out of the spectacular failure of the Paisley-inspired 1977 Loyalist strike and was based fundamentally on a strong belief on the part of its organisers in an independent Ulster. It led to the document 'Beyond the Religious Divide' (1978), which proposed a bill of rights, a president chosen from outside the major political parties and an executive selected from the worlds of academia, the professions and Trade Unions overseen by elected representatives. This document was the high-water mark of the UDA's political mobilisation, and was symptomatic of the decline of residual Unionism as I have defined it – a process that led to many of the cultural initiatives central to the UDA during this period. Perhaps most notable among this activity was the publication, one year after *Concrete Whirlpools of the Mind*, of a classically identitarian play, *This is It!*,[55] about the abortive Loyalist Day of Action in 1981, written by Duddy, Tyrie and the community theatre director Michael Hall. *This is It!* explored perceptions of identity as inheritance with the desire to 'get away from the obsessions with the past'.[56] Appropriately, the play concludes with a song (performed to the tune of 'The Sash') that proposes some form of generic and formal alternative:

> It's a land of many contrasts,
>> Not just in the beauty all around;
> For hidden behind all the bitterness,
>> A friendlier people couldn't be found.
> Will we ever find our citizens,
>> Whose sons and daughters languish in jail,
> Together rebuild Old Ulidia,
>> And unite the Cruthin and Gael?

The strained sense of optimism evinced by *This is It!* proved to be short-lived. On 11 March 1988, following the discovery of a bomb under his car, Tyrie lost a vote of confidence in the UDA inner council. He resigned his chairmanship of the UDA and younger, more militant, elements took over. The 'progressivist' strands in Ulster Loyalism he came to represent were not totally extinguished but were, instead, marginalised by an increased and revitalised programme of sectarian killings.[57]

The danger with this kind of reading is that it can take us back to a dubious version of Northern Irish history as based upon the politics of missed opportunity. In these terms, Duddy's particular reformulation of an identity position recognised the dissociation in this period between working-class Loyalism and its traditional affiliation, sought in vain for a new order of allegiance, but was ultimately extinguished by material circumstances. Such an interpretation constitutes a mode of cultural fantasy too easily seduced by the seeming emergence of the 'progressive' out of the residual and monolithic. Indeed, perhaps lurking behind the identification of a progressivist strand in Loyalist identity is a covert hope that some kind of discreet *embourgeoisement* is taking place. What this example of identity politics does illustrate, however, is its ability to reformulate its strategic affiliations while seeming to retain its essential form. This has important implications. By concentrating on identity's capacity for agency, and in perceiving it as a formation whose subversive function seeks to replace dominant political groupings, we can see how aspects of Ulster Loyalism in this period embody a knowing, parodic and performative function. This awareness, in turn, can challenge common and misleading readings of the movement as inherently reactive, reactionary or retrogressive. Understood as such, this activity is far from any desire to 'unite the Cruthin and Gael'. Rather the rhetoric of despair that dominates 'Our Way' (and the politics of the UDA it embodies) constitutes a Gramscian mode of 'fragmented and episodic'[58] consciousness seeking to rise out of its status through 'active or passive affiliation'[59] to dominant formations. Identitarian consciousness is, in this example, something at war with itself, something that can be both subversive and complicit in its 'active or passive affiliations', and it is within this framework that the crucial distinctions and discords that exist between the various class interests of what is euphemistically called the 'Unionist family' can be identified.

This accords in a number of interesting ways with the structures of camp sensibility as I have previously detailed them. As I have already suggested, Duddy's use of analogy to articulate an identity position requires the simultaneous ability to view the external symptoms of that position. This is because the momentum of analogy derives in the first and final instance from a congruence of *formal* patterns. As with other modes of camp, this is a position that demands an attempted objectification of a subject position, an emptying out of content and a willingness to read contingent allegiances and negotiations as part of a universal pattern. In this way, the efficacy of Duddy's analogy is ultimately dependent on aesthetic criteria. Just as the activities of Duddy and Tyrie in this period are reliant on a perceived dissociation within Unionism, so the poem's mobilisation of externality proposes a more radical dissociation in the self-delighting terms of its fetishisation of an identity position. As such, it can be argued that 'Our Way', in its ellipses and taboos, its use of analogy and intervention, can be seen not simply as a way of justifying the process of continued sectarian murder but also as a recognition of irreversible loss, a morbid rehearsal of the symptoms of dispossession.

Nationalist Camp

If the camp sensibility represented by Duddy and Tyrie manifests itself in a prioritisation of form, an attempt to objectify the identity of popular Loyalism in its relationship to power, then Nationalist camp can be said to make the reverse journey, seeking instead to relocate its claim for historical redress in terms of vernacular sentimentality. This takes the guise of a turning inward, a reorientation of grievance through the retrieval of a personal history and, therefore, a repositioning of the subject in relation to material forces. By placing emphasis on the individual as the means through which perceived historical oppression is countenanced, Nationalist camp reads against the bourgeois depoliticisation of the individual as I have identified it elsewhere in this study. Rather, the sentimentality of Nationalist camp has an effect closer to Lloyd's conception of kitsch in so far as it offers a reduplication of affect. It constitutes an *attempt* to remember rather than the act of remembrance itself.

The tendency of nationalism to maintain and renew itself through the retrospective examination of the particular individual who comes to exemplify the project suggests why the novel and the autobiography play significant roles within its mediation. In this Irish Nationalism is, of course, little different from other modern nationalist movements across Europe, as its reliance on the dissemination of paradigms of self-formation corresponded with the growth of print culture across the continent. While, in these terms, the autobiography and the *Bildungsroman* can be perceived as forms through which narratives of significance can be constructed, narratives in which essential knowledge declares itself irresistibly from the midst of unpromising origins, this tendency can also be understood as the process whereby a putative heterogeneous self is subtended by the creation of a coherent political identity. One effect of this is the creation of a totalitarian sensibility, a world-view that implicates all the various details of quotidian existence and reads them as essential aspects of a narrative of understanding that will culminate in the achievement of the full Nationalist project. As this suggests, the ingenuity of the form lies not with its selectivity, its capacity to identify which aspects of the life were of significance in the creation of the paradigmatic individual, but rather in its ability to locate significance in disparate and usually unpromising material. The major risk attendant on this project is, therefore, that the high seriousness through which it is conducted and upon which it is reliant can easily become self-parodic. It becomes not merely ludicrous but a form of high camp in its need to demonstrate the possibilities for learning implicit in ever more unlikely personal experience. This urge is a necessary part of the process of self-formation because of identity's reliance upon repetition. In order to mediate convincingly the aspirations and desires of a particular social grouping, identity has to continually redeclare itself, renew the images by which it is constituted, and offer as many ways of reforming the self as possible. The significance of this moment of subject formation lies, then, with its ability to mediate between conceptions of itself as both unique and yet reproducible. As with the other modes of camp I have been discussing, it is in the formal progression from innocence to experience that its pedagogic status resides.

The complexities of this manoeuvre can be readily understood by consideration of an exemplary text, Bernadette Devlin's autobiography *The Price of My Soul*.[60] Advertising itself on its front cover in these terms: 'The fighting Irish girl MP tells her personal story – and what is really happening inside Ulster', the work offers itself as both a justification and an explanation. It charts the narrative of Devlin's astonishing rise to political significance and the lessons she assimilated in order to arrive at that position. At the same time, the narrative evinces a slightly appalled perception of the cost of this to her own fragile sense of individuality. Devlin signals this apprehension in the foreword to the text, which is written, she notes, in order 'to explain how the complex of economic, social, and political problems of Northern Ireland threw up the phenomenon of Bernadette Devlin'.[61] The objectification implicit in her self-perception as a 'phenomenon' indicates something of identitarianism's primary aim: the creation of an identity position that is fully explicable by seemingly abstract historical and material forces and one that, as a result, demands the rejection of extraneous personal detail as an irrelevance. As with Hewitt's creation of himself as a symbol of dissenting non-conformism and Paisley's self-conscious inheritance of the role of Protestant martyr, Devlin's paradigmatic status requires an elimination of the self and a concomitant belief that a historical narrative can be embodied. As I have suggested, while *The Price of My Soul* appears uneasy with this construction – in the foreword Devlin insists 'before I get submerged in all the Joans of Arc and Cassandras and other fancy labels people stick on me, I want to put the real flesh-and-blood Bernadette Devlin on record'[62] – at the same moment the nominal status of this disquiet is signalled by the autobiography's determination to reconstruct experience as fable in the manner that I have already identified as central to the creation of the identitarian text:

> Once when I was seven or eight I came in late to tea, to discover that my sisters had eaten up all but one of the square ends of the slices of bread, which I – and they – preferred to the round ends. The one remaining square end was at the bottom of the plate, and I began flicking through the bread like the pages of a book in search of the piece I wanted. Whereupon my father slapped my hand from the table, looked at me, and said, 'What have you done?'
>
> 'Nothing,' I said, big tears standing in my eyes.
>
> 'Do you expect any other human being to eat the food you have rejected as not fit for your consumption?'
>
> 'But, daddy,' I said, horror dawning, 'I can't eat five slices of bread – not with my tea as well.'
>
> My father removed my meal, set down one empty plate, put the five slices of bread on it, and said, 'You can have butter on them. You can have jam on them. You can have anything you like on them. But nobody is going to eat that bread but you. And if you can't eat it tonight – don't make yourself sick! – it will be there for your breakfast tomorrow.' And I ate every one of those slices of bread.[63]

The presence of this extraordinary episode within the narrative of dawning political consciousness that the text as a whole represents illustrates well the various strategies of the Nationalist autobiography as a paradigm of self-formation. The granting of immanent meaning to quotidian detail creates a totality of effects in which it becomes strictly unnecessary to explain the significance of the event itself. In these terms, the self-recognition of childhood greed constitutes an implicit motivation for the Republican socialism that the text will ultimately proclaim. The assumption of this connection, however, demands a certain dissociation between the identity that is writing and the self that is being examined: the carefully observed sentimentality of 'big tears standing in my eyes' forces a distinction between the event and its recollection and so fetishises the subject as one fit only for subsequent transformation. The combination of naïve if loveable child, stern and yet caring father ('don't make yourself sick!') and the finality of the ultimate resolution ('And I ate every one of those slices of bread') is assumed to be self-evident. In these terms the primary purpose of the anecdote accords with the wider strategies of the form in that it signals Bernadette's distinctiveness: the depth of her folly is matched only by the knowledge she ultimately takes from it and thus she learns to reject the attitudes she shares with her sisters at the start of the passage.

The only problem here, however, is that this process simply does not work. As the episode illustrates what I have identified previously as identity's narcissism of eternal self-recognition, so the high serious-ness of this passage, its delight in the contemplation of a former self, constitutes only a camp form of obsessive self-regard. At some point within the recollection of the anecdote its didactic function becomes subordinate to an impulse that finds pleasure in the minutiae of the moment itself. As camp prioritises form over content, so Devlin's aestheticisation of the moment in 'flicking through the bread like the pages of a book' undercuts her primary purpose. This is all the more marked in that the motivation for the entire event – the preference for square over round ends of bread – is at once crucial yet ineffable. It is the hole in the heart of the story that nevertheless, or perhaps as a result, comes to overwhelm the subsequent moral. Camp in these terms accords with Dyer's perception of the concept as a 'revelling in the style' of a moment or artefact, the moment when high seriousness is forgotten and form becomes pleasure.

This anecdote establishes the tone of the rest of the volume and illustrates the considerable significance placed upon the self-evident nature of the moment of individual recollection. It is out of these moments that the reader must construct the overall narrative. Senti-mentality is a crucial aspect of this process, for it is its role in this context to mediate between the child and the adult, to see the instinctive actions of the child as ultimately constitutive of the mature political process. In this way sentimentality becomes the most narcis-sistic of emotions in that its efficacy is dependent on a recognition that what is being presented is no more than a (slightly) flawed version of what we have ultimately come to be. *The Price of My Soul*'s investment in this technique is so extensive that its effect can become unnerving. In poring obsessively over the mundane details of her school days in the hope of finding signifying traces, Devlin transforms the Catholic education she endures into a political education. This is a recurring trope in Catholic accounts of selfhood and is predicated on a perception that the certainties of faith and doctrine will be initially assimilated with enthusiasm and then rejected as the educated subject recognises their inherently oppressive aspects. In this way, a Catholic school's 'best pupils' inevitably become its most troublesome – the template followed being, of course, James Joyce's *A Portrait of the Artist as a Young Man*. Devlin's perception of her progression through school accords closely with this model:

> I was head girl at that time by popular acclaim, and the next year I was elected head girl by the prefects. Mother Benignus didn't want me to be head girl the second year: she thought it was making me big-headed and that I was taking over the school from under her feet. In fact, there were three of us – Aideen Mallon, Sheila O'Farrell, and myself. For two years we made ourselves responsible for behaviour in the school and in that time took it from the brink of chaos and made of it a reasonably civilized society. [...] We used to make children stay in after school and anyone who broke the silence merely prolonged the detention period by another three minutes.[64]

This 'little syndicate of Stalinism', as even Devlin herself refers to it, represents a rejection of the Church on its own terms in that it illustrates a more stringent commitment to the Church's own strictures than the Church itself displays. Once this stage has been achieved, Devlin then confronts and vanquishes Mother Benignus ('Mother, you *are* a bigot, I'm very sorry you're a bigot. But you *are* a bigot'[65]) and can thus move on. It is through the details of this account that Devlin's later adventures can be read as components of an essential identity: her rejection of Mother Benignus displays her instinctive hostility to power, the careful naming of her co-conspirators indicates something of her later belief in the power of combination, while her act of seizing control reinforces the militancy that it is the book's purpose as a whole to proclaim.

The identification of this technique inevitably raises questions about the ability of Nationalist autobiography to present a sense of the subject as in process, as developing towards a finished state. For Sontag, as I have previously noted, one key aspect of camp is the pleasure it finds in the concept of 'instant character', the sense of an individual as 'being one, very intense thing',[66] and it is for this reason that camp gravitates towards cultural forms (such as opera) that offer this possibility. Nationalist autobiography such as *The Price of My Soul* is also dependent on this essence: Devlin's instinctive militancy is apparent at all times – it is her own 'very intense thing' – and cannot be compromised by the possibilities of experience. In these terms sentimentality gains even greater significance, for it is all that can be offered as a means of indicating the boundary between 'what was' and 'what is'. This can be illustrated by the manner in which the text negotiates one obvious boundary of this type: the re-emergence of social violence in the

North, as represented by the 1956 IRA border campaign and its coincidental significance as an event that marks the transition from Devlin's childhood certainties to her adult responsibilities:

> As soon as the sirens started, doors in our neighbourhood would open and our neighbours would appear, pulling on their heavy coats and shouldering their sten guns. Most of the Protestant men in our district were B-men, or Specials – members of the civilian militia in Northern Ireland which was formed to fight the IRA. So while some of my friends' daddies were disappearing into their houses to lie low, other peoples' daddies were setting out armed after them.[67]

The tension here between registers, between the adult who understands the sectarian affiliations of the community and the weapons at their disposal, and the child who sees only the involvement of her friends' 'daddies', is negotiated only through sentimentality. Its significance, in these terms, lies in the fact that it forces the reader to make the connection between innocence betrayed and the cynicism of ultimate knowledge and it is in this that its pedagogic status resides. More significantly again, the trajectory of this technique moves beyond the development of Devlin herself and sets in process the inevitable tendency to read the event in terms of the calcification of an entire community. The fact that Devlin subsequently reinforces this point ('At times like these the tragic division in Northern Ireland split even wider'[68]) only indicates a slight lack of confidence in the efficacy of the form she has mobilised. It is for this reason that the text finds it necessary to underwrite the opposition through the assertion of a distinction between the putative cross-communal decency implicit in pre-violence Northern Ireland and the sectarian hatred that will typify it afterwards: a distinction that, as I will discuss, is also important to the fiction of Gerry Adams. For Devlin this division is encapsulated in the transformation of a 'wee Protestant woman' she knew who, in the years before the violence, would 'bake us cakes, and so on', but, after 1969, was more content to call her 'Fenian scum'.[69]

As *The Price of My Soul* develops, Devlin's argument becomes increasingly structured around the distinction between theory and practice, between the value of lived experience and the pointlessness of what she considers abstruse political discourse. As she notes: 'I'm not a socialist because of any high-flown intellectual theorizing: life has made me one.'[70] Of course, this conviction would re-emerge famously when Devlin, as MP for Mid-Ulster, physically attacked the British home secretary Reginald Maudling on the floor of the House of

Commons following the Bloody Sunday massacre in 1972; an event she justified on the grounds that 'If I am not allowed to inform the House of what I know, I'll inform Mr Maudling of what I feel.'[71] This distinction between knowing and feeling, as with that between theory and practice, is not unusual but its significance to *The Price of My Soul* lies with the instinctive force it grants to Devlin's arguments and chimes with the text's more pointedly justifying function. Most crucially, in terms of the book's ideal readership, it is the strategy that allows her to explicate her complex attitude towards Republican terrorism, in that the Devlin who 'wandered about by myself making terrorist plans'[72] (fantasies of complex strategic operations that she shares with the reader) is presented as a figure bewildered by false consciousness: 'Those were my militant Republican days. But I got over these dreams of violence, and told myself it didn't matter if the people who kept us in poverty were called British or not. It wasn't simply getting Britain out of Ireland that mattered: it was the fact that we were economically depressed, and I couldn't see terrorism solving that.'[73] This is, perhaps, the most sensitive moment in the text as it gestures towards the divisions within the Nationalist project she had previously presented as unified. In order to reconfigure its implications Devlin reimagines the role of violence in Nationalist struggle as acceptable if motivated by life experience but unacceptable if harnessed to an ideological strategy. As she observes in regard to the siege of the Bogside:

> We had an influx of foreign revolutionary journalists searching for illumination on the Theory of Petrol Bomb Fighting. The people of the Bogside thought it was fantastic: they didn't know how to spell revolution, never mind work it out, but they were really delighted with themselves, that people should come from the Sorbonne to ask the unemployed of Bogside where they learned to fight so well.[74]

As the queasy humour of this account indicates, the obvious contradiction of this opposition lies with the fact that the articulation of this instinctive response requires the assertion of a intellectual distance uncomfortably close to the 'high-flown intellectual theorizing' Devlin has been careful to reject. It is for this reason that Devlin's treatment of the Bogsiders is nearly identical to her treatment of her classmates at school, as she sets them to barricade building in order to give them 'something to do which would take their minds off wrecking Derry and slaughtering Policemen'.[75] As the autobiography shows patterns re-emerging so the opposition between theory and practice is blurred by the unalterable and absolute assertion that Devlin *knows better*.

Ultimately *The Price of My Soul* attempts to resolve the contradiction it has created between the call of political destiny and the demands this makes on the ethical self. Stressing at all times her unhappiness with the role that has been allotted to her, Devlin describes herself as 'muggins', somebody 'dumped into Parliament',[76] a sacrificial figure who will inevitably be betrayed. Read in these terms it is appropriate that Devlin compares herself with Michael Collins, if only because the autobiography as the exemplary Nationalist text of self-formation will always locate itself historically through the use of analogies. As she notes: 'I feel a kindred spirit with the arrogant personality of Collins, and I believe that I'm in much the same situation as him. Basically, I have no place in organized politics. By coming to the British Parliament, I've allowed the people to sacrifice me at the top and let go the more effective job I should be doing at the bottom.'[77] This is not a comfortable moment within the text (how could any autobiographical analogy with Collins be comfortable?) but it is significant in that it allows Devlin to recontextualise what she has previously written of as her political idiosyncrasies in terms of a recurring pattern. In this, the perception of Collins as 'totally undiplomatic, so arrogantly honest', 'basically an aggressive, bullying type of person'[78] is compared to the machinations of Eamon De Valera – an unfair struggle because 'De Valera was a politician and politicians always win'[79] – and through this opposition Devlin's own instincts towards 'action' as opposed to 'theory' are reinscribed. For this reason it is perhaps appropriate that it is 'instinct' that is granted the last word: 'For half a century it [Unionist Party government] has misgoverned us, but it is on the way out. Now we are witnessing its dying convulsions. And with traditional Irish mercy, when we've got it down we will kick it into the ground.'[80]

The vernacular sentimentality that underwrites the emotional impact of *The Price of My Soul* is not, however, exclusively the domain of Nationalism. Rather its presence, and formations similar to it, can be identified in the wide variety of regional studies and excavations of the local across the North. The resurgence of interest in townlands in Ulster[81] is one symptom of this, as is the number of locally produced magazines, such as the Falls Road's *Rushlight*, which confirm and renew a sense of regional solidarity through the recovery and dissemination of significant local archives. Nostalgia would be too crude a term for this activity, although the artefacts it reproduces are, in Lloyd's terms, kitsch in that they gesture to an irretrievable loss (the photograph of the local shop that no longer exists, a turn-of-the-century newspaper account of a church trip) and find their largest readership in the diaspora. The sentimental poetry of 'John O'the North' published in the *Belfast Telegraph* during the 1940s,[82] which contrasts the beauty of Ulster with the horrors of modern warfare, constitutes another example, as does the more exhaustive gathering of Belfast stories, myths and popular history undertaken by Cathal O'Byrne and collected in *As I Roved Out: A Book of the North*.[83] This impulse towards the local – and the concomitant assumption that it is the specificities of the local environment that create the identity position – delineates the contours of Northern Ireland's distinctive regionalist sensibility. Moreover, if regionalism is defined in terms of its concentration on the 'surface' of shared inheritance and a concomitant relegation of the 'content' of material, sectarian or communal histories then its camp potential is clear. It is in this form that Nationalism's sporadic appeals to those beyond its own community revisits the tropes of the regionalist instinct, priding those qualities of the indigenous, the distinctive, and the rooted with the hope of locating – or at least gesturing towards – a shared inheritance.

An exemplary instance of this mode of appeal is Gerry Adams' collection of short stories from 1992, *The Street and Other Stories*.[84] Ostensibly a series of parables of political awakening, the book describes itself as 'stories of ordinary lives lived in extraordinary circumstances, of everyday life in a community subjected to exceptional pressures'. As this goes some way towards suggesting, the strategy of the collection appears to work in two different ways. At one level, the stories explore the minutiae of life for marginalised individuals in West Belfast, demonstrating how they survive and often flourish in the context of what the collection insists throughout is a civil war, and, through this, how they arrive at a richly realised sense of their individuality. At another narrative level, however, these idiosyncratic figures are read as part of a recurring paradigm, fragments of the ongoing narrative of growing Republican consciousness. The formal tension that this creates is not, in itself, unusual – indeed it can be seen as the defining dilemma of Northern Irish bourgeois realist fiction – but the extent to which *The Street* invests in the possibilities of identity politics as a means of reconciling such dissidence makes it more remarkable. This can be most obviously identified in the way the large majority of the stories conclude with the achievement of an identity position. For instance, in 'The Rebel', Margaret, a respectable middle-aged mother, discovers Republicanism and feminism and reconciles this to the material conditions of her life, while in 'Up the Rebels', Seamus, an ordinary criminal long since reconciled to his life cycle of petty crime and imprisonment, comes to recognise the nature of state oppression with the help of Republican prisoners incarcerated alongside him in jail.

This suggests the organising principle of the collection. Rather than asserting a distinction between life and political theory in the manner of *The Price of My Soul*, *The Street* seeks to demonstrate how theory arises organically out of life and, with this, insists that resistance is the inevitable response to oppression. The effectiveness of this technique is dependent on the reading strategies demanded by the short story form Adams utilises. As each story in *The Street* remakes in differing ways the overall progression from naïvety to knowledge which it is the larger purpose of the text to proclaim, so the collection promises both diversity and unity of purpose: the 'everyday' (each individual life in each story) is reconciled with the development of collective Republican consciousness (the collection as a whole). Similarly, Adams' use of a technique recognisably derived from the stylistic 'scrupulous meanness'[85] deployed by Joyce in *Dubliners* demands a mode of reading that searches for moments of signification in fleeting details and passing remarks. The larger narrative of political significance is rendered implicit in each fragment and the reader's necessary recognition of this constitutes a commitment to the collection's overall theme. For these reasons, the short story form is a particularly effective vehicle for conveying the Nationalist ideal of the self-realising individual. As the creation of an identity position effectively constitutes a full stop in the development of the individual subject, the point beyond which nothing else can be said, so the intense rhythms of the form can enable its manifestation without the novel's tiresome insistence on narrative. In these terms the short story meets and recognises Sontag's sense of the camp individual as 'being one, very intense thing' and, concomitantly, recoils in horror from the messiness of a novelistic perception of the individual as a site of revision, disillusionment and emotional evolution.

However, while *The Street* is clearly fascinated by the various ways in which what can be termed 'good Republican subjects' are created, at the same time it seeks to appeal to a constituency beyond Republicanism. In this way, it is strikingly different to *The Price of my Soul*, which, by comparison, reads as a kind of *samizdat* literature, a secret document to be circulated only among believers. The broader appeal of *The Street* is based on its investment in what I have termed 'vernacular sentimentality': it seeks to capture the circling and self-reflexive rhythms of the storyteller, finds playful humour in what is seen as typically Protestant intransigence, and opens up the North (albeit nominally) as a site of shared inheritance. In this way, the text is both a Nationalist paradigm of self-formation and a slightly timid exploration of the ways in which Nationalism might extend into hostile territory. The most vivid example of this in the collection is the story 'The Mountains of Mourne'. Set in 1969 during the early phases of the 'Troubles' it tells of the narrator's encounter with Geordie Mayne, a Shankill Orangeman, and their brief life together delivering alcohol to bars in the run-up to Christmas. As a new experience, the episode is understood as a holiday from commitment, a brief freedom from the identitarian imperative that usually obsesses the narrator. Prior to gaining the job he had been 'one of a dozen young men and women who were up to their necks in trying to sort things out'[86] and the earnestness of this task contrasts with the admission that he is soon so preoccupied by his new work that 'I hadn't even seen, read or heard any news all that week'. As he notes, 'both I and the struggle appeared to be surviving without each other',[87] 'familiar scenes might as well have been in another country'.[88] Described as such the story constitutes a recognisable trope within a factional culture. The encounter with the putative enemy in a friendly context is seen to cast in sharp relief the binary sterilities of the conflict and thus offers a dream of transcendence through carnivalesque inversion: a Northern Irish version of the Christmas Day football match during the trench warfare of the First World War. Indeed, the major risk of such inversions – that they merely reinscribe the oppositions that they seemingly parody – is a danger that ultimately threatens Adams' story.

It is through this technique, however, that 'The Mountains of Mourne' seeks to appeal to a new constituency while functioning as another instance of dawning Republican consciousness. But the price that the story must pay in order to balance these demands is identifiable in the tension implicit in the narrator's uneasy mix of registers as Republican orthodoxies rub uncomfortably against the attempt to capture the rhythms of the storyteller:

> How could a house be Catholic or Protestant? Yet when it comes to writing about the reality it's hard to find other words. Though loath to do so, I use the terms Catholic and Protestant here to encompass the various elements who make up the Unionist and non-Unionist citizens of this state.
> It wasn't my intention to tell you all this. I could write a book about the

craic I had as a child making my way in and out of all those wee streets on the way back and forth to school or the Boys' Confraternity in Clonard or even down at the Springfield Road dam fishing for spricks, but that's not what I set out to tell you about.[89]

By placing phrases such as 'to encompass the various elements', 'the Unionist and non-Unionist citizens of this state', '*craic*', 'wee' and 'spricks' in such agonising proximity, a peculiar sense is created that the story is policing itself, that imaginative reality cannot be reconciled to political discourse. In the same way, the vernacular elements of the story, its mobilisation of local speech patterns and precise references to long since disappeared aspects of Northern culture, are constructed as modes of fetish, temporary and knowing excursions into the realm of camp.

The friendship between the narrator (who assumes the false name 'Joe Moody') and Geordie develops as their deliveries take them across the city, up the Shankill Road (where the narrator visits Geordie's house and notes that 'only for the picture of the British Queen, I could have been in my own street') and ultimately into County Down. Here the two men, who had previously built their relationship around the avoidance of political discussion, find a new way of relating to each other. With the help of a guidebook they immerse themselves in the history of the area and through this discover a new series of contexts for their lives realised by the redemptive powers of the landscape itself. The narrator's sabbatical from the Republican struggle and Geordie's brief release from Orange ideology become a shared holiday in regionalism and in these terms it is appropriate that they begin to construct themselves as tourists in their own state – sectarian division, it is implied, having rendered them remote from their true inheritance.

Inevitably perhaps, political tensions re-emerge. On Christmas Eve, the last day of their deliveries, they offer a lift to a local man. While initially they both delight in his embodiment of an eccentric rural Ulster mindset, it is he who introduces the theme of political division through a politicisation of the landscape they had previously constructed as benign:

> 'That's some view,' Geordie said in disbelief.
> Paddy hardly heard as he looked pensively ahead at the open road.
> 'There's only one thing you can't see from Donard, and many people can't see it anyway although it's the talk of the whole place, and even if it jumped up and bit you it's not to be seen from up there among all the sights. Do yous know what I am getting at, boys? It's the cause of all our

cursed troubles, and if you were twice as high as Donard you couldn't see it. Do yous know what it is?'

We both waited expectantly, I with a little trepidation, for him to enlighten us.

'The bloody border,' he announced eventually. 'You can't see that awful bloody imaginary line that they pretend can divide the air and the mountain ranges and the rivers, and all it really divides is the people. You can see everything from Donard, but isn't it funny you can't see that bloody border?'[90]

Geordie's initial dislike of such sentiments is increased when Paddy and the narrator begin speaking in Irish ('that bloody foreign language of yours'[91]) and it is of no surprise when the anxieties that had been sublimated for the sake of their friendship ultimately explode as Geordie attacks the narrator (symbolically shattering the peace of Silent Valley in the process):

'Who do you think I am? Who do you think you are is more like it,' he snapped back, 'with all your bright ideas about history and language and all that crap. You and that oul' eejit Paddy are pups from the same Fenian litter, but you remember one thing, young fella-me-lad, yous may have the music and songs and history and even the bloody mountains, but we've got everything else; you remember that!'

His outburst caught me by surprise.

'All that is yours as well, Geordie. We don't keep it from you. It's you that rejects it all. It doesn't reject you. It's not ours to give or take. You were born here same as me.'[92]

It is significant in the context of the story's overall strategy that Joe's response to Geordie's frustrated rage at this point again ventriloquises Republican orthodoxy. While this constitutes another example of the story's uneasy mix of registers, it also indicates that this is the essential message of the parable, a moral reinforced by Joe in a different register when he insists that Geordie has 'Fuck all except a two-bedroomed house in Urney Street and an identity crisis.'[93] As their fragile alliance crumbles, the story acknowledges that the imperatives of an identity position will always impose themselves, will always constitute a form of closure and, therefore, the end of a narrative. For this reason the possibilities inherent in their relationship are re-read sentimentally as a moment of missed opportunity. Their encounter concludes without resolution but with a recognition of difference: Geordie acknowledges that Joe is 'dead on [...] for a Fenian', and the narrator, recalling the event twenty years later, is assured of the fact that Geordie 'wasn't such a bad fella, for an Orangeman'.[94]

It is tempting to read the irresolvable tensions of 'The Mountains of Mourne' within the context of Adams' political role since its publication. As his political future is dependent on his ability, if not to reconcile, at least to hold in a creative tension the various antagonistic strands within the Republican movement so as to maintain a coherent position from which to negotiate, so the story articulates an identity that is similarly Janus-faced: the narrator must tell one story to Geordie the Orangeman while maintaining a secret dialogue with the historical imperative of Nationalism represented by Paddy. In these terms, it is, perhaps, not unreasonable to note that Sinn Féin has made little effort to articulate its case to working-class Protestants beyond the platitudes of shared regional inheritance and the assumed reality of economic equivalence that the narrator of 'The Mountains of Mourne' offers Geordie. However, what 'The Mountains of Mourne' does demonstrate in an exemplary manner is the role of identity as a means of expressing political agency. As I began this book by discussing, for Spivak this involves 'a distancing from oneself', a way of 'trying to generalise myself, make myself a representative, trying to distance myself from some kind of inchoate speaking *as such*'. It is through this positioning that, as she notes, 'a political consciousness comes in'.[95] The political consciousness of *The Street* is similarly unified around this principle but the act of distancing it dramatises is one that proposes a continuum, rather than a distinction, between the vague contradictions of everyday life and the ultimate expression of a coherent world-view. In this way, the collection, like *The Price of My Soul*, can be understood as another paradigmatic text of self-formation. This progression, however, exacts a price. While identity offers itself as a mode of salvation (and thus every other aspect of the text is rendered subordinate to its realisation), unfortunately it can suggest nothing of what might take its place if, and when, it fails. Even at the point when the limits of a particular identity's political agency are revealed, it cannot contemplate its own obsolescence, nor imagine a world without its presence. Instead identity retreats into itself, fetishises its own symptoms, and becomes a camp rehearsal of its existence, fully expecting the moment when it will re-remerge as a significant force. As this suggests, while identity denies history, it is, at the same time, necessarily enslaved to it and so becomes ultimately no more than a metaphor for a relationship it seeks to conceal. In the final analysis, then, identity politics, like Adams' story, constitute an imaginative dead end: Geordie and the narrator part with mutual respect but nothing else.

The implications of this awareness are disquieting and suggest that the overwhelming question 'what comes after the identity parade?' is, almost by definition, unanswerable. As Barthes observes, 'history never ensures the triumph pure and simple of something over its opposite: it unveils while making itself, unimaginable solutions, unforeseeable syntheses'.[96] This is not, however, a criticism of any utopian strain within bourgeois ideology but instead is an attempt to suggest the limits of that which proposes itself as an anti-bourgeois analysis. Such theory, as Barthes insists, 'cannot see the Promised Land' because 'tomorrow's positivity is entirely hidden by today's negativity'. The despairing overtones of this statement should not obscure the fact that it also constitutes a mode of commitment to historical process – a resistance to bourgeois ideology's domination of the 'now'. In this way, Barthes' thought chimes with Guy Debord's perception that 'the abstract desire for immediate effectiveness accepts the laws of the ruling thought, the exclusive point of view of the *present'*. Overwhelmed as we are by the identitarian imperatives of the present, we cannot yet transcend the totalitarian nature of identity's response to history, cannot, in other words, enact the utopian political critique as it is often desired;[97] but then, as Debord insists, 'the critique which goes beyond the spectacle must *know how to wait'*.[98]

Notes

Introduction

1 Gayatri Chakravorty Spivak and Sneja Gunew, 'Questions of Multiculturalism', in Spivak, *The Post-Colonial Critic: Interviews, Strategies, Dialogues*, ed. Sarah Harasym, London, Routledge, 1990, p. 60.
2 'Nationalism: Irony and Commitment', *Field Day Pamphlet*, No. 13, Derry, Field Day Theatre Company, 1988, p. 7.
3 'Nationalism', pp. 7–8.
4 'Escaping from Belfast: Class, Ideology and Literature in Northern Ireland', *Race and Class*, Vol. 20, No. 1, 1978, pp. 41–62.
5 Rethinking the role of identity in these terms prompts necessary revisions. For instance, a government-funded body such as the Cultural Traditions Group does not, as I have previously argued, seek to provide 'interpellation into the practices of the bourgeois state' for dissident and residual sectarian cultural formations (see R. Kirkland, *Literature and Culture in Northern Ireland since 1965: Moments of Danger*, London, Longman, 1996, p. 114). Instead, the activity of such reconciliation agencies is one that searches for, recognises, and colludes with the dissident and the residual across a pre-existent identitarian matrix through which these latter groups have already constituted themselves.
6 *Mythologies*, London, Grafton, 1987, p. 138.
7 *Mythologies*, p. 139.
8 Joseph Ruane and Jennifer Todd, '"Why Can't You Get Along with Each Other?" Culture, Structure and the Northern Ireland Conflict', in *Culture and Politics in Northern Ireland*, ed. Eamonn Hughes, Buckingham, Open University Press, 1991, pp. 27–43.
9 At such moments it is worth remembering that the Joycean model of Irish cultural plurality to which so many of these readings ultimately subscribe has as one of its crucial elements what Joyce termed 'the new bourgeois conventions'. See James Joyce, 'Ireland, Island of Saints and Sages' (1907), in *The Field Day Anthology of Irish Writing*, ed. Seamus Deane and Andrew Carpenter, Derry, Field Day, 1991, III, p. 8.
10 'The Politics of the Possible', in *The Nature and Context of Minority Discourse*, ed. Abdul R. JanMohamed and David Lloyd, Oxford, Oxford University Press, 1990, p. 245.

11 In *Rethinking Northern Ireland*, ed. David Miller, London, Longman, 1998, pp. 199–210.
12 Bennett, 'Don't Mention the War', in Miller, ed., *Rethinking Northern Ireland*, p. 199.
13 *Culture and the State*, London, Routledge, 1996, p. 5.
14 See, for instance, Norman Vance's *Irish Literature: A Social History*, Oxford, Blackwell, 1990, pp. 209–260, or Patrick Grant's *Breaking Enmities: Religion, Literature and Culture in Northern Ireland, 1967–97*, Basingstoke, Macmillan, 1999, pp. 32–71.
15 *Mythologies*, p. 139.
16 For the liveliest account of this debate see Stephen Howe's *Ireland and Empire: Colonial Legacies in Irish History and Culture*, Oxford, Oxford University Press, 2000.
17 'The Politics of Literary Postcoloniality', *Race and Class*, Vol. 36, No. 3, 1995, pp. 1–20 (p. 7).
18 For specifically Northern Irish institutional responses to this crisis see my *Literature and Culture in Northern Ireland since 1965*, pp. 85–120.
19 Although what Edward Larrissy has described as Terry Eagleton's 'thoroughly orthodox Marxism' (review of *Heathcliff and the Great Hunger, Journal of Victorian Culture*, Vol. 2, No. 2, Autumn 1997, pp. 332–36 [p. 336]) in *Heathcliff and the Great Hunger: Studies in Irish Culture* (London, Verso, 1995), *Crazy John and the Bishop and Other Essays on Irish Culture* (Cork, Cork University Press, 1998) and *Scholars and Rebels in Nineteenth-Century Ireland* (Oxford, Blackwell, 1999) suggests a welcome intervention.
20 'Modernization and Aesthetic Ideology in Contemporary Irish Culture', in *Writing in the Irish Republic: Literature, Culture, Politics 1949–1999*, ed. Ray Ryan, Basingstoke, Macmillan, 2000, pp. 105–29 (p. 127).
21 'Bhabha, the Post/Colonial and Glenn Patterson's *Burning Your Own*', *Irish Studies Review*, Vol.7, No.1, April 1999, pp. 65–71 (p. 66).
22 Terry Eagleton, *Literary Theory: An Introduction*, Oxford, Blackwell, 1983, p. 197.
23 'Introduction: Rethinking Northern Ireland', in Miller, ed., *Rethinking Northern Ireland*, p. xix.
24 *Writing to the Moment: Selected Critical Essays 1980–96*, London, Faber & Faber, 1996, pp. 312–15 (p. 315).
25 'Notes on "Camp"', in *Against Interpretation*, London, Vintage, 1994 (1966), pp. 275–92 (p. 277).

1. Cultural Identity and the Bourgeois Spectacle

1 *Irish News*, 2 July 1998, p. 5.
2 Terence O'Neill's televised address to Northern Ireland of December 1968 is, in retrospect, perhaps the most striking of such moments:

> What kind of Ulster do you want? I will accept whatever your verdict may be. If it is your decision that we should live up to the words 'Ulster is British', which is part of our creed, then my services will be at your disposal to do what I can. But if you should want a separate, inward-looking, selfish and divided Ulster, then you must seek for others to lead you along the road, for I cannot and will not do it.

3 *Crazy John and the Bishop*, p. 326.
4 For instance (and in no particular order): the Cultural Traditions Group, Education for Mutual Understanding, the Community Relations Council, the Central Community Relations Unit, and, it can be argued, the Arts Council of Northern Ireland.
5 *The Novel and the Nation: Studies in the New Irish Fiction*, London, Pluto Press, 1997, p. 4.
6 Smyth, *The Novel and the Nation*, p. 5.
7 Ed. Andy Pollak, Dublin, Lilliput Press, 1993.
8 *Mistaken Identities: Poetry and Northern Ireland*, Oxford, Clarendon Press, 1997, p. 2.
9 *Gender Trouble: Feminism and the Subversion of Identity*, London, Routledge, 1990, p. 128.
10 'Cultural Identity and Diaspora', in *Colonial Discourse and Post-Colonial Theory*, ed. Patrick Williams and Laura Chrisman, Hemel Hempstead, Harvester Wheatsheaf, 1993, pp. 392–403 (p. 395).
11 *Gender Trouble*, p. 17.
12 Perhaps the broadest definition of the bourgeois in terms of its enduring existence comes in Nicholas Berdyaev's *The Bourgeois Mind and other Essays* (London, Sheed and Ward, 1934, p. 11). Berdyaev notes (p. 11): 'In the very depths of his being, or non-being, the bourgeois is distinguishable from the not bourgeois; he is a man of a particular spirit, or particular soullessness. The state of being bourgeois has always existed in the world, and its immortal image is for ever fixed in the Gospels with its equally immortal antithesis, but in the nineteenth century it attained its climax and ruled supreme.' More helpful for our purposes is Tom Nairn's account of Northern Ireland in terms of bourgeois capitalism in *The Break-Up of Britain: Crisis and Neo-Nationalism* (London, Verso, 1981), in which he observes (p. 235): 'This settlement had evolved into a bourgeois society. Although on a small scale (more like a 'city-state' than a territorial nation) it possessed the whole range of classes and most of the institutions that typify such a society. Yet this evolution had occurred under the most universal conditions. The economic integration it rested on was accompanied and modelled by that double isolation already referred to – by the politics and the culture of an especially insecure frontier.'
13 *Bourgeois Morality*, trans. G.L. Campbell, London, Routledge, 1986, pp. 7–8.
14 *Mythologies*, pp. 138–39.
15 *Mythologies*, p. 139.
16 *Mythologies*, p. 139.
17 *Mythologies*, p. 140.
18 *Mythologies*, p. 140.
19 *Imagined Communities: Reflections on the Origin and Rise of Nationalism*, London, Verso, 1991.
20 *The Society of the Spectacle*, Detroit, Black and Red, 1983, section 55. First published as *La Société du Spectacle*, 1967.
21 *The Society of the Spectacle*, section 56.
22 'Cultural Identity and Diaspora', in Williams and Chrisman, eds., *Colonial Discourse*, p. 392.

23 *Gender Trouble*, p. 136.
24 *Selections from the Prison Notebooks*, ed. and trans. Quintin Hoare and Geoffrey Nowell Smith, London, Lawrence and Wishart, 1971, p. 52.
25 *Mythologies*, p. 140.
26 'Broadcasting in a Divided Community', in *Culture, Identity and Broadcasting in Ireland: Local Issues, Global Perspectives*, ed. Martin McLoone, Belfast, Institute of Irish Studies, 1991, pp. 99–103 (p. 102).
27 Butler, 'Broadcasting', in McLoone, ed., *Culture, Identity and Broadcasting*, p. 103.
28 *Nationalism, Colonialism and Literature*, ed. Seamus Deane, Minneapolis, University of Minnesota Press, 1990, p. 11.
29 'Nationalism'.
30 See Eagleton, 'Nationalism', p. 7.
31 *Material Conflicts: Parades and Visual Displays in Northern Ireland*, Oxford, Berg, 1997, p. 11.
32 *Anomalous States*, p. 55.
33 *Anomalous States*, p. 56.
34 *The Location of Culture*, London, Routledge, 1994, p. 1.
35 *Gender Trouble*, p. 148
36 *The Location of Culture*, p. 86.
37 *The Location of Culture*, p. 86.
38 *Postcolonial Theory*, Edinburgh, Edinburgh University Press, 1998, p. 149.
39 'Excess: Post-Colonialism and the Verandahs of Meaning', in *De-Scribing Empire: Post-Colonialism and Textuality*, ed. Chris Tiffin and Alan Lawson, London, Routledge, 1994, pp. 33–44 (p. 33).
40 'Cultural Identity and Diaspora', in Williams and Chrisman, eds., *Colonial Discourse*, p. 397.
41 'Nationalism', p. 7.
42 *Gender Trouble*, p. 17.
43 *Strange Country: Modernity and Nationhood in Irish Writing since 1790*, Oxford, Clarendon Press, 1997, p. 163.
44 *The Wretched of the Earth*, trans. Constance Farrington, Harmondsworth, Penguin, 1985 (1965), pp. 164–65.
45 David Lloyd, 'Nationalisms against the State: Towards a Critique of the Anti-Nationalist Prejudice', in *Re-Examining and Reviewing the Philippine Progressive Vision: Papers and Proceedings of the 1993 Conference of the Forum for Philippine Alternatives (FOPA), San Francisco Bay Area, California, April 2–4, 1993*, ed. Forum for Philippine Alternatives, Quezon: FOPA, 1993, pp. 27–38.
46 *Strange Country*, p. 163.

2. Identity, Image and Ideology in Film

1 *The Society of the Spectacle*, section 167.
2 Kevin Rockett, Luke Gibbons and John Hill, *Cinema and Ireland*, Syracuse, Syracuse University Press, 1988, p. 184.
3 In *Film Theory and Criticism: Introductory Readings*, ed. Gerald Mast and Marshall Cohen, Oxford, Oxford University Press, 1979, pp. 610–20 (p. 617).

4 Jean-Pierre Oudart, Jean Narboni and Jean-Louis Comolli, 'Readings of Jancsó: Yesterday and Today', in *Cahiers du Cinéma: Volume III 1969–1972: The Politics of Representation* (An anthology from *Cahiers du Cinéma* Nos. 210–239, March 1969–June 1972), ed. Nick Browne, London, Routledge/British Film Institute, 1990, pp. 89–111 (pp. 93–94).

5 'Toward a Non-Bourgeois Camera Style', in Mast and Cohen, eds., *Film Theory and Criticism*, pp. 839–55 (p. 847).

6 'Cinema, the Ceasefire and "the Troubles"', *Irish Studies Review*, No. 20, Autumn 1997, pp. 2–8 (p. 3).

7 'Cinema, the Ceasefire and "the Troubles"', p. 8.

8 Collected in Browne, ed., *Cahiers du Cinéma: Volume III*.

9 *Cahiers du Cinéma: Volume III*, p. 14.

10 *Cahiers du Cinéma: Volume III*, p. 15.

11 *Cahiers du Cinéma: Volume III*, p. 15.

12 Pascal Bonitzer, Jean-Louis Comolli, Serge Daney, Jean Narboni and Jean-Pierre Oudart, '*La Vie est à nous*: A militant film', in Browne, ed., *Cahiers du Cinéma: Volume III*, pp. 68–88 (p. 77).

13 *Cahiers du Cinéma: Volume III*, p. 19.

14 One recent example of this tendency is Brian McIlroy's *Shooting to Kill: Filmmaking and the 'Troubles' in Northern Ireland* (Trowbridge, Flicks Books, 1998), which is built around what the author identifies as the lack of adequate representations of Northern Irish Protestants/Unionists in Northern Irish film and television. While this argument can be justified (and while it gives the book a certain rhetorical momentum) the nature of its dominance in the work tends to overwhelm possible analyses of form and image. Moreover, as Lance Pettitt astutely observes in review, it lends to the book a slightly paranoid tone, as when McIlroy observes: 'The Unionist case is not put and, ironically, cannot be trusted to be put, by Protestants themselves' (p. 145) (*Irish Studies Review*, Vol. 7, No. 1, April 1999, pp. 104–106).

15 Jean-Louis Comolli, 'Film/Politics (2): *L'Aveu*: 15 Propositions', in Browne, ed., *Cahiers du Cinéma: Volume III*, pp. 163–73 (p. 170).

16 'Film/Politics (2)', in Browne, ed., *Cahiers du Cinéma: Volume III*, p. 171.

17 London, Penguin, 1991.

18 The Remains of Empire: Conflicting Representations in Contemporary Film', *Irish Studies Review*, No. 7, Summer 1994, pp. 23–27 (p. 27).

19 Brian Neve, 'Film and Northern Ireland: Beyond "the Troubles"?', in *European Identity in Cinema*, ed. Wendy Everett, Exeter, Intellect Books, 1996, pp. 83–92 (p. 86).

20 '*In the Name of the Father*', *Cineaste*, Vol. 20, No. 4, October 1994, p. 47.

21 *Shooting to Kill*, p. 60.

22 *Shooting to Kill*, p. 60.

23 *Anomalous States*, p. 134.

24 'The Remains of Empire', p. 27.

25 The publicity on the video cover of *Hidden Agenda* tempts the viewer with murder... torture... corruption' and quotes the *Sunday Correspondent*'s judgment that the film is 'a fine political thriller'.

26 For a useful definition of docudrama see Seth Feldman, 'Footnote to Fact: The

Docudrama', in *Film Genre Reader*, ed. Barry Keith Grant, Austin, University of Texas Press, 1986, pp. 349–50. In relation to this argument, a brief comparison with Loach's Spanish Civil War film *Land and Freedom* (1995) is illustrative. While this later film employs many of the formal techniques also found in *Hidden Agenda*, most notably the many scenes containing explicitly didactic dialogue, its perception of the Left as having agency (despite its ultimate defeat) posits a residual optimism which allows for both a resolution of knowledge and formal closure.

27 In *Odd Man Out* the text superimposed over this shot is entirely illustrative of this desire in its emphasis on 'background': 'This story is told against a background of political unrest in a city of Northern Ireland. It is not concerned with the struggle between the law and an illegal organisation, but only with the conflict in the hearts of the people when they become unexpectedly involved.' *Hidden Agenda* employs a similar technique, presenting the viewer with quotations from James Fintan Lalor and Margaret Thatcher.

28 Rockett, Gibbons and Hill, *Cinema and Ireland*, p. 235.

29 Brian McIlroy, 'The Repression of Communities: Visual Representations of Northern Ireland during the Thatcher Years', in *British Cinema and Thatcherism*, ed. Lester Friedman, London, University College London Press, 1993, pp. 92–108 (p. 98).

30 The circularity of this quest narrative is reminiscent of Paul Muldoon's long poem *Immram*, a work that similarly explores the hereditary nature of violence from a Northern Irish perspective (*Why Brownlee Left*, London, Faber & Faber, 1980, pp. 38–47).

31 'Readings of Jancsó', in Browne, ed., *Cahiers du Cinéma: Volume III*, pp. 89–111.

32 'Readings of Jancsó', in Browne, ed., *Cahiers du Cinéma: Volume III*, p. 16.

33 'Readings of Jancsó', in Browne, ed., *Cahiers du Cinéma: Volume III*, p. 97.

34 It is interesting to note that the roughly contemporaneous Brian Friel play *Translations* (1980) adopts a similar device in the mute victim figure of Sarah, a young woman who metonymically represents the linguistic repression of the Ballybeg community. The first production of *Translations* had Stephen Rea and Ray McAnnally in the cast (*Translations*, London, Faber & Faber, 1981).

35 Rockett, Gibbons and Hill, *Cinema and Ireland*, pp. 183–84.

36 See Rockett, Gibbons and Hill, *Cinema and Ireland*, pp. 181–84.

37 *World Cinema 4: Ireland*, Trowbridge, Flicks Books, 1989, p. 72.

38 An image revisited interestingly in Alan Parker's Dublin film *The Commitments* (1991). In this film the redemptive powers of soul music are shown as capable of penetrating even this symbol of Ireland as brutal killing house.

39 Rockett, Gibbons and Hill, *Cinema and Ireland*, p. 174.

40 London, Methuen, 1982.

41 See Martin Dillon, *The Shankill Butchers: A Case Study of Mass Murder*, London, Hutchinson, 1989. The methods by which these films draw on this material are of some interest. The character of Ginger (Ian Hart) in *Nothing Personal* refers us to Lenny Murphy through his habit of mutilating his victims with a knife. This activity, while placing Ginger outside the conventions of the 'decent Loyalism' to which other characters in the film subscribe, is strictly incidental to the overall plot and is merely referred to through brief glimpses rather than framed

as a symbol of ultimate evil. *Resurrection Man*, by contrast, is an adaptation of a novel of the same name by Eoin McNamee (London, Picador, 1994), who wrote the screenplay for the film. McNamee's novel, in turn, can be described without undue simplification as a fictionalised account of Dillon's original work. In both the novel and the film this is suggested not only through the close rendering of events described in *The Shankill Butchers*, but also through the subplot, which concentrates on Ryan, a journalist who becomes obsessed with the murders and who exhibits the same contradictions of voyeurism and repulsion illustrated in Dillon's original work. In the progression from original act to journalistic study to novel and on ultimately to film what remains constant, like a malign genetic trait, is the assumption that the murders are so essentially evil as to defy representation. For this reason they become explicable only as symbols.

42 McNamee's choice of 'Victor Kelly' as a name for the Lenny Murphy character is significant. While the character has to have a Catholic-sounding surname in order to represent the Catholicism that was assumed to be a part of Murphy's own psychological profile, the choice of Victor suggests a possible reference to Victor Frankenstein – a figure with a similar predilection for finding bodies and dissecting them. In both instances it should be noted that these characters commit such acts convinced that they are for the long-term benefit of their community. Similarly, the transformation of the 'Shankill Butchers' to the 'Resurrection Men' further emphasises the activity of body snatching and ultimate dissection. I am grateful to Simon Bainbridge for drawing my attention to this parallel.

43 'An Irish Intelligentsia: Reflections on its Desirability', *The Honest Ulsterman*, No. 46–47, November 1974, pp. 27–34 (pp. 31–32).

44 A consideration of such images inevitably begins, as with so many analyses of Northern Ireland and cinema, with Carol Reed's *Odd Man Out* (1947), which mobilised the conventions of noir in order to understand the motivations of IRA terrorism as a force arising out of the very fabric of a malign Belfast itself. However, in terms of *Nothing Personal* and, to a lesser extent, *Resurrection Man*, Reed's later film *The Third Man* (1949) appears a more direct ancestor. The post-war Vienna of *The Third Man*, while again the paradigm of a noir location, has been 'bombed about a bit' and the sense this lends of an exhausted battle-ground no longer worth fighting over informs the later films' vision of violent ideologies devoid of political vision.

45 'Women in Film Noir', in *Women in Film Noir*, ed. E. Ann Kaplan, London, British Film Institute, 1980, pp. 38–50 (p. 41).

46 Ginger notes in response to Kenny's post-interrogation realisation that Liam is 'not IRA', 'Well, he'll join after this.' Indeed, Ginger's philosophy of sectarian hate, while presented as securely within the realms of psychopathic insanity, is the only coherent and consistent ideological position in the film.

47 Later in this scene Ginger will place the bullets from his gun in Liam's mouth in order to 'wash' them. Similarly, in both films guns are continually inserted into mouths both as a symbol of absolute humiliation and, if the gun is placed in the protagonist's own mouth, to suggest something of the terrorist's own emotional anarchy (Ginger in *Nothing Personal*, Victor in *Resurrection Man*).

48 It is of interest to note that John Lynch, the actor who plays Liam, is also the eponymous anti-hero of *Cal* and plays the role of Bobby Sands in *Some Mother's Son* (1996). In these films, as with his role in *Nothing Personal*, he plays characters who seem to invite and subsequently to welcome the violence perpetrated upon them.

49 This progression is also central to the construction of Maurice Leitch's Loyalist thriller *Silver's City* (London, Secker and Warburg, 1981).

50 James W. McAuley, 'Cuchullain and an RPG-7: The Ideology and Politics of the Ulster Defence Association', in Hughes, ed., *Culture and Politics in Northern Ireland*, p. 53.

51 *Derry Journal*, Friday 28 September 1990, p. 6.

52 Bonitzer et al., '*La Vie est à nous*: A Militant Film', in Browne, ed., *Cahiers du Cinéma: Volume III*, p. 77. See discussion above.

53 In McLoone, ed., *Culture, Identity and Broadcasting*, p. 80.

54 Sleeve notes to the video release of *Hush-a-Bye Baby*.

55 McLoone, ed., *Culture, Identity and Broadcasting*, p. 145.

56 *Derry Journal*, Friday 24 November 1989, p. 11.

57 The same age of course as Goretti Friel in *Hush-a-Bye Baby*.

58 See Nell McCafferty, 'The Death of Ann Lovett', in *The Abortion Papers: Ireland*, ed. Ailbhe Smyth, Dublin, Attic Press, 1992, pp. 99–106 for an account of how the Granard community responded to her death.

59 See Harry Barnes, 'Break the Taboo', *Fortnight*, No. 367, December 1997–January 1998, p. 9.

60 See Noreen Byrne, 'Cases X, Y, Z', *Fortnight*, No. 367, December 1997–January 1998, p. 8.

61 Barnes, 'Break the Taboo', p. 9.

62 Laura Friel, 'Intense Debate on Abortion', *An Phoblacht/Republican News*, 28 March 1996, p. 5.

63 Rita O'Reilly, *An Phoblacht/Republican News*, 23 May 1996, p. 12.

64 Monica McWilliams, 'Women in Northern Ireland: An Overview', in Hughes, ed., *Culture and Politics in Northern Ireland*, pp. 81–100 (pp. 94–95).

65 Luke Gibbons, 'On the Beach: Abortion and Divorce in Irish Cinema', *Artforum*, Vol. 31, No. 2, 1992, p. 13.

66 For a fuller analysis of the significance of this poem to *Hush-a-Bye Baby* see Elizabeth Butler Cullingford's 'Seamus and Sinéad: From "Limbo" to *Saturday Night Live* by way of *Hush-a-Bye Baby*', *Colby Quarterly*, Vol. 30, No. 1, 1994, pp. 43–62.

67 Geraldine Wilkins, 'Film Production in Northern Ireland', in *Border Crossing: Film in Ireland, Britain and Europe*, ed. John Hill, Martin McLoone and Paul Hainsworth, Belfast, Institute of Irish Studies/London, British Film Institute, 1994, pp. 140–45 (p. 142).

68 See McLoone, ed., *Culture, Identity and Broadcasting*, p. 116.

69 As a way of indicating just how complete this segregation of news is it is worth noting that during the *Hush-a-Bye Baby* controversy an article in the *Londonderry Sentinel* (26 September 1990, p. 8) introduced the work of Derry poet Seamus Heaney to its readers.

70 C. McKeever, *Derry Journal*, Friday 28 September 1990, p. 6.

71 Sean Carr, *Derry Journal*, Tuesday 25 September 1990, p. 10.
72 *Derry Journal*, Friday 28 September 1990, p. 6.
73 *Derry Journal*, Friday 28 September 1990, p. 17.
74 *Derry Journal*, Tuesday 9 October 1990, p. 11.
75 Sleeve notes to the video release of *Hush-a-Bye Baby*.
76 'Seamus and Sinéad', p. 46.
77 Bonitzer et al., *'La Vie est à nous*: A Militant Film', in Browne, ed., *Cahiers du Cinéma: Volume III*, p. 77.
78 Later in the film what can be termed the ideological state apparatus of medicine is also brought to bear upon Goretti as she is unable to inform her doctor of her pregnancy for fear he will tell her parents.
79 'Lear's Fool and Goya's Dilemma', *Circa*, No. 50, March–April 1990, p. 55.
80 'Lear's Fool', p. 56.
81 As Gibbons points out, the film's focus on a blue plastic fertiliser bag washed up on the beach in front of Goretti connects immediately to the case of Joanne Hayes ('On the Beach', p. 13). Similarly, while Goretti is baking in the farm-house in Donegal she listens to a radio debate on abortion that invokes the plight of Ann Lovett. Alongside these cases Margo Harkin notes that just before filming started, a baby was washed up at Culmore Point in Derry (see McLoone, ed., *Culture, Identity and Broadcasting*, p. 113).
82 'Shamrocks and Shillelaghs: Idyll and Ideology in Irish Cinema', *Film Comment*, Vol. 30, No. 3, May 1994, pp. 24–40 (p. 40).
83 In Kennedy's terms this is a cinema that 'acknowledges the tragedies of [Ireland's] past and the agonies of its present while insisting that humanity can coexist with history, myth with reality, poetry with prose. And that the fluidity of personal destiny can be both example and weapon against the obdurate imperatives of political destiny' ('Shamrocks and Shillelaghs', p. 40).
84 Rockett, Gibbons and Hill, *Cinema and Ireland*, p. 184.
85 'Film and Northern Ireland', in Everett, ed., *European Identity in Cinema*, p. 92.
86 *Shooting to Kill*, p. 59.
87 Cambridge, Cambridge University Press, 1997.
88 *Cinema, Theory and Political Responsibility*, p. 88.
89 'Pigs and Provos, Prostitutes and Prejudice: Gay Representation in Irish Film, 1984–95', in *Sex, Nation and Dissent in Irish Writing*, ed. Éibhear Walshe, Cork, Cork University Press, 1997, pp. 252–84 (p. 273).
90 '"Forked-Tongued on the Border Bit": Partition and the Politics of Form in Contemporary Narratives of the Northern Irish Conflict', *The South Atlantic Quarterly*, Vol. 95, No. 1, Winter 1996, pp. 227–76.
91 '"Forked-Tongued on the Border Bit"', p. 263
92 Browne, ed., *Cahiers du Cinéma: Volume III*, p. 17.
93 Jordan acknowledges these influences in his introduction to the screenplay of the film (*The Crying Game: An Original Screenplay*, London, Random House, 1993, p. viii).
94 Browne, ed., *Cahiers du Cinéma: Volume III*, p. 19.
95 Browne, ed., *Cahiers du Cinéma: Volume III*, p. 19.
96 'Film and Northern Ireland', in Everett, ed., *European Identity in Cinema*, p. 92.
97 Browne, ed., *Cahiers du Cinéma: Volume III*, p. 20.

3. Violence, History and Bourgeois Fiction

1 Robert McLiam Wilson, *Eureka Street*, London, Secker and Warburg, 1996, p. 379.
2 In *Peripheral Visions: Images of Nationhood in Contemporary British Fiction*, ed. Ian A. Bell, Cardiff, University of Wales Press, 1995, pp. 128–48.
3 *The Novel and the Nation*, p. 114.
4 *The Novel and the Nation*, p. 123.
5 'Fiction in Conflict', in Bell, ed., *Peripheral Visions*, p. 146.
6 'Introduction: Northern Ireland – Border Country', in Hughes, ed., *Culture and Politics in Northern Ireland*, p. 7.
7 *Culture and Politics in Northern Ireland*, p. 1.
8 *Culture and Politics in Northern Ireland*, p. 3.
9 'Fiction in Conflict', in Bell, ed., *Peripheral Visions*, p. 129.
10 *Culture and Politics in Northern Ireland*, p. 9.
11 'Fiction in Conflict', in Bell, ed., *Peripheral Visions*, p. 130.
12 It should be noted, though, that Hughes recognises the fact that 'thrillers can often articulate a rich response to a morally and politically complex world'. There is an irony implicit to this observation, however, as he notes that it has been in the poetry of Paul Muldoon that the possibilities of the thriller form have been 'best mobilised' (*Culture and Politics in Northern Ireland*, p. 7).
13 'Fiction in Conflict', in Bell, ed., *Peripheral Visions*, p. 146.
14 'Escaping from Belfast', p. 42.
15 'Escaping from Belfast', p. 54.
16 'Escaping from Belfast', p. 55.
17 'Escaping from Belfast', p. 62.
18 'Escaping from Belfast', p. 62.
19 'Don't Mention the War', in Miller, ed., *Rethinking Northern Ireland*, p. 199.
20 'Don't Mention the War', in Miller, ed., *Rethinking Northern Ireland*, p. 201.
21 'Don't Mention the War', in Miller, ed., *Rethinking Northern Ireland*, p. 200.
22 In 'Don't Mention the War' Bennett refers to Ulster Protestant culture as 'a barren, angry, schizophrenic world' (p. 208), the art that emerges from it is 'spawned', and it is usually 'an angry reaction to the prevalence of bigotry, claustrophobia and paranoia' (p. 209). Ultimately, it 'is restricted to little more than flute bands, Orange marches and the chanting of sectarian slogans at football matches' (p. 210).
23 *Mythologies*, pp. 150–55.
24 Dublin, Poolbeg, 1993.
25 'Form and Ideology in the Anglo-Irish Novel', *Bullán: An Irish Studies Journal*, Vol. 1, No. 1, Spring 1994, pp. 17–26 (p. 17).
26 *The Novel and the Nation*, p. 30.
27 'Form and Ideology in the Anglo-Irish Novel', p. 25.
28 *A Wreath Upon the Dead*, pp. 152–53.
29 Patrick Kavanagh, *The Collected Poems*, Newbridge, Goldsmith Press, 1990, pp. 148–49.
30 *A Wreath Upon the Dead*, p. 466.
31 *A Wreath Upon the Dead*, p. 272.
32 Friel, *Translations*, p. 38.

33 *A Wreath Upon the Dead*, p. 98.

34 *Poetry in the Wars*, Newcastle, Bloodaxe, 1986, p. 191.

35 *Heathcliff and the Great Hunger*, p. 21.

36 'Form and Ideology in the Anglo-Irish Novel', p. 17.

37 *A Wreath Upon the Dead*, pp. 113–14.

38 'Don't Mention the War', in Miller, ed., *Rethinking Northern Ireland*, p. 209.

39 *The Novel and the Nation*, p. 120.

40 *The Novel and the Nation*, p. 121.

41 For further reflections on the significance of Victor Kelly's name see the discussion of the film adaptation of this novel in Chapter 2.

42 Joseph Conrad, *Heart of Darkness*, London, Penguin, 1989 [1902], p. 113.

43 McNamee, *Resurrection Man*, p. 44.

44 Conrad, *Heart of Darkness*, p. 112.

45 *The Great Tradition: George Eliot, Henry James, Joseph Conrad*, London, Chatto and Windus, 1948, p. 226.

46 *The Novel and the Nation*, p. 122.

47 McNamee, *Resurrection Man*, p. 16.

48 *Resurrection Man*, p. 22.

49 *Resurrection Man*, p. 83. The uncomfortable space between the violent event and its subsequent codification within the language of the news media that the novel identifies at this point is one occupied also by Seamus Heaney's poem 'Whatever you say say nothing' (*North*, London, Faber & Faber, 1975, pp. 57–60), where the inadequacies of 'Backlash' and 'crack down', 'the Provisional wing', 'Polarization' and 'long-standing hate' similarly indicate the more profound inarticulacy of being 'besieged within the siege, whispering morse'.

50 I am grateful to James Daniel for drawing my attention to the significance of this opening.

51 *Culture and Imperialism*, London, Chatto and Windus, 1993, p. 33.

52 For a discussion of the way this idea is made manifest within a specific text see the analysis of Neil Jordan's film *Angel* in Chapter 2.

53 McNamee, *Resurrection Man*, p. 183.

54 As Seamus Deane argues in 'An Irish Intelligentsia', pp. 31–32. See the discussion of this essay in Chapter 2.

55 McNamee, *Resurrection Man*, p. 3.

56 *Resurrection Man*, p. 4.

57 *Resurrection Man*, p. 6.

58 *Resurrection Man*, p. 233.

59 See 'The Dead', in *Dubliners*, London, Granada, 1981 [1914], p. 201: 'His soul swooned slowly as he heard the snow falling faintly through the universe and faintly falling, like the descent of their last end, upon all the living and the dead.'

60 London, Harper Collins, 1995.

61 The novel was subsequently retitled *Cross ma heart* by Harper Collins in 1999.

62 Bateman's rise to fame following the publication of his first novel *Divorcing Jack* (London, Harper Collins, 1994) can be described, without hyperbole, as a phenomenon. His subsequent novels have been *Cycle of Violence* (London, Harper Collins, 1995), *Of Wee Sweetie Mice and Men* (London, Harper Collins,

1996), *Empire State* (London, Harper Collins, 1997), *Maid of the Mist* (London, Harper Collins, 1999), *Turbulent Priests* (London, Harper Collins, 1999) and *Shooting Sean* (London, Harper Collins, 2001). As well as a continued interest in exploring the muddled interaction of direct intervention and blind chance through the thriller format, the novels also share a distinctive, and immediately recognisable, packaging featuring an image of the protagonist of each novel at a point of dramatic crisis. For instance, the cover of *Cycle of Violence* depicts Miller tied to a chair having his hair permed. To his right there is aimed a hairdryer, to his left a gun. This image illustrates well the combination of the violent and the ludicrous that has become Bateman's trademark.

63 Bateman, *Cycle of Violence*, p. 245.

64 The obvious comparative text here is Forster's *Howards End* (1910), with its vision of a creeping London modernity overwhelming all the tenuous human relationships that stand in its way.

65 Bateman, *Cycle of Violence*, p. 26.

66 *Cycle of Violence*, p. 204.

67 *The Novel and the Nation*, pp. 123–24.

68 Interestingly Bateman has discussed his own writing practices as 'based on risk', a form of 'typing with my fingers crossed'. As he notes: 'I don't plan any of the books in advance. I have a basic idea for the story and the first chapter and then I just start writing. I just have no idea how my books are going to end.' (http://www.harpercollins.co.uk/authors/64.htm)

69 Bateman, *Cycle of Violence*, p. 242.

70 *Cycle of Violence*, p. 106.

71 *Cycle of Violence*, p. 72.

72 *Cycle of Violence*, pp. 115–16.

73 *Mythologies*, p. 153.

74 Annie Dunlop, *Kissing the Frog*, Dublin, Poolbeg, 1996, p. 63.

75 Dunlop, *Kissing the Frog*, p. 82.

76 *Kissing the Frog*, p. 15.

77 *Kissing the Frog*, p. 104.

78 *Kissing the Frog*, p. 15.

79 *Kissing the Frog*, p. 5.

80 *Kissing the Frog*, p. 16.

81 *The Novel and the Nation*, p. 125.

82 Bateman, *Cycle of Violence*, p. 10.

83 It should also be noted that the hero of Bateman's earlier novel *Divorcing Jack*, Dan Starkey, is practically identical to *Cycle of Violence*'s Miller. Smyth notes the similarity of the fictional Starkey to the real Bateman in that he is also 'a young journalist with novelistic aspirations who writes a satirical column for an Ulster newspaper' (*The Novel and the Nation*, p. 125).

84 Smyth, in his reading of *Divorcing Jack*, identifies a similar transgression at work and finds in this the message that 'there has to be a space within the imagination of Northern Ireland for non-bigoted, politically sceptical, Protestant atheists'. At the same time, it is difficult not to have sympathy with his perception that the 'collapsing of the barriers between narrative and reality' that this requires 'can sometimes be an irritation' (*The Novel and the Nation*, p. 125).

85 Richard Mills, '"All Stories are Love Stories": Robert McLiam Wilson Inter-viewed by Richard Mills', *Irish Studies Review*, Vol. 7, No. 1, April 1999, pp. 73–77 (p. 76).

86 'The Formalist School of Poetry and Marxism', in *Literature and Revolution*, Ann Arbor, MI, Ann Arbor Paperbacks, 1960, p. 179.

87 *Literature and Revolution*, p. 234.

88 London, Chatto and Windus, 1992.

89 See Patten, 'Fiction in Conflict', in Bell, ed., *Peripheral Visions*, pp. 128–48.

90 Fermanagh, Armagh, Tyrone, Londonderry, Antrim, Down.

91 *Fat Lad*, p. 127.

92 For further thoughts about this triangular structure see my *Literature and Culture in Northern Ireland since 1965*, pp. 48–49.

93 'Fiction in Conflict', in Bell, ed., *Peripheral Visions*, p. 145.

94 Belfast, Blackstaff Press, 1989.

95 See Hughes, *Culture and Politics in Northern Ireland*; Candida Crewe, 'Belfast Slabbers Pave a Literary Way', *The Guardian*, 18 February 1992, p. 32; Patten, 'Fiction in Conflict', in Bell, ed., *Peripheral Visions*; Kirkland, *Literature and Culture in Northern Ireland since 1965*.

96 *A Theory of Literary Production*, trans. Geoffrey Wall, London, Routledge, 1978, p. 93.

97 *Literary Production*, p. 83.

98 *Literary Production*, p. 87.

99 Terry Eagleton, *Ideology: An Introduction*, London, Verso, 1991, p. 193.

100 'Violence and the Constitution of the Novel', in *Anomalous States*, p. 133.

101 *Anomalous States*, p. 134.

102 *Anomalous States*, p. 134.

103 *Anomalous States*, p. 134.

104 Wilson, *Eureka Street*, p. 359.

105 *Eureka Street*, p. 96.

106 For further development of this idea see Eagleton, *Ideology: An Introduction*, p. 154.

107 Wilson, *Eureka Street*, p. 163.

108 *Eureka Street*, p. 27.

109 *Eureka Street*, p. 187.

110 *Eureka Street*, p. 186.

111 See Candida Crewe, 'Biting the Bullet', *The Times Magazine*, 7 September 1996, p. 18, and Shawn Pogatchnik, *Associated Press* syndicated interview, 13 May 1992. However, see also Wilson's own satiric poem 'The way Forward for Ireland', *Fortnight*, No. 303, February 1992, p. 40.

112 One might compare the banality of this opposition with Wilson's earlier novel *Ripley Bogle*, which delights in dissolving the contract of trust between reader and novel through a series of sustained and increasingly complex 'lies' (as the novel terms them), deceptions and narrative suspensions. Here, as opposed to *Eureka Street*, the concept of narrative veracity is seen to have an economic basis quite beyond the means of the impoverished Bogle.

113 For instance Jake's account of an early encounter with Aoirghe: ' "You're from West Belfast, then?" she asked me, a new glitter in her eyes. I nearly laughed.

Nobody in Belfast says West Belfast. That was TV news talk' (*Eureka Street*, p. 94).

114 *The Historical Novel*, London, Penguin Books, 1969, p. 285.

115 *Marxism and Form: Twentieth-Century Dialectical Theories of Literature*, Princeton, Princeton University Press, 1974, p. 195.

116 *Marxism and Literary Criticism*, London, Methuen, 1976, p. 30.

117 Wilson, *Eureka Street*, pp. 50–51.

118 *Eureka Street*, p. 61.

119 *Eureka Street*, p. 62.

120 Patterson, *Fat Lad*, p. 8.

121 I am grateful to Clare Anderson for drawing my attention to this idea.

122 Patterson, *Fat Lad*, p. 66.

123 *Fat Lad*, p. 182.

124 *Fat Lad*, p. 249.

125 Lukács, *The Historical Novel*, p. 239.

126 *The Historical Novel*, p. 239.

127 *The Historical Novel*, p. 239.

128 *Marxism and Form*, p. 197.

129 Patterson, *Fat Lad*, p. 9.

130 *Fat Lad*, p. 46.

131 *Fat Lad*, p. 258.

132 Wilson, *Eureka Street*, p. 118.

133 *Eureka Street*, p. 154.

134 *Eureka Street*, p. 139.

135 Patterson, *Fat Lad*, p. 4.

136 *Fat Lad*, p. 4.

137 London, Chatto and Windus, 1988.

138 Patterson, *Fat Lad*, p. 11.

139 See Patten, 'Fiction in Conflict', in Bell, ed., *Peripheral Visions*, p. 143; Kirkland, *Literature and Culture in Northern Ireland since 1965*, p. 49.

140 See especially Carson's *The Irish For No* (Dublin, Gallery Press, 1987), *Belfast Confetti* (Dublin, Gallery Press, 1989), *First Language* (Dublin, Gallery Press, 1993) or his collection of Belfast prose memories and stories *The Star Factory* (London, Granta, 1997). Neil Corcoran's 'One Step Forward, Two Steps Back: Ciaran Carson's *The Irish For No*', in *The Chosen Ground: Essays on the Contemporary Poetry of Northern Ireland*, ed. Neil Corcoran, Bridgend, Seren Books, 1992, pp. 213–33 charts Carson's progression away from modernist poetic stabilities (represented by his rejection of Heaney's *North*) towards a more provisional awareness 'of how much may ooze and slip and spill' (p. 232).

141 Patterson, *Fat Lad*, p. 207.

142 Again, one can think here of Forster's *Howards End* and the contrast it insists upon between the stability of place (most obviously Howards End itself) and the shifting vagaries of ideologically motivated individuals (most obviously the Wilcox family). In an Irish context such an opposition is well represented by J.C. Beckett's comment that 'We have in Ireland an element of stability – the land, and an element of instability – the people. It is to the stable element we must look for continuity.' See John Wilson Foster, *Colonial Consequences: Essays in Irish Literature and Culture*, Dublin, Lilliput Press, 1991, p. 149.

143 Patterson, *Fat Lad*, p. 214.

144 Wilson, *Eureka Street*, p. 180.

145 *Eureka Street*, p. 294.

146 Louis Althusser, 'Ideology and the State', in *Essays on Ideology*, London, Verso, 1984, pp. 1–60 (p. 49).

147 Wilson, *Eureka Street*, p. 214.

148 Patterson, *Fat Lad*, p. 277.

149 *Fat Lad*, p. 269.

150 *The Historical Novel*, p. 287.

151 Duffaud, *A Wreath Upon the Dead*, p. 112.

4. Three Forms of Camp

1 *Bourgeois Morality*, p. 25.

2 *Gender Trouble*, p. 139.

3 *Gender Trouble*, pp. 140–41.

4 *Gender Trouble*, p. 141.

5 *Gender Trouble*, p. 141.

6 In *Only Entertainment*, London, Routledge, 1992, pp. 135–47. It is necessary to place Dyer's cheerful analysis in the context of other more militant reclamations of camp by queer theory. For instance, Moe Meyer's utopian aspiration to cleanse the concept of inappropriate usage insists that 'Camp embodies a specifically queer cultural discourse' and for this reason 'the un-queer do not have access to the discourse of Camp, only to derivatives constructed through the act of appropriation' ('Introduction: Reclaiming the Discourse of Camp', in *The Politics and Poetics of Camp*, ed. Moe Meyer, London, Routledge, 1994, p. 1).

7 *Only Entertainment*, p. 135.

8 In *Against Interpretation*, pp. 275–92. Sontag is unusual in choosing to capitalise 'Camp' throughout her essay. Dyer opts for the lower case and I have followed his example.

9 For Sontag these include Tiffany lamps, Scopitone films, *The Enquirer* (headlines and stories), Aubrey Beardsley drawings, *Swan Lake*, old Flash Gordon comics and 'stag movies seen without lust' (*Against Interpretation*, pp. 277–78). Dyer includes Nelson Eddy and Jeanette MacDonald, Aubrey Beardsley, Vienna Waltzes, most classical ballet, the Queen Mother, velvet and brocade curtains and Marlene Dietrich (*Only Entertainment*, pp. 137–38).

10 *Against Interpretation*, p. 277.

11 *Against Interpretation*, p. 277.

12 *Against Interpretation*, p. 285.

13 *Against Interpretation*, p. 288.

14 *Against Interpretation*, p. 288.

15 *Against Interpretation*, p. 286.

16 Wilson, *Eureka Street*, p. 396.

17 *Only Entertainment*, p. 138.

18 *Mythologies*, p. 109.

19 'The Recovery of Kitsch', in *Distant Relations: Chicano, Irish, Mexican Art and Critical Writing*, ed. Trisha Ziff, New York, Smart Art Press, 1995, pp. 146–54 (p. 147).

20 'The Recovery of Kitsch', in Ziff, ed., *Distant Relations*, p. 148.
21 'The Recovery of Kitsch', in Ziff, ed., *Distant Relations*, p. 150.
22 In *Liberty Tree*, London: Faber & Faber, 1983, p. 33.
23 Sontag, *Against Interpretation*, p. 277.
24 In *Aspects of Irish Studies*, ed. Myrtle Hill and Sarah Barber, Belfast, Institute of Irish Studies, 1990, p. 56.
25 Paisley was imprisoned for three months for his part in a demonstration held outside the General Assembly of the Presbyterian Church. However, Paulin could also be referring to the letters Paisley produced during a subsequent incarceration in 1969. This is of little significance to my argument in that Paisley's response to his imprisonment was the same in each instance.
26 *Against Interpretation*, p. 276.
27 In *The Collected Poems of John Hewitt*, ed. Frank Ormsby, Belfast, Blackstaff Press, 1991, p. 60.
28 *Ancestral Voices: The Selected Prose of John Hewitt*, ed. Tom Clyde, Belfast, Blackstaff Press, 1987, p. 28.
29 The fact that Hewitt, for a period, also invested some hope in the regionalist project demonstrates the ways in which the various manifestations of non-aligned identitarianism can bleed into each other. See his essays 'The Bitter Gourd: Some Problems of the Ulster Writer' (*Ancestral Voices*, pp. 108–21) and 'Regionalism: The Last Chance' (*Ancestral Voices*, pp. 122–25). I consider these essays and the regionalist project as a whole in more detail in *Literature and Culture in Northern Ireland since 1965*, pp. 27–33.
30 Mills, '"All Stories are Love Stories"', pp. 74–75.
31 Belfast, Northern Ireland Office, 1989.
32 *The Day of the Men and Women of Peace...*, p. 1.
33 *The Day of the Men and Women of Peace...*, p. 72.
34 It should be noted that *The Day of the Men and Women of Peace...* cannot be considered in isolation but rather takes its place within a series of government initiatives developed during this period to facilitate social and cultural exchange, such as Education for Mutual Understanding and the Central Community Relations Unit. I consider the implications of these quasi-institutions in more detail in *Literature and Culture in Northern Ireland since 1965* (pp. 111–16). See also Richard English, 'Cultural Traditions and Political Ambiguity', *Irish Review*, No. 15, 1994, pp. 97–106, and Steve Bruce, *The Edge of the Union: The Ulster Loyalist Political Vision*, Oxford, Oxford University Press, 1994. Similarly, such developments need to be read in the context of the British government's repeated declaration since 1990 that it has 'no selfish strategic or economic interest in Northern Ireland' (see Paul Bew, Peter Gibbon and Henry Patterson, *Northern Ireland 1921–1994: Political Forces and Social Classes*, London, Serif, 1995, p. 228).
35 *Collected Poems*, pp. 200–202. In light of the poem's exploration of dissident sexual identities it is appropriate that it first appeared in *The Honest Ulsterman* (No. 50, Winter 1975, pp. 138–40), a magazine edited initially by James Simmons that began its life proclaiming sexual liberation as a means of achieving social liberation. I am grateful to Jeff Dudgeon for drawing this poem to my attention.

36 *Against Interpretation*, p. 290. The other force, incidentally, is 'Jewish moral seriousness'.
37 *Only Entertainment*, p. 135.
38 *Only Entertainment*, p. 138.
39 *Gender Trouble*, pp. 140–41.
40 See, for instance, the views of Andy Tyrie, then commander of the Ulster Defence Association, in Robert Bell's interview 'Culture – the Voice of the UDA', *The Belfast Review*, No. 10, March–May 1985, pp. 2–4.
41 Belfast, Ulidia Press, 1983.
42 See Damian Gorman, 'The Way of the Killer Ant', *The Belfast Review*, No. 4, Autumn 1893, pp. 2–3 (p. 2).
43 Quoted in Martin Dillon and Denis Lehane, *Political Murder in Northern Ireland*, London, Penguin, 1973, p. 286. It is significant that similar comparisons and justifications have been taken up with enthusiasm by a series of militant Loyalist journals.
44 Indeed, while Duddy was prepared to imagine the experience of Northern Irish Protestants as akin to that of the Jews, James Simmons, in the roughly contemporaneous poem 'Ulster Says Yes', recognised that, for many, Protestants could be more closely identified with the Nazis:

> However, we weren't Nazis or Yanks,
> so measure your fuss
> who never suffered like Jews or Blacks,
> not here, not with us.

See James Simmons, *Poems 1956–1986*, ed. Edna Longley, Dublin, Gallery Press, 1986, p. 197.
45 Oxford, Blackwell, 1995, p. 254.
46 Of this tension, Jonathan Stevenson notes: 'Tyrie [...] saw his job as keeping a respectable – that is a marginally political – face on an organisation which couldn't help but stay essentially paramilitary. Unfortunately he couldn't sustain the effort' (*We Wrecked the Place: Contemplating an End to the Northern Irish Troubles*, New York, The Free Press, 1996, p. 87).
47 It is worth noting that Mahon is, of course, another Belfast Protestant writer, although Duddy had never heard of him at the time of writing *Concrete Whirlpools of the Mind* (Gorman, 'The Way of the Killer Ant', p. 2).
48 See 'Rage for Order', in *Poems 1962–78*, Oxford, Oxford University Press, 1979, p. 44.
49 One might think here of Mahon's use of the word 'home' in the second section of his poem 'Afterlives' (*Poems 1962–78*, p. 58):

> Perhaps if I'd stayed behind
> And lived it bomb by bomb
> I might have grown up at last
> And learnt what is meant by home.

Or, more notoriously, Seamus Heaney's recognition of the temptation posed by 'exact and tribal, intimate revenge' in 'Punishment' (*North*, pp. 37–38).
50 *A Rage for Order: Poetry of the Northern Ireland Troubles*, Belfast, Blackstaff Press, 1992.
51 For a fuller analysis of this process see McAuley, 'Cuchullain and the RPG-7', in

Hughes, ed., *Culture and Politics in Northern Ireland*, pp. 45–68.

52 '[The] introduction [of Direct Rule] represented the definitive end of the "Orange State". It allowed the British government the space to introduce a strategy of reform "from above".' Paul Bew and Gordon Gillespie, *Northern Ireland: A Chronology of the Troubles 1968–1993*, Dublin, Gill and Macmillan: 1993, pp. 50–51.

53 See Tim Pat Coogan, *The Troubles*, London, Random House, 1995, p. 286.

54 'Identity and its Discontents: Women and the Nation', in Williams and Chrisman, eds., *Colonial Discourse*, pp. 376–91 (p. 379).

55 Sam Duddy, Andy Tyrie and Michael Hall, *This is It!*, *Theatre Ireland*, No. 7, Autumn 1984, pp. 19–34.

56 *This is It!*, p. 20.

57 Stevenson notes (*We Wrecked the Place*, p. 88) that during the five years following Tyrie's resignation the UFF carried out 72 political murders – substantially more than the UVF during the same period. It can, however, be proposed that such progressivist strands re-emerged in the formation of the Ulster Democratic Party – which took the NUPRG document *Common Sense* (1987) as its manifesto.

58 Gramsci, *Selections from the Prison Notebooks*, p. 55.

59 *Selections from the Prison Notebooks*, p. 52.

60 London, Pan Books, 1969.

61 *The Price of My Soul*, p. 9.

62 *The Price of My Soul*, p. 9.

63 *The Price of My Soul*, pp. 33–34.

64 *The Price of My Soul*, pp. 66–67.

65 *The Price of My Soul*, p. 69.

66 *Against Interpretation*, p. 286.

67 *The Price of My Soul*, p. 40.

68 *The Price of My Soul*, p. 42.

69 *The Price of My Soul*, p. 51.

70 *The Price of My Soul*, p. 49.

71 *Irish Times*, 1 February 1972, p. 1.

72 *The Price of My Soul*, p. 77.

73 *The Price of My Soul*, p. 78.

74 *The Price of My Soul*, p. 205.

75 *The Price of My Soul*, p. 173.

76 *The Price of My Soul*, p. 170.

77 *The Price of My Soul*, p. 89.

78 *The Price of My Soul*, p. 88.

79 *The Price of My Soul*, p. 89.

80 *The Price of My Soul*, p. 205.

81 See *Every Stoney Acre has a Name: A Celebration of the Townland in Ulster*, ed. Tony Canavan, Belfast, Federation for Local Studies, 1991.

82 See *Various Verses by John O'the North*, Belfast, Derek McCord, 1945.

83 Belfast, Blackstaff Press, 1982.

84 Dingle, Brandon Books, 1992.

85 *The Letters of James Joyce*, II, ed. Richard Ellmann, London, Faber & Faber, 1964, p. 134.

86 Adams, *The Street*, p. 49.
87 *The Street*, p. 55.
88 *The Street*, p. 51.
89 *The Street*, p. 48.
90 *The Street*, pp. 59–60.
91 *The Street*, p. 61.
92 *The Street*, pp. 62–63.
93 *The Street*, p. 63.
94 *The Street*, p. 66.
95 Spivak and Gunew, 'Questions of Multiculturalism', in Spivak, *The Post-Colonial Critic*, p. 60.
96 *Mythologies*, p. 157.
97 As an example of such utopian criticism see Spurgeon Thompson's 'The Commodification of Culture and Decolonisation in Northern Ireland' (*Irish Studies Review*, Vol. 7, No. 1, 1999, pp. 53–63), where he notes: 'In short, the danger that Northern Ireland faces in this moment of decolonisation is that culture will be stripped of its social and political meanings and changed into a set of objects like chocolates in a box, set out for selection and consumption. Quietly dropped in this transformation is political agency' (p. 62).
98 *The Society of the Spectacle*, section 220.

Bibliography

Adams, G., *The Street and Other Stories*, Dingle, Brandon Books, 1992.

Ahmad, A., 'The Politics of Literary Postcoloniality', *Race and Class*, Vol. 36, No. 3, 1995, pp. 1–20.

Althusser, L., *Essays on Ideology*, London, Verso, 1984.

Anderson, B., *Imagined Communities: Reflections on the Origin and Rise of Nationalism*, London, Verso, 1991.

Barnes, H., 'Break the Taboo', *Fortnight*, No. 367, December 1997– January 1998, p. 9.

Barthes, R., *Mythologies*, trans. Annette Lavers, London, Grafton, 1987.

Bateman, C., *Cycle of Violence*, London, Harper Collins, 1995.

— *Divorcing Jack*, London, Harper Collins, 1994.

— *Empire State*, London, Harper Collins, 1997.

— *Maid of the Mist*, London, Harper Collins, 1999.

— *Shooting Sean*, London, Harper Collins, 2001.

— *Turbulent Priests*, London, Harper Collins, 1999.

— *Of Wee Sweetie Mice and Men*, London, Harper Collins, 1996.

Bell, I.A., ed., *Peripheral Visions: Images of Nationhood in Contemporary British Fiction*, Cardiff, University of Wales Press, 1995.

Bell, R., 'Culture – the Voice of the UDA', *The Belfast Review*, No. 10, March–May 1985, pp. 2–4.

Berdyaev, N., *The Bourgeois Mind and Other Essays*, London, Sheed and Ward, 1934.

Bew, P., P. Gibbon and H. Patterson, *Northern Ireland 1921–1994: Political Forces and Social Classes*, London, Serif, 1995.

Bew, P., and G. Gillespie, *Northern Ireland: A Chronology of the Troubles 1968–1993*, Dublin, Gill and Macmillan, 1993.

Bhabha, H., *The Location of Culture*, London, Routledge, 1994.

Browne, N., ed., *Cahiers du Cinéma: Volume III 1969–1972: The Politics of Representation* (An anthology from *Cahiers du Cinéma* Nos. 210–239,

March 1969–June 1972), London, Routledge/British Film Institute, 1990.

Bruce, S., *The Edge of the Union: The Ulster Loyalist Political Vision*, Oxford, Oxford University Press, 1994.

Butler, J., *Gender Trouble: Feminism and the Subversion of Identity*, London, Routledge, 1990.

Butler Cullingford, E., 'Seamus and Sinéad: From "Limbo" to *Saturday Night Live* by way of *Hush-a-Bye Baby*', *Colby Quarterly*, Vol. 30, No. 1, 1994, pp. 43–62.

Byrne, N., 'Cases X, Y, Z', *Fortnight*, No. 367, December 1997–January 1998, p. 8.

Canavan, T., ed., *Every Stoney Acre has a Name: A Celebration of the Townland in Ulster*, Belfast, Federation for Local Studies, 1991.

Carson, C., *Belfast Confetti*, Dublin, Gallery Press, 1989.

— *First Language*, Dublin, Gallery Press, 1993.

— *The Irish For No*, Dublin, Gallery Press, 1987.

— *The Star Factory*, London, Granta, 1997.

Churchill, C., *Top Girls*, London, Methuen, 1982.

Cleary, J., '"Forked-Tongued on the Border Bit": Partition and the Politics of Form in Contemporary Narratives of the Northern Irish Conflict', *The South Atlantic Quarterly*, Vol. 95, No. 1, Winter 1996, pp. 227–76.

Coogan, T.P., *The Troubles*, London, Random House, 1995.

Conlon, G., *Proved Innocent*, London, Penguin, 1991.

Conrad, J., *Heart of Darkness*, London, Penguin, 1989 [1902].

Corcoran, N., ed., *The Chosen Ground: Essays on the Contemporary Poetry of Northern Ireland*, Bridgend, Seren Books, 1992.

Crewe, C., 'Belfast Slabbers Pave a Literary Way', *The Guardian*, 18 February 1992, p. 32.

— 'Biting the Bullet', *The Times Magazine*, 7 September 1996, p. 18.

Deane, S., 'An Irish Intelligentsia: Reflections on its Desirability', *The Honest Ulsterman*, No. 46–47, November 1974, pp. 27–34.

— *Strange Country: Modernity and Nationhood in Irish Writing since 1790*, Oxford, Clarendon Press, 1997.

Deane, S., ed., *Nationalism, Colonialism and Literature*, Minneapolis, University of Minnesota Press, 1990.

Deane, S., and A. Carpenter, eds., *The Field Day Anthology of Irish Writing*, 3 vols., Derry, Field Day, 1991.

Debord, G., *The Society of the Spectacle*, Detroit, Black and Red, 1983 [1967].

Devlin, B., *The Price of My Soul*, London, Pan Books, 1969.

Dillon, M., *The Shankill Butchers: A Case Study of Mass Murder*, London, Hutchinson, 1989.

Dillon, M., and D. Lehane, *Political Murder in Northern Ireland*, London, Penguin, 1973.

Duddy, S., *Concrete Whirlpools of the Mind*, Belfast, Ulidia Press, 1983.

Duddy, S., A. Tyrie and M. Hall, *This is It!*, *Theatre Ireland*, No. 7, Autumn 1984, pp. 19–34.

Duffaud, B., *A Wreath Upon the Dead*, Dublin, Poolbeg, 1993.

Dunlop, A., *Kissing the Frog*, Dublin, Poolbeg, 1996.

Dyer, R., *Only Entertainment*, London, Routledge, 1992.

Eagleton, T., *Crazy John and the Bishop and Other Essays on Irish Culture*, Cork, Cork University Press/Field Day, 1998.

— 'Form and Ideology in the Anglo-Irish Novel', *Bullán: An Irish Studies Journal*, Vol. 1, No. 1, Spring 1994, pp. 17–26.

— *Heathcliff and the Great Hunger: Studies in Irish Culture*, London, Verso, 1995.

— *Ideology: An Introduction*, London, Verso, 1991.

— *Literary Theory: An Introduction*, Oxford, Blackwell, 1983.

— *Marxism and Literary Criticism*, London, Methuen, 1976.

— 'Nationalism, Irony and Commitment', *Field Day Pamphlet*, No. 13, Derry, Field Day Theatre Company, 1988.

— *Scholars and Rebels in Nineteenth-Century Ireland*, Oxford, Blackwell, 1999.

English, R., 'Cultural Traditions and Political Ambiguity', *Irish Review*, No. 15, 1994, pp. 97–106.

Everett, W., ed., *European Identity in Cinema*, Exeter, Intellect Books, 1996.

Fanon, F., *The Wretched of the Earth*, trans. C. Farrington, Harmonds-worth, Penguin, 1985 [1965].

Forum for Philippine Alternatives, ed., *Re-Examining and Reviewing the Philippine Progressive Vision: Papers and Proceedings of the 1993 Conference of the Forum for Philippine Alternatives (FOPA), San Francisco Bay Area, California, April 2–4, 1993*, Quezon, FOPA, 1993.

Forster, E.M., *Howards End*, London, Penguin, 1992 [1910].

Foster, J.W., *Colonial Consequences: Essays in Irish Literature and Culture*, Dublin, Lilliput Press, 1991.

Friedman, L., ed., *British Cinema and Thatcherism*, London, University College London Press, 1993.

Friel, B., *Translations*, London, Faber & Faber, 1981.

Friel, L., 'Intense Debate on Abortion', *An Phoblacht/Republican News*, 28 March 1996, p. 5.

Gandhi, L., *Postcolonial Theory*, Edinburgh, Edinburgh University Press, 1998.

Gibbons, L., 'On the Beach: Abortion and Divorce in Irish Cinema', *Artforum*, Vol. 31, No. 2, 1992, p. 13.

Goodby, J., 'Bhabha, the Post/Colonial and Glenn Patterson's *Burning Your Own'*, *Irish Studies Review*, Vol. 7, No. 1, April 1999, pp. 65–71.

Gorman, D., 'The Way of the Killer Ant', *The Belfast Review*, No. 4, Autumn 1893, pp. 2–3.

Gramsci, A., *Selections from the Prison Notebooks*, ed. and trans. Q. Hoare and G. Nowell Smith, London, Lawrence and Wishart, 1971.

Grant, B.K., ed., *Film Genre Reader*, Austin, University of Texas Press, 1986.

Grant, P., *Breaking Enmities: Religion, Literature and Culture in Northern Ireland, 1967–97*, Basingstoke, Macmillan, 1999.

Heaney, S., *North*, London, Faber & Faber, 1975.

Hewitt, J., *Ancestral Voices: The Selected Prose of John Hewitt*, ed. T. Clyde, Belfast, Blackstaff Press, 1987.

— 'As You Like It', *The Honest Ulsterman*, No. 50, Winter 1975, pp. 138–40.

— *The Collected Poems of John Hewitt*, ed. F. Ormsby, Belfast, Blackstaff Press, 1991.

Hill, J., M. McLoone and P. Hainsworth, *Border Crossing: Film in Ireland, Britain and Europe*, Belfast, Institute of Irish Studies/London, British Film Institute, 1994.

Hill, M., and S. Barber, eds., *Aspects of Irish Studies*, Belfast, Institute of Irish Studies, 1990.

Howe, S., *Ireland and Empire: Colonial Legacies in Irish History and Culture*, Oxford, Oxford University Press, 2000.

Hughes, E., ed., *Culture and Politics in Northern Ireland*, Buckingham, Open University Press, 1991.

Jameson, F., *Marxism and Form: Twentieth-Century Dialectical Theories of Literature*, Princeton, Princeton University Press, 1974.

JanMohamed, A.R., and D. Lloyd, eds., *The Nature and Context of Minority Discourse*, Oxford, Oxford University Press, 1990.

Jarman, N., *Material Conflicts: Parades and Visual Displays in Northern Ireland*, Oxford, Berg, 1997.

'John O'the North', *Various Verses by John O'the North*, Belfast, Derek McCord, 1945.

Jordan, N., *The Crying Game: An Original Screenplay*, London, Random House, 1993.

Joyce, J., *Dubliners*, London, Granada, 1981 [1914].

— *The Letters of James Joyce*, II, ed. R. Ellmann, London, Faber & Faber, 1964.

Kaplan, E.A., ed., *Women in Film Noir*, London, British Film Institute, 1980.

Kavanagh, P., *The Collected Poems*, Newbridge, Goldsmith Press, 1990.

Kennedy, H., 'Shamrocks and Shillelaghs: Idyll and Ideology in Irish Cinema', *Film Comment*, Vol. 30, No. 3, May 1994, pp. 24–40.

Kirkland, R., *Literature and Culture in Northern Ireland since 1965: Moments of Danger*, London, Longman, 1996.

Larrissy, E., review of *Heathcliff and the Great Hunger* by T. Eagleton, *Journal of Victorian Culture*, Vol. 2, No. 2, Autumn 1997, pp. 332–36.

Leavis, F.R., *The Great Tradition: George Eliot, Henry James, Joseph Conrad*, London, Chatto and Windus, 1948.

Leitch, M., *Silver's City*, London, Secker and Warburg, 1981.

Lloyd, D., *Anomalous States: Irish Writing and the Post-Colonial Moment*, Dublin, Lilliput, 1993.

Lloyd, D., and P. Thomas, *Culture and the State*, London, Routledge, 1996.

Longley, E., *Poetry in the Wars*, Newcastle, Bloodaxe, 1986.

Lukács, G., *The Historical Novel*, London, Penguin Books, 1969.

Macherey, P., *A Theory of Literary Production*, trans. G. Wall, London, Routledge, 1978.

Mahon, D., *Poems 1962–78*, Oxford, Oxford University Press, 1979.

Mast, G., and M. Cohen, eds., *Film Theory and Criticism: Introductory Readings*, Oxford, Oxford University Press, 1979.

McDonald, P., *Mistaken Identities: Poetry and Northern Ireland*, Oxford, Clarendon Press, 1997.

McGarry, J., and B. O'Leary, *Explaining Northern Ireland*, Oxford, Blackwell, 1995.

McGee, P., *Cinema, Theory and Political Responsibility in Contemporary Culture*, Cambridge, Cambridge University Press, 1997.

McIlroy, B., *Shooting to Kill: Filmmaking and the 'Troubles' in Northern Ireland*, Trowbridge, Flicks Books, 1998.

— *World Cinema 4: Ireland*, Trowbridge, Flicks Books, 1989.

McLoone, M., ed., *Culture, Identity and Broadcasting in Ireland: Local Issues, Global Perspectives*, Belfast, Institutute of Irish Studies, 1991.

— 'Lear's Fool and Goya's Dilemma', *Circa*, No. 50, March–April 1990, pp. 54–57.

— 'In the Name of the Father', Cineaste, Vol. 20, No. 4, October, 1994, p. 47.

McNamee, E., Resurrection Man, London, Picador, 1994.

Meyer, M., ed., The Politics and Poetics of Camp, London: Routledge, 1994.

Miller, D., ed., Rethinking Northern Ireland, London, Longman, 1998.

Mills, R., '"All Stories are Love Stories": Robert McLiam Wilson Interviewed by Richard Mills', Irish Studies Review, Vol. 7, No. 1, April 1999, pp. 73–77.

Muldoon, P., Why Brownlee Left, London, Faber & Faber, 1980.

Nairn, T., The Break-Up of Britain: Crisis and Neo-Nationalism, London, Verso, 1981.

Neve, B., 'Cinema, the Ceasefire and "the Troubles"', Irish Studies Review, No. 20, Autumn 1997, pp. 2–8.

Northern Ireland Office, The Day of the Men and Women of Peace Must Surely Come..., Belfast, Northern Ireland Office, 1989.

Nugent, J., 'The Remains of Empire: Conflicting Representations in Contemporary Film', Irish Studies Review, No. 7, Summer 1994, pp. 23–27.

O'Byrne, C., As I Roved Out: A Book of the North, Belfast, Blackstaff Press, 1982.

Ormsby, F., ed., A Rage for Order: Poetry of the Northern Ireland Troubles, Belfast, Blackstaff Press, 1992.

Ossowska, M., Bourgeois Morality, trans. G.L. Campbell, London, Routledge, 1986 [1956].

Patterson, G., Burning Your Own, London, Chatto and Windus, 1988.

— Fat Lad, London, Chatto and Windus, 1992.

Paulin, T., Liberty Tree, London, Faber & Faber, 1983.

— Writing to the Moment: Selected Critical Essays 1980–96, London, Faber & Faber, 1996.

Pettitt, L., review of Shooting to Kill by B. McIlroy, Irish Studies Review, Vol. 7, No. 1, April 1999, pp. 104–106.

Pogatchnik, S., Associated Press syndicated interview with Robert McLiam Wilson, 13 May 1992.

Pollak, A., ed., A Citizens' Inquiry: The Opsahl Report on Northern Ireland, Dublin, Lilliput Press, 1993.

Rockett, K., L. Gibbons and J. Hill, Cinema and Ireland, Syracuse, Syracuse University Press, 1988.

Rolston, B., 'Escaping from Belfast: Class, Ideology and Literature in Northern Ireland', Race and Class, Vol. 20, No. 1, 1978, pp. 41–62.

Ryan, R., ed., *Writing in the Irish Republic: Literature, Culture, Politics 1949–1999*, Basingstoke, Macmillan, 2000.

Said, E., *Culture and Imperialism*, London, Chatto and Windus, 1993.

Simmons, J., *Poems 1956–1986*, ed. E. Longley, Dublin, Gallery Press, 1986.

Smyth, A., ed., *The Abortion Papers: Ireland*, Dublin, Attic Press, 1992.

Smyth, G., *The Novel and the Nation: Studies in the New Irish Fiction*, London, Pluto Press, 1997.

Sontag, S., *Against Interpretation*, London, Vintage, 1994 [1966].

Spivak, G.C., *The Post-Colonial Critic: Interviews, Strategies, Dialogues*, ed. S. Harasym, London, Routledge, 1990.

Stevenson, J., *We Wrecked the Place: Contemplating an End to the Northern Irish Troubles*, New York, The Free Press, 1996.

Thompson, S., 'The Commodification of Culture and Decolonisation in Northern Ireland', *Irish Studies Review*, Vol. 7, No. 1, 1999, pp. 53–63.

Tiffin, C., and A. Lawson, *De-Scribing Empire: Post-Colonialism and Textuality*, London, Routledge, 1994.

Trotsky, L., *Literature and Revolution*, Ann Arbor, MI, Ann Arbor Paperbacks, 1960 [1957].

Vance, N., *Irish Literature: A Social History*, Oxford, Blackwell, 1990.

Walshe, É., ed., *Sex, Nation and Dissent in Irish Writing*, Cork, Cork University Press, 1997.

Williams, P., and L. Chrisman, eds., *Colonial Discourse and Post-Colonial Theory*, Hemel Hempstead, Harvester Wheatsheaf, 1993.

Wilson, R.M., *Eureka Street*, London, Secker and Warburg, 1996.

— *Ripley Bogle*, Belfast, Blackstaff Press, 1989.

— 'The Way Forward for Ireland', *Fortnight*, No. 303, February 1992, p. 40.

Ziff, T., ed., *Distant Relations: Chicano, Irish, Mexican Art and Critical Writing*, New York, Smart Art Press, 1995.

Index